Think this is one of the least interesting California places to visit? Think again...Flynn will show you how wrong you were.
Booklist

A fine guide to California's state capital....the best in bargains and attractions for savvy visitors.
Bookwatch

Lively and spirited.
The Sacramento Bee

Written in a clear and simple fashion, comprehensive in its coverage...get an inside look at Sacramento with Dan Flynn.
Sacramento News and Review

Informative, opinionated, comprehensive -- it's a great guide book.
The Oregonian

Has the scoop on Sacramento's secrets.
Orange County Register

Capital ideas for just hanging out in our state capital.
The Fresno Bee

Neat places to go, fun things to do.
The Davis Enterprise

An ideal gift for a friend.
The Press Tribune

To Karen, John and Jimmy. Family is everything.

Publisher's Cataloging-in-Publication Data

Flynn, Dan, 1961-
    Inside Guide to Sacramento : The Hidden Gold of California's Capital / by Dan Flynn. --3rd ed.
        p.   cm.
    Bibliography: p.
    Includes index.
    ISBN 0-9643150-7-6 : $15.00
    1. Sacramento (Calif.)--Description--Guide-books. 2. Historic Sites--California--Sacramento--Guide-books.   I. Title.
    F869.S12 F59 1994
    917.9454

                                                                    94-61195
                                                                    CIP

Printed in Canada by Printcrafters, Inc.

Third Edition

Embarcadero Press
P.O. Box 188325
Sacramento, California 95818-8325

INSIDE GUIDE TO SACRAMENTO

The Hidden Gold of California's Capital

Dan Flynn

Design by Richard Tolmach
Photography by James A. Browning, Jr., Dan Flynn and Richard Tolmach
Editing by Karen M. Flynn and John Gilroy

Embarcadero Press
Sacramento, California

CONTENTS

PART I
QUICK GLANCE
TRIVIA

- The Gold Rush brought financial ruin to Sacramento founder John Sutter.
- In response to frequent flooding, many of Sacramento's streets were raised 12 feet between 1864 and 1873.
- Old Sacramento was considered the worst slum west of Chicago in the 1950s.
- Interstate 5 and the development of Capitol Mall destroyed many of Sacramento's early historic buildings.
- The middle of Sacramento's Tower Bridge is mechanically lifted at the rate of one foot per second.
- The oldest firehouse building in California, built in 1853, houses Sacramento's Firehouse Restaurant.
- Sacramento pioneer Sam Brannan was California's first leader of the Mormon Church and the state's first millionaire.
- Sacramento's K Street was converted to a pedestrian mall in 1969.
- *The Sacramento Bee's* mascot, Scoopy, was designed by Walt Disney.
- Julia Morgan, architect of Hearst Castle, designed Sacramento's Public Market Building, which is now the lobby of the Sheraton Grand Hotel.
- The State Capitol Building originally was to have been built in what is now known as Sacramento's César Chavez Plaza.
- The State Capitol Building's first architect, Reuben Clark, went insane before the building was completed.
- Some legislators wanted to abandon the State Capitol Building in the 1970s and build two modern towers instead.
- The California State Fair was held near 15th and N Streets in Sacramento from 1884 to 1905.
- President Gerald Ford survived an assassination attempt after walking across the street from Sacramento's Senator Hotel in 1975.
- The Stanford Window in Sacramento's St. Paul's Episcopal Church is one of the most valuable stained-glass windows in the world.
- The Rolling Stones' Keith Richards was knocked unconscious by an electrical shock at a Sacramento Memorial Auditorium performance in 1965.
- Nancy Reagan considered the Old Governor's Mansion to be depressing.

- Governor Jerry Brown lived in an apartment building across the street from Capitol Park.
- President Harry S Truman spoke at Sacramento's WPRR depot during his 1948 whistle-stop campaign.
- Sacramento's St. Francis Catholic Church's organ loft and stairway feature original stair railings from the State Capitol Building.
- The Alkali Flat neighborhood's J. Neely Johnson House, built in 1854, is the oldest residence in Sacramento.
- Sacramento's Boulevard Park neighborhood was once the site of the State Fair's horse races.
- The Grace Day Center, established 1920, is Sacramento's oldest day care center.
- The first drink was poured in Sacramento's Old Ironsides saloon in 1895.
- The Oak Park neighborhood is Sacramento's first suburb, established in 1889.
- Sacramento's Curtis Park, with its unusual oval shape, was the site of a racetrack in the 1860s.
- U.S. Supreme Court Justice Anthony Kennedy lived in Sacramento's Land Park neighborhood.
- Tower Records was established by Russ Solomon at 15th and Broadway in Sacramento in 1960.
- North Sacramento was a separate city before a controversial annexation to Sacramento in 1964.
- *The Sporting News* once described Sacramento as "possibly the best baseball town of its size in the country."
- Western Swing legend Bob Wills operated a Sacramento roadhouse named Wills' Point in the 1950s.
- Rancho Seco Park surrounds a deactivated nuclear power plant.
- The City of Sacramento operates such unusual recreational amenities as a trapshooting club, bocce ball courts and a Sierra family camp.
- Davis was known as Davisville until 1907.
- Freeport was established so that shippers could avoid a Sacramento tax.
- Courtland is the most productive pear-growing region in the United States.
- Locke once had five brothels and five gambling houses.
- Locke's absentee landlord wanted to transform the historic town into a Chinese theme park in the 1970s.
- Long-time patrons smear peanut butter on their steaks at Locke's Al the Wop's restaurant.
- Giusti's restaurant in the Delta has been open since 1910.
- Rio Vista's Foster's Big Horn, a bar and grill, features more than 300 wild game trophies.

- The Isleton Crawdad Festival attracts more than 200,000 people each year.
- Before 1931, Fair Oaks was spelled Fairoaks.
- Folsom State Prison was known by prisoners as "the end of the world."
- Folsom's Ashland Freight Depot, built in the late 1850s, is the oldest train station west of the Mississippi.
- Folsom's St. John the Baptist Catholic Church, built in 1857, is the oldest church in the Sacramento region.
- The Lodi/Woodbridge area produces more tons of the premium winegrape varietals than any other region in the state.
- A&W root beer was invented by a pharmacist in Lodi in 1919.
- Rocklin lost the Southern Pacific Railroad's headquarters to Roseville and a state prison to Folsom.
- Roseville's oldest building is the I.O.O.F. Hall, built in 1878.
- Large cargo vessels can dock in West Sacramento, 85 miles from the Pacific Ocean.
- Creedence Clearwater Revival's "Green River" was written about Yolo County's Putah Creek.
- The Yolo County Historical Museum is housed in a structure built in 1849.
- Elk Grove Brewing Company was named best small brewery in the nation in 1999 and 2000.
- Frank Fat's restaurant in Sacramento was known as Frank's 806 when it debuted in 1939.
- Biba Caggiano, owner of Biba restaurant in Sacramento, once hosted a nationally broadcast cooking show.
- Darrell Corti, of Corti Bros. supermarket in Sacramento, is one of the world's foremost food and wine experts.
- Royal Hong King Lum is Sacramento's oldest restaurant, opened in 1906.
- The Sunday farmers' market at 8th and W Streets in Sacramento is the largest in Northern California.
- Gunther's Ice Cream in Sacramento has been scooping since 1940.
- Ronald Reagan enjoyed eating Merlino's orange freeze at the stand on Stockton Boulevard in Sacramento.
- The Sacramento Natural Food Co-op is among the five largest in the United States.
- Dirk Mueller of Morant's Sausage in Sacramento studied sausage making in Germany for five years.
- Poor Red's in El Dorado is the world's largest buyer of Galliano liqueur, a key ingredient in the house specialty, the Golden Cadillac.
- Sacramento's lowest recorded temperature was 17 F. on Dec. 11, 1932.
- Sacramento's highest recorded temperature was 114 F. on July 17, 1925.

TOP 10 LISTS

THINGS TO DO IN A HURRY
State Capitol
Capitol Park
Old Sacramento
McKinley Park
Boulevard Park tour
Midtown restaurants and cafes
Downtown Plaza shopping
Esquire IMAX Theatre
Golden State Museum
California State Railroad Museum

BEST SACRAMENTO HANGOUTS
Fox and Goose
Tower Cafe
Virgin Sturgeon
Bonn Lair
Simon's
Vic's Ice Cream
Freeport Bakery
César Chavez Plaza Farmers' Market
New Helvetia Roasters and Bakers
33rd Street Bistro

BEST PLACES TO TAKE THE KIDS
Sacramento Zoo
Fairy Tale Town
Funderland
California State Railroad Museum
McKinley Park Playground
Sutter's Fort
Davis Farmers' Market
Effie Yeaw Nature Center
Explorit Science Center
State Capitol

SINCERE SACRAMENTO SLOGANS
Selected from reader responses solicited by Sacramento Bee Columnist Steve Wiegand:
Where It All Began
A Capital Place
City of Rivers
The Outdoor City

City of Trees
Heart of the Valley
Gateway to the Goldfields
'Tween Seaside and Sierra
Heart of California
Two Rivers Run Through It

IRREVERENT SACRAMENTO SLOGANS

Selected from reader responses solicited by Sacramento Bee Columnist Steve Wiegand:
You Have To Live Somewhere
We Would If We Could But We Can't So We Won't
We Just Don't Get It
Tulsa of the West
Home of the Dry Heat
Close Enough for Government Work
How Would You Like It If We Sent All Our Crappy Politicians To Your Town?
Together, We Still Suck
You're Halfway There
Just A Bladder From Tahoe

PLACES TO FIND POLITICIANS WHEN YOU CAN'T FIND THEM ANYWHERE ELSE

Frank Fat's
Simon's
Brannan's
Fox and Goose
Marilyn's
The Broiler
Centro
Esquire Grill
Morton's
Biba

QUIRKS AND ODDITIES

Gov. Jerry Brown's wildly expressionistic official portrait
Tiny K Street key shop
Tile House at 2816 22nd Street in Curtis Park
Subterranean State Office Building
Referring to Goethe Park as "Gay-tee" Park
Dollar-bill ceiling in Locke's Al the Wop's
Pedal-driven carousel in Davis Central Park
R.U.O.F. the cow messenger (215 N. 16th Street, Sacramento)
Spoof of "Sunday Morning in the Mines" mural (Sacramento Masonic Temple)
Free auto ferries in the Delta

BEST OF THE REGION

DELI
David Berkley There are few better ways to assemble a picnic than from Berkley's well-stocked gourmet deli.

OUTDOOR DINING
Paragary's Midtown Designer David Yakish has created a stunning dining setting with waterfalls, vines, mature olive trees and a river rock fireplace.

DIVE RESTAURANT
Squeeze Inn Those with a taste for trivia contests, quirky humor, cramped quarters and big burgers can't do better than the Squeeze Inn.

UNUSUAL RESTAURANT
Foster's Big Horn You never dine alone when seated under the watchful gaze of 300+ big-game trophies in Foster's dining room.

BURGER
Nationwide Meats Harris Ranch beef makes the difference in Nationwide's superb French Steakburger.

ITALIAN
Biba Biba features authentic Italian food prepared with quality ingredients. You pay dearly, but this is the real thing.

BREAKFAST
Fox and Goose This British pub will get your day off to a satisfying start.

STEAKHOUSE
Buckhorn Buckhorn's serves dry-aged beef of big-city quality.

SPANISH
Tapa the World Tapa the World taps the exuberant spirit of Spain.

PIZZA
Giovanni's This new pizzeria in South Land Park produces great New York-style pie.

VIETNAMESE
Hoa Viet The Stockton Boulevard location is where the Vietnamese go to eat.

BARBEQUE
MacQue's MacQue's is off the beaten path but worth the hunt.

REGIONAL MEXICAN
Centro Cocina Mexicana Centro lets you enjoy regional specialties, super-premium tequilas and chips fried to order.

VEGETARIAN
Sunflower Drive-In Sunflower is the nutburger capital of the valley.

BAKERY
Freeport Bakery Walter Goetzeler uses generations of know-how to produce delicious European and American treats.

ICE CREAM
Vic's Ice Cream Vic's has been a friendly Land Park gathering spot since 1947.

COFFEEHOUSE
Weatherstone Sac's oldest coffeehouse features a pleasant outdoor courtyard.

PUB
Fox and Goose Fox and Goose has the comfortable feel of a century-old pub.

BREWPUB
Elk Grove Brewing Company Housed in a 19th Century general store building in old Elk Grove, this brewpub has been recognized as the best in U.S.

BAR & GRILL
Jamie's Enjoy crab cakes, lamb shanks and smoked prime rib in this friendly neighborhood bar.

INDEPENDENT BOOKSTORE
Avid Reader A good selection, helpful staff and special events have allowed Avid Reader to compete with the big boxes.

MOM AND POP MARKET
Taylor's Market Taylor's features a quality butcher shop, fine wine selection and friendly service.

CONCERT VENUE
The Palms Playhouse Top acts love to play this rickety barn with 120 seats.

POLITICAL HANGOUT
Simon's Lots of the Capitol's top dogs unwind here.

FRUIT FREEZE
Merlino's Nothing goes down easier or tastes better than a Merlino's freeze on a Sacramento summer day.

HOT DOG
Wiener Works These giant dogs have top quality ingredients.

MARTINI
Bandera Double portions, premium spirits and a variety of four jumbo olives go into Bandera's house martini.

FARMERS' MARKET
Davis The Davis market blooms with community spirit and great produce.

NATURAL FOODS MARKET
Sacramento Natural Foods Co-op There's no better place in the region for organic produce and bulk foods.

NEIGHBORHOOD PARK
McKinley Park A jogging track, duck pond, library, playground, swimming pool, basketball court and tennis courts are among the attractions in this historic park.

FOOD FESTIVAL
Isleton Crawdad Festival Enjoy a bit of Louisiana alongside the Sacramento River Delta.

MUSIC FESTIVAL
Sacramento Jazz Jubilee A world class festival, with an emphasis on Dixieland.

GOURMET MARKET
Corti Brothers The Cortis know food and wine and everything Italian.

SAUSAGE
Morant's Discover the difference that five years of German training makes.

PART II
FOOD LOVER'S GUIDE
RESTAURANTS

Price code is keyed to the cost of the majority of dinner entrees on the menu: $ = under $6, $$ = $6-$12, $$$ = $12-$18 and $$$$ = $18 and up. Breakfast and lunch will cost less.

AMERICAN/CALIFORNIAN

Alexander's Meritage Vincent Paul Alexander, who trained under Wolfgang Puck and other culinary luminaries, established his local reputation as the head chef at Slocum House. When Christophe's old location became available, Alexander decided to strike out on his own. Alexander serves traditional entrées with an updated flair. The menu includes roast breast of marinated pheasant wrapped in a vegetable mousseline and sauteed Atlantic king salmon served with braised fennel and lentil cream sauce. There also is a prix fixe option, with a choice of four or five courses matched with appropriate wines. *6608 Folsom-Auburn Road, Folsom; 916/988-7000; dinner Tuesday-Sunday, brunch Sunday; $$$$*

Bandera Bandera's menu offers assertively flavorful selections inspired by the American South and West. As you sit in the broad, open dining room, you can admire the chickens slowly turning on the spit in a wood-fired stone oven. Appetizers include a split artichoke grilled over hardwood and served with remoulade sauce, as well as black bean chicken chili, caesar salad and jumbo gulf shrimp cocktails. The juicy prime rib merits high marks, as do the rotisserie selections, mashed potatoes and slightly-sweet corn bread. Get there early — Bandera often fills up with the cocktail crowd (notable house specialties include the Bandera Cosmo and the Dean Martin Martini) and reservations are not taken. *2232 Fair Oaks Boulevard, Sacramento; 916/922-3524; dinner nightly; $$$; www.banderarestaurants.com*

Esquire Grill A great addition to Randy Paragary's local restaurant empire, Esquire Grill evokes the aura of the classic American downtown grill. The stylish Art Deco dining room features a curving bar, leather banquettes and a view to the kitchen. Esquire Grill skillfully modernizes traditional menu favorites, such as adding paper-thin red onion and radishes to the Shrimp Louie salad, setting a thick grilled burger on a house-baked bun and serving top-shelf french fries with the skins on. The mixed drinks are handled with similar care and appropriately emphasize the

cocktail shaker rather than the blender. The restaurant brings sorely needed pizazz to the downtown restaurant scene, and nearby Capitol types have rewarded Esquire Grill with a full reservation book. *1213 K Street, Sacramento; 916/448-8900; lunch Monday-Friday, dinner nightly; $$$; www.paragarys.com/esquire.html*

The Kitchen Your dinner at The Kitchen quite possibly will be the best meal of your life. The restaurant specializes in "demonstration dinners" that allow each of the 42 lucky customers to observe the meal's preparation. Talking loudly and at rapid-fire speed, Chef Randall Selland makes the evening fun, informal and accommodating. Selland also delivers an Ivy League education in seasonal cooking (one night a salad of perfect, first-growth baby organic greens was dressed with spicy fried rock shrimp, lemongrass cream and truffle oil); quality control (he makes his own ice cream, dries his own habanero peppers and drives long distances to find choice produce) and culinary creativity (such as one night's entrée choice of grilled filet of beef tenderloin with fresh morel and shiitake mushrooms that had been tossed in foie gras butter and peppered bacon; or sesame-crusted Hawaiian ono with grilled asparagus, lobster-soybean broth and a salsa of rock crab, avocado and croutons). Reservations are taken on the first weekday of the month for dates two months out. Bring your own wine or order from the extensive wine list that offers hard-to-find California selections at reasonable prices. *2225 Hurley Way, Sacramento; 916/568-7171; one seating at 7:00 p.m. Thursday-Saturday; $$$$*

Mace's Grill Mace's is decorated in an upscale safari motif — you half-expect the waiter to speak with a British accent. The restaurant focuses on local, fresh ingredients, offering inventive daily specials such as fish tacos with scallops and fideo. The phyllo-wrapped cambozola with roasted garlic is the signature appetizer, and the menu offers fresh fish, pasta and meat entrées. Mace's fires the grill with almond wood. Service is friendly and attentive. The restaurant features an adjoining wine shop where you may wish to select a bottle before heading for the dining room. *11773 Fair Oaks Boulevard, Fair Oaks; 916/863-0400; dinner Tuesday - Saturday; $$$*

Silva's Sheldon Inn Doug Silva has served up hearty fare in this rural former grocery store since 1988. With its country furnishings of doilies, quilts and fresh flowers, Silva's Sheldon Inn exudes a cozy, home-like ambiance. The menu also joins in the family-friendly spirit, with inexpensive child plate selections and Sunday evenings devoted to family-style dinners. Start with Beef Skewers Portuguese (marinated in garlic, bay leaf and red wine) or perhaps a cup of Portuguese bean soup. The entrées include roast duckling, grilled lamb chops marinated with garlic and rosemary and filet mignon with Béarnaise sauce. Finish off with one of Silva's belly-comforting desserts, such as apple bread pudding or fruit cobbler. *9000 Grant Line Road, Elk Grove; 916/686-8330; dinner Tuesday-Sunday; $$$*

Slocum House Slocum House is located in a former residence built in 1925 on the edge of the old Fair Oaks Village. Don't be put off by the cheap-looking aggregate concrete steps and wrought iron railing that lead up to the restaurant, because this is one of the region's finer dining establishments. Be sure to reserve a table on the delightful patio when weather allows. The menu incorporates

European, Latin and Asian influences and all entrées come with soup or salad, homemade bread and fresh vegetables. Jim LePerriere, formerly of Enotria and Biba, handles the executive chef honors. For an appetizer, try the ahi spring roll, stuffed with bok choy, carrots, scallions and jicama; or the smoked tomato and roasted poblano soup. Consider as a main course the wood-grilled filet mignon served with hearty cabernet-white cheddar mashed potatoes, or ahi tuna seared rare with a crunchy sesame seed crust. *7992 California Avenue, Fair Oaks; 916/961-7211; lunch Tuesday-Friday, dinner Tuesday-Sunday, brunch Sunday; $$$$; www.slocum-house.com*

AUSTRIAN-GERMAN

Cafe Vienna If the mayor of Salzburg found Cafe Vienna's cuisine to be authentic, that should be good enough for the rest of us. We're talking hearty, stick-to-your-ribs fare, with an emphasis on meat, fried potatoes, spaetzle and dumplings. Check out the Viennese Onion Roast – a six ounce roasted New York strip steak, steeped in its own juices and topped with browned onions, or the hassenpfeffer, chunks of rabbit baked in a wine sauce. Entrées, breads, sides and desserts are all prepared on the premises with authentic ingredients. The wine list features selections from Austria, Germany, Sierra Foothills and Mendocino; and no bottle exceeds $30. Cafe Vienna features monthly buffet dinner and dancing events and has a patio and banquet room. Located just five minutes from the Capitol Building in West Sacramento. *1229 Merkley Way, West Sacramento; 916/371-9560; lunch buffet Monday-Friday, dinner, Monday-Saturday; $$$; www.viennatonight.com*

BAR AND GRILL

Fox and Goose Allyson Dalton, daughter of Fox and Goose founders Bill and Denise Dalton, now has the reins at Sacramento's favorite British pub. Thankfully, she has not tinkered with success. Breakfast still features classical music, great coffee and a wonderful soft light from the warehouse windows. Lunch includes such pub favorites as welsh rarebit and the "ploughman's lunch" of cheddar, warm bread, fruit and chutney, not to mention a fine selection of soups, salads, sandwiches and specials. Evenings still find British and Irish accents at the bar and a lively music scene. The only changes Allyson has allowed have been for the better: credit cards are finally accepted, weekend breakfast begins earlier and the vegetarian selections are more plentiful. As for dessert, your physician undoubtedly would frown upon the silky burnt cream; but your mental health will benefit from the indulgence. *1001 R Street, Sacramento; 916/443-8825; breakfast, lunch and light dinner daily; $; www.foxandgoose.com*

Jamie's Bar and Grill Jamie Bunnell insists that everything on his menu be made from scratch, including onion ring batter, salad dressings, potato salad and mayonnaise. He cures bacon and roasts turkeys for his fine clubhouse sandwiches and Cobb salads. Don't hesitate to order any of the daily specials, which may include smoked prime rib, crab cakes, lamb shanks or Chinese chicken salad. Friday evenings feature a popular all-you-can eat barbecue for $12. The bar itself has a friendly, neighborhood vibe; but it is Jamie Bunnell's attention to the kitchen that allows this establishment to rise above the crowd. *427 Broadway, Sacramento; 916/442-4044; lunch and dinner Monday-Friday; $$*

Old Ironsides Located in Sacramento's oldest bar (established 1895), Old Ironsides has been owned within the same family since 1934. Soak up the atmosphere in the deco-era booths in the bar, or head for the dining room. The lunch features very good daily soups and specials, such as fried calamari. The steak sandwich and Italian meatloaf sandwich are solid bets. *1901 10th Street, Sacramento; 916/443-9751; lunch Monday-Friday; $; www.theoldironsides.com*

Plainfield Station This former gas station, located on a quiet rural road outside Woodland, has sated hungry motorists since 1934. The burgers are just okay, but with cheap draft beer and a jukebox of country music, Plainfield Station is well worth a visit. *Corner of Roads 29 and 98 (Take Interstate 80 west to Pedrick Road, turn west and go about five miles, or take Highway 113 to Covell Boulevard, turn west and go to Road 98, turn right), Woodland; 530/668-0207; $*

Virgin Sturgeon The Virgin Sturgeon was a favorite hangout during the Jerry Brown Administration and is still popular with the locals. The bar and grill occu-

pies a barge docked along the Sacramento River, which you access by walking down a recycled airline boarding ramp. If you have a boat, you can dock right outside. The peaceful river setting is only a short distance from downtown, but you feel like you are much further from civilization. There is a menu featuring burgers, seafood and  sandwiches, though your best bet is to order the smoked fish as an appetizer (ask for extra bread), have a drink and enjoy the river view. *1577 Garden Highway, Sacramento; 916/921-2694*

BARBECUE

MacQue's MacQue's industrial location belies the top-notch barbecue that can be found inside. Owners Mack and Charlie Thomas know how to make a robust sauce, and they have discovered the right smoky balance for the slow-cooked ribs, chicken, hot links, tri-tip, pork and ham. The excellent side dishes include three different kinds of beans (baked, western and red beans and rice), four salads (cole slaw, potato, pasta and macaroni) and two vegetables (green beans and corn). MacQue's clean and inviting dining room offers several tables and a friendly staff. *8101 Elder Creek Road (at Power Inn Road, across from Jack in the Box), Sacramento; 916/381-4119; lunch and dinner Monday-Saturday; $$*

BREWPUBS

Elk Grove Brewing Company In the center of South Sacramento suburbia stands the old Elk Grove General Store building, a two-story brick structure that dates from 1885. Inside is the Elk Grove Brewing Company, a welcome find in a land of chain restaurants. In fact, this small brewery and its brewmaster were named the best in the nation at the 1999 and 2000 Great American Brewfest in Denver. The food here is of the hearty variety: beer-battered onion rings, sausage platters, burgers, pasta, chili, sandwiches and salads. The brews are excellent; go for a sampler or try the Wrangler Red Ale, a reddish brown, full-bodied ale with a slightly bitter finish. *9085 Elk Grove Boulevard, Elk Grove; 916/685-ALES; lunch and dinner daily; $$; www.elkgrovebrewery.com*

Rubicon Brewing Company

Rubicon's popularity has not waned since it opened in 1986. Owner Ed Brown has maintained a lively Midtown people-watching spot, as well as a casual place to hang out to catch up with friends or watch a ballgame. Rubicon features burgers, fish and chips, sandwiches and salads, but the main attraction is the beer. The amber ale is particularly fine, a copper-colored, well-balanced brew with a gentle bitter finish. *2004 Capitol Avenue, Sacramento; 916/448-7032; lunch and dinner daily, breakfast Saturday and Sunday; $; sacweb.com/rubicon*

Sacramento Brewing Company The walls of Sacramento Brewing Company proudly display the many awards that the brewpub has won in commercial beer judging competitions. Standouts from the tap room include the extra pale ale, which will appeal to the Bud drinkers, as well as the amber ale, a bold red brew with an appealing, roasted-malt character. The menu complements the beer with hearty, flavorful selections such as fried calamari, grilled skirt steak marinated in roasted chilies and braised pork ribs marinated in ale. The Citrus Heights location, known as Sacramento Brewing Company's Oasis, features a striking Egyptian decor. *2713 El Paseo Lane (Town and Country Village), Sacramento; 916/485-4677; 7811 Madison Avenue, Citrus Heights; 916/966-6274; lunch and dinner daily, brunch Sunday; $$$; www.sacbrew.com*

Sudwerk The enormous copper kettles dominating the dining room and the heady aroma of steaming wort leave no doubt that Sudwerk is a working brewery. The owners developed the original location, in Davis, with an eye toward authenticity in the brewery equipment, the restaurant design and the delicious food. You cannot go wrong with the (Morant's) sausage platter, or the wiener schnitzel or a host of other German specialties. The huge portions are just right with a liter of your favorite style of German beer. Sudwerk features plenty of non-German menu selections as well, such as crab cakes and brick-oven pizza. *1375 Exposition Drive, Sacramento; 916/925-6623; 2001 2nd Street, Davis; 530/758-8700; lunch and dinner daily; $$; www.sudwerk.com*

CAFES

Cafe Bernardo Randy Paragary brought to Sacramento what might be called "casual fine dining" when he opened Cafe Bernardo back in 1992. At Bernardo's you order and pay as at a fast food restaurant, but get bistro-quality food served at your table, for not much more than fast food prices. The kitchen will treat you well here, whether it's a breakfast of Eggs Bernardo or waffles with pecan butter, a lunch of a sampler of three wonderful salads or a dinner of grilled polenta and mixed greens. The menu also features decent wine by-the-glass and microbrews. The Sacramento midtown location also offers fresh-squeezed juices at the adjoining Juice-O-Rama. *2726 Capitol Avenue, Sacramento; 916/443-1180; 234 D Street, Davis; 530/750-5101; 1563 Eureka Road, Roseville; 916/773-3778; breakfast, lunch and dinner daily; $$; www.paragarys.com/bernardo.html*

Jack's Urban Eats Jack's menu showcases sandwiches and salads in a cafeteria format (with striking similarities to the popular Pluto's chain). As you move through the line, you get to watch the staff grill flank steak and herbed chicken, slice freshly roasted turkey, and prepare french fries and salads to order. The sandwiches include such luxuries as housemade aioli and caramelized onions. For salads, the customer specifies spinach, mixed greens or caesar, and then may order up to six additions from the likes of marinated mushrooms, caramelized walnuts and roasted potatoes. The place can get terribly noisy, though there is quieter seating outside. Jack's satisfies a yuppie palate on a blue-collar budget. *20th and Capitol, Sacramento; 916/444-0307; 2535 Fair Oaks Boulevard, Sacramento; 916/481-5225; lunch Monday-Friday, dinner daily; $; www.paesanospizzeria.com*

Luna's Cafe and Juice Bar Brother and sister Art and Chris Luna have operated this laid-back gathering place for many years. The simple, inexpensive menu evokes memories of the natural food eateries of the 1970s, with quesadillas, salads, sandwiches, soup and fresh fruit liquados. The cafe is decorated with the work of local artists. The mood is coffeehouse casual and Luna's often features poetry readings and other events. *1414 16th Street, Sacramento; 916/441-3931; breakfast and lunch, Monday-Saturday; $*

River Rock Cafe Steve Priley, one of the original founders of Java City, branched out to beer and food at River Rock Cafe. After putting in a few years on Sunrise Boulevard, Priley moved to a distinctive atrium dining room that he had constructed within walking distance of the new Century Theatres in Roseville. The 50 beers on tap should satisfy the most demanding connoisseur and the salads, sandwiches and entrées make for a tasty, quick meal before or after the show. *1595 Eureka Road, Roseville; 916/780-2739; breakfast, lunch and dinner; $$*

33rd Street Bistro Chef Fred Haines served an eight-year stint as a chef in Seattle, and the Northwest influence is evident at 33rd Street Bistro. Check out the grilled panini sandwiches such as "Pike Street Market" (cambozola, artichoke hearts, marinated red pepper), the lovely salads (try the wood-roasted salmon salad) and the entrées such as smoked chicken ravioli. Breakfast selections include smoked brook trout hash served over roasted red potatoes and a vegetable frittata topped with roasted red pepper cream and asiago cheese. The bistro is noisy, with its bare maple floors, brick walls, throngs of chatty diners and busy chefs putting it all together right in the middle of the room. Altogether one of Sacramento's best places for excellent food at a moderate price. The Arden Fair Mall location offers some of the same dishes in a food court setting. *3301 Folsom Boulevard, Sacramento; 916/455-2233; breakfast, lunch and dinner daily; $$*

Tower Cafe Tower Cafe owner Jim Seaman has labored tirelessly to transform Broadway into a lively entertainment area. The cafe sits in the shadow of the landmark Tower Theatre, with outdoor seating spilling into the triangular space at the corner of Broadway and Land Park Drive. Tower has borne criticism for slow service and inconsistent execution in the kitchen, but there's no denying that the cafe is one of Sacramento's best places for people watching. You have your choice of the dining room, which features a variety of artifacts from around the world and the big glass windows, or the patio, which Seaman has enhanced with landscaping, lighting and other amenities. *1518 Broadway, Sacramento; 916/441-0222; breakfast, lunch and dinner daily; $$; towercafe.com*

CARIBBEAN/CREOLE

Celestin's Buoyant Caribbean culture permeates Celestin's, one of midtown Sacramento's longest-lived restaurants. Haitian-born Patrick Celestin brings forth the spicy, colorful flavors of his homeland with a menu of gumbos (which you tailor to your preference of chicken, red snapper, salmon, shrimp, andouille, kielbasa, scallops or some combination), each made with a dark roux and spiked with the flavor of tomato and sassafras. The menu also includes coconut-lime scallops or chicken, a variety of seafood dishes and an array of deep-fried appetizers. The wine list offers an inexpensive, Beaujolais-style Zinfandel made from organic Mendocino County grapes that makes a fine partner with the spicy cuisine. Vivid colors and rhythmic music of the islands enfold the dining room, assuring that a meal at Celestin's will lift your spirits. *18th and K Streets, Sacramento (November 2001); 916/444-2423; lunch Tuesday-Saturday, dinner Tuesday-Sunday; $$$*

CHINESE

Capital Tea Garden Many Sacramentans consider Capital Tea Garden to serve the area's best dim sum. The restaurant also offers a variety of Mandarin and Cantonese dishes as well as live seafood. *1100 T Street, Sacramento; 916/448-1218; lunch Monday-Friday, dinner nightly; $*

Chinois City Wok The three SooHoo brothers, Alvin, Terry and David, once operated at the upper end of the restaurant spectrum with Chinois East/West, featuring Asian/European/California fusion cuisine that achieved great popularity over its 10-year life span. Weary of playing at that elite level, the brothers closed down the restaurant; and Alvin and Terry later opened Chinois City Wok.

Now with its smaller dining room and lower prices, you can still enjoy some of the dishes that made the old place so popular. Specialties include the Mongolian Grilled Beef Laughing Buns, prawn potstickers and the Phoenix and Dragon — prawns, chicken, mushrooms and avocado in a Provencale herb cream sauce. Despite the smaller scale, the restaurant still exhibits the SooHoo panache, from the lively interior design to the white chocolate-dipped fortune cookie that finishes the meal. *3535 Fair Oaks Boulevard, Sacramento; 916/485-8690; lunch Monday-Friday, dinner nightly; $$*

Eastern Empire Eastern Empire features dishes from China and the South Pacific. The classy dining room offers sleek furniture, subdued lighting and bow-tied waiters. The bar offers those wonderful Polynesian cocktails, like the Zombie, served in a tiki glass. As for the food, try the minced chicken with let-tuce cups — minced chicken breast tossed with stir-fried mint, red pepper, onion and cilantro, which you wrap up in iceberg lettuce and eat like a taco. Also con-sider the tantalizing seafood dishes, such as prawns with crabmeat sauce and the prawns and scallops in a spicy garlic wine sauce. *460 Howe Avenue (in the University Village Shopping Center), Sacramento; 916/646-1698; lunch and dinner daily; $$*

Far East Cafe To get a sense of how much work it is to run a restaurant, drop into Far East Cafe. Owner Sammy Leong races through his business performing every possible task: seating people, cleaning up spills, shouting orders to the kitchen, fetching lollipops for children and delivering unrequested napkins. He also manages to maintain a cheerful demeanor, probably because the place does consistently heavy business. Sammy has acknowledged that his food is not the best in town, though it is good and very cheap. One of the best items on the menu is the spicy chow fun (with onions, bell peppers, black bean sauce, your choice of meat or chicken and plenty of seared chow fun noodles). *5014 Freeport Boulevard, Sacramento; 916/456-9835; lunch and dinner daily; $*

Frank Fat's Chinese immigrant Frank Fat opened a restau-rant, known as Frank's 806, in 1939. Showing a keen under-standing of the business potential of a location two blocks from the male-dominated State Capitol, he advertised that the restaurant would feature "charming, beautiful and cour-teous Chinese waitresses." During its heyday, Fat's would be packed with legislators and lobbyists, with possibly a card game in the back room. Frank died at age 92 in 1997, and his son Wing carries on the tradition of making the politicos welcome. Legislative term limits have somewhat dimin-ished the restaurant's status as the unofficial home of the Legislature, but the restaurant's opulence, the New York Steak Frank Fat Style (grilled sirloin smothered in sauteed  onions and oyster sauce) and the outstanding banana cream pie are reasons enough to visit this local institution. *806 L Street, Sacramento; 916/442-7092; lunch Monday-Friday, dinner nightly; $$$; www.fatsrestaurants.com/frankfats/index.html*

Louie's Frank and Gloria Louie have been offering solid food and service at the right price since 1988. The place is particularly crowded at lunch due to its close proximity to the Department of Motor Vehicles, the U.C. Davis Medical Center and the Shriners Hospital; but Louie's moves customers right along with a cafeteria-style format. Dinner features table service. The restaurant has built a strong following within the Legislature, where Louie's decadent honey prawns with pecans fuel many a late-night session. *4605 Broadway (at Stockton Boulevard), Sacramento; 916/739-8646; lunch and dinner daily; $*

COFFEE SHOPS

Market Club The Market Club serves cheap breakfasts and lunches, either at the counter or in the simple dining room. One of the restaurant's main attractions is its location, hidden away in a produce-shipping yard. Just drive right into the loading yard off 5th Street — don't worry, nobody will throw you out. The menu offers American as well as Japanese selections. One of the best breakfast dishes in town is the Oki Special (served Sunday only), which is a fried egg served over fried rice. Lunches offer daily specials and gigantic portions. The Market Club is popular with Sacramento police officers, the Japanese-American community and early-morning golfers. *2630 5th Street, Sacramento; 916/498-9953; breakfast and lunch Sunday-Friday; $*

Original Perry's Original Perry's may not get you to believe the old maxim that truckers always know the best places to eat, but the food here ain't bad. Original Perry's has been an authentic truck stop restaurant since 1968 (originally known as Richfield Trukadero Coffee Shop), where big rigs fuel up while truckers fortify themselves for the long haul. Owner Perry Potiris has been in the business for 50 years, succeeding on a formula of low prices, large portions and above-average grub (soups, sauces, gravies and salads are made on the premises). Dinner prices crest at the seven-dollar level, and include soup and salad. Breakfast is served at any time, with three eggs the standard (except for the omelets, which contain four). *7895 Stockton Blvd, Sacramento; 916/423-1103; breakfast, lunch and dinner daily; $$; www.elkgrove.net/Original.Perrys/menu.htm*

CONTINENTAL

La Boheme La Boheme offers plenty for the traditionalist who enjoys classic continental cuisine, as well as for the patron desiring a more contemporary meal. For the traditionalist, there are classics like duck à l'orange, filet of beef aux poivres and steak diane, cherries jubilée and baked Alaska. For those wanting a break from tradition, there is swordfish in tequila lime sauce, grilled salmon with a lemon herb sauce and vegetarian pasta with tomato basil sauce. La Boheme also offers an impressive selection of game entrées, including moose, elk, buffalo and venison. Chef Daniel Alizeau brings out the best in each entrée with his exceptional sauce-making skills. The dining room is cozy with rich wood-paneled walls, small vases of fresh flowers, candlelight and a fireplace. The admirable wine list provides a diverse selection of California and European producers, with moderate prices. *9634 Fair Oaks Boulevard, Fair Oaks; 916/965-1071; dinner Monday-Saturday; $$$*

EAST EUROPEAN

Cafe Marika The menu is exceedingly simple at humble Cafe Marika: about seven choices at lunch, six at dinner. The restaurant serves some of the most comforting food imaginable, such as lean pieces of pork simmered in a paprika sauce and served over rice, or skinless chicken thighs in a mild creamy paprika sauce served over homemade spaetzle. The owners, Eva and Louie, are from Prague, with Louie doing the cooking and Eva the serving. You won't go to Cafe Marika looking for cutting edge cuisine – what you get are consistent, satisfying, inexpensive meals, in a setting that is so intimate that you may even leave having gained some new friends. *2011 J Street, Sacramento; 916/442-0405; lunch Monday-Friday; dinner Thursday-Saturday; $$*

Little Prague Bohemian Restaurant Proprietors Eva and Vaclav Burger offer delicious housemade Czech specialties such as grilled, smoked pork chops, hunter-style beef goulash and chicken leek stew. Sausages come from Sacramento's Morant's, and Pilsner Urquell is on tap. Lunch features broader international selections that vary with the season. Be sure to sample some of the luscious desserts produced by the Farmer's Wife Bakery. The dining room offers cozy, pillow-strewn banquettes, small-paned windows and classical music. *330 G Street, Davis; 530/756-1107; breakfast, lunch and dinner daily, except brunch served weekends and restaurant closed Monday after 2:30 p.m.; $$$*

GREEK

Greek Village Inn A recent change in ownership has transformed the old Greek Village Inn into perhaps the best Greek restaurant in Sacramento. The menu is crammed with authentic dishes such as makaronada (imported macaroni with grilled eggplant, browned butter, mizithra cheese, roasted garlic and fresh herbs) and saganaki (kefalograviera cheese flamed at the table). The weekends feature breakfast through which you can satisfy your urge for feta, grilled eggplant, gyros meat and kalamata olives, accompanied by eggs and garlic potatoes. *65 University Avenue, Sacramento; 916/922-6334; lunch and dinner daily, breakfast Saturday and Sunday; $$*

Symposium Restaurant Perhaps the best testimonial to the excellence of this restaurant was its selection by Sacramento developer Angelo Tsakapoulos as the caterer for an event featuring the President of the United States. Since 1977 Symposium has been serving Davis residents a variety of Greek specialties, sweetbreads, fish dishes and salads. The restaurant also bakes an excellent pizza and has a full bar. *1620 E. 8th Street, Davis; 530/756-3850; lunch Monday-Friday, dinner Monday - Saturday; $$$; www.davis411.com/re/symposium/*

HAMBURGERS, HOT DOGS, PASTIES

Jim-Denny's Lunch Opened during the Depression, this 12-stool joint is worth a visit for nostalgia alone. The ancient pine paneling, burnished by age and decades of hamburger grease, has more character than a dozen fast food chains. The burgers sizzle before your eyes, and are constructed to the same specifications as those of original owner, Jim Van Nort. Former Lieutenant Governor and Assembly

Speaker Leo McCarthy liked the place so much he announced his candidacy for U.S. Senate here. *816 12th Street, Sacramento; 916/443-9655; breakfast and lunch, Monday-Friday; $*

Nationwide Meats Nationwide's French Steak Burger is the pinnacle of the burger maker's art. Father and son team Frank and John Gonzales hand-form a one-third pound patty of Harris Ranch beef, grill it, set it on a sturdy Muzio French roll and lay on the fresh lettuce, tomato, pickles, onions and secret sauce. An order of fries consists of a large potato that has been cut into fat wedges, deep fried, salted and served in wax paper. To top off the oversized experience, the salt shakers are simply 20-ounce salt boxes that have been perforated with an ice pick. Nationwide had to vacate their funky J Street location in 2001, but their new home on H Street has a lot more leg room. *1930 H Street, Sacramento; 916/444-3286; lunch and early dinner Monday-Saturday; $*

Pasty Shack Some people say that the Pasty Shack doesn't make pasties in the traditional British manner, which may be all for the best. The four varieties of pasties (Cornish, Bavarian, Chicken and Veggie and Mexican) have a light, flaky crust; and the fillings, such as the Cornish pasty's steak and potato, are seasoned just right. With only four tables, the Pasty Shack obviously cannot host big parties; and most patrons get their order "to go." *4746 J Street, Sacramento; 454-9630; lunch and early dinner Monday-Friday, lunch Saturday; $*

Squeeze Inn The Squeeze Inn smells of hot grease, is more cluttered than a used bookstore and would be a serious contender for the dive hall-of-fame. Although the inimitable original owner, Ken Noblett, recently retired and moved out of state, the new owners have kept the Squeeze's charms intact. The burger is among the large and sloppy variety, with a toothpick that barely keeps it assembled. The fresh-cut fries are among the best in the region. *7918 Fruitridge Road, Sacramento; 916/386-8599; lunch and early dinner, Monday-Saturday; $*

The Wienery The Wienery gets its dogs from Alpine Meats in Stockton. The dogs are 60 percent beef and 40 percent pork from high-grade trim, smoked over hardwood and contain no preservatives. You can have yours served in myriad combinations, from the Fiesta Dog (served open face with refried beans) to the Paisano Dog (served with Italian tomato sauce). Of course, you can also get a plain dog with traditional condiments. Soup, chili and salads are made from scratch; and the beer is served in a frosted mug. *715 56th Street (Elvas Shopping Center), Sacramento; 916/455-0497; lunch Tuesday-Saturday; $*

Wiener Works The folks at Wiener Works treat the hot dog with the kind of care that would make a German engineer proud. The dog is crafted to their specifications, then stuffed into a natural casing (like a sausage) and smoked over hickory and oak. The dog undergoes a proper beer steaming and is served in a fresh bun. Fries receive the same level of attention — unskinned russet potatoes sliced pencil thin, then deep-fried to perfection. Admirably, the portions reflect a Costco mentality. Ask for a "tiny" portion of fries and the basket that you receive will equal two "super-size" portions at the big chains. *5207 Madison Avenue, Citrus Heights; 916/334-8711; lunch daily, dinner Monday-Saturday; $*

Willie's Burgers and Chiliburgers Fast food is an art form in Los Angeles, and among L.A.'s oldest and most revered institutions is Tommy's Hamburgers.

Former L.A. resident Bill Taylor paid homage to Tommy's by opening Willie's in 1991. Compare Willie's chili cheeseburger (called The Slammer) to Tommy's and you may agree that Willie's has the superior chili. Just add a few yellow peppers, yank some paper towels from the wall dispenser and you are ready for the Willie's/Tommy's experience. Willie's is open until midnight, except on Friday and Saturday, when it stays open until after the bars close. *2415 16th Street, Sacramento; 916/444-2006; 823 Wales Drive, Folsom; 916/983-6755; lunch and dinner daily; $*

INDIAN

Kaveri Madras Cuisine Kaveri claims to be the only restaurant in the region that serves South Indian dishes such as dosas (crepes made with a variety of exotic flours and often stuffed with vegetable curry). The restaurant also offers the more common tandoori oven, curry and rice dishes found in North India. All dishes are prepared with care, and if you cannot settle on one item, Kaveri offers a $6-7 lunch buffet as well as an $11-12 multiple-course dinner. The restaurant is clean and simply appointed, with Indian tapestries and art gracing the walls. *1148 Fulton Avenue, Sacramento; 916/481-9970; lunch and dinner daily; $$*

ITALIAN

Biba Italian-born Biba Caggiano has written several cookbooks, hosted a cooking show on The Learning Channel and received honors from some of the most prestigious culinary institutions in the world. Unlike many celebrity chefs, she is talented not in flash and fad, but in simplicity and authenticity. The restaurant uses fine, imported Italian ingredients; makes the sausage, gnocchi, pasta and breads from scratch; and seeks out top-quality seafood, meats and poultry. Dishes that you may find on the menu — grilled rabbit tenderloins wrapped in pancetta; pasta with porcini mushrooms, sausage, tomato and cream; marinated and grilled pork loin with sausage, pancetta, roasted red peppers and fresh sage — will taste as good as they sound. Ms. Caggiano no longer spends much time at the stove, but she does oversee the entire operation and often finds time to chat with the customers. *2801 Capitol Avenue, Sacramento; 916/455-2422; lunch Monday-Friday, dinner Monday-Saturday; $$$$; biba-restaurant.com*

Club Pheasant This West Sacramento favorite has been serving up hearty Italian fare since 1935. The food isn't the world's greatest, although some  folks rave about the Pheasant's fried ravioli. The real appeal is the lively chatter, authentic character and no-nonsense manner of this bonafide institution. The wine list appropriately focuses on the cheap stuff, and a strong cocktail to start the meal almost goes without saying. *2525 Jefferson Boulevard, West Sacramento; 916/371-9530; lunch and dinner daily; $$*

Español Yes, Español is an Italian restaurant – the Spanish name comes from this eatery's beginnings as a Basque boarding house in Old Sacramento. Another remnant of that heritage is the family-style dinner, with several courses of simple, hearty food served to the entire table. At Español, the Italian entrées change nightly, providing each member of your party with from two to four selections. You don't have to order family style, but it is among the best values on the menu. *5723 Folsom Boulevard, Sacramento; 457-1936; lunch and dinner Tuesday-Sunday; $$*

Il Fornaio Il Fornaio in downtown Sacramento warrants a visit for the dining room alone. The soaring ceiling, classical arches, marble floors, crisp tablecloths, jacketed waiters and tall windows would be right at home in the most sophisticated city. But this is Sacramento, after all; and if you want to enjoy all this splendor on the cheap, go during lunch, order something from the bakery and grab a seat at the bar. To get the full treatment, make a reservation for a table in the dining room or in the airy, enclosed patio along the sidewalk. The sizable staff generally takes good care of the clientele, lavishing attention as well as a basket of crusty bread and extra virgin olive oil. The extensive menu features wood-fired brick oven pizzas, rotisserie chicken, various pastas, entrées and daily specials. Execution from the kitchen can be spotty (this is a very large restaurant) but generally is of very good quality. *400 Capitol Mall, Sacramento; 916/446-4100; lunch Monday-Friday, dinner nightly; 1179 Galleria Road (Roseville Galleria), Roseville; 916/728-1200; lunch and dinner daily; $$$; www.ilfornaio.com*

Paragary's Bar and Oven Randy Paragary opened the original Paragary's in midtown in 1983, introducing many Sacramentans to the wonders of the wood-fired oven, mesquite grill and extra virgin olive oil. Meals come with plenty of brick oven bread and sweet butter. Try a pizza from the wood-fired oven, or a pasta of hand-cut rosemary noodles with seared chicken and pancetta. The midtown location offers a lush courtyard with mature olive trees, three waterfalls and a river rock fireplace. *1401 28th Street, Sacramento; 916/457-5737; 2220 Gold Springs Court, Gold River; 916/852-0214; lunch Monday-Friday, dinner nightly; $$$; www.paragarys.com*

Piatti Piatti is a small restaurant chain that got its start in the late 1980s in the Napa Valley. The wine country influence shows in the crusty, country Italian bread; dipping oil spiked with balsamic vinegar, chili flakes and chopped garlic; mesquite-grilled meats; housemade pastas, wood-fired oven pizza; thoughtful wine list; Tuscan-rustic interior and lively dining room. *569 Pavilions Lane, Sacramento; 916/649-8885; 3003 Douglas Boulevard, Roseville; 916/786-5678; lunch and dinner daily, $$$; www.piatti.com*

JAPANESE

Aomi's Aomi's is a teppan-style restaurant, where a chef personally cooks for your table, à la Benihana. You sit on stools at a high table (maximum seating of eight), with much of the table occupied by a large griddle. Each member of the party orders an entrée, such as New York steak, lobster, salmon steak, scallops, shrimp or chicken. Then your chef takes over. Sporting white waiter's jackets and red toques, the chefs are personable and skilled, with the cooking demonstration punctuated by the clacking of the knife and spatula. Dinners include soup, salad, shrimp appetizers, seasonal vegetables, rice and green tea. Aomi's promises a fun evening and particularly is enjoyable with large parties. *2623 Fulton Avenue, Sacramento; 916/481-1850; lunch and dinner daily; $$$*

Edokko Noodle restaurants, where one can get cheap and gratifying bowls of soup, are the Japanese version of fast food. Edokko serves big, steaming bowls of udon and ramen, with various meats, seafood and vegetables, at fast food prices. Be warned – when the menu indicates "spicy," expect blistering. *358 Florin Road, Sacramento; 916/395-0632; 1724 Broadway, Sacramento; 916/448-2828; lunch and dinner, Monday-Saturday; $*

Hana Tsubaki A popular East Sacramento restaurant where the tables start filling up once the doors swing open. The square dining room exhibits the quiet elegance of Japanese design with its natural wood-paneled walls and back-lit rice-paper screens. The lunch special offers a stomach-filling value — miso soup, cucumber salad, steamed rice and an entrée (sometimes a combo) for less than $6. *5006 J Street, Sacramento; 916/456-2849; lunch Tuesday-Friday; dinner Tuesday-Saturday; $$*

Megami The line often extends to the door at lunchtime at Megami, but rest assured that you will be served quickly and you somehow will get a seat. Among the more dependable downtown lunch haunts, Megami cranks out big plates of char-broiled chicken teriyaki, crispy sesame chicken and spicy chicken yakiniku for about five bucks. Owner Alan Honda cheerfully oversees the operation — he estimates that he runs through about 80 chicken lunches per day. The small sushi bar offers good value and is the place to sit if you are really in a hurry. The restaurant gets pretty quiet in the evening hours and is a favorite hangout for Sacramento police officers. *1010 10th Street, Sacramento; 916/448-4512; lunch and dinner, Monday-Friday; $$*

Mikuni Mikuni's sushi bar is often jammed with diners enjoying the more than 200 traditional and original varieties of sushi, including "I can't believe I ate the whole thing" rolls with names like Japanese Burrito and Big Al. Mikuni recently unveiled perhaps the world's first sushi bus, which can be booked for a mobile sushi party. *4323 Hazel Avenue, Fair Oaks; 916/961-2112; lunch and dinner Monday-Saturday; 1565 Eureka Road, Roseville; 916/797-2112; lunch and dinner nightly; $$; www.mikunisushi.com*

Taka's Sushi Taka's cozy little Midtown location jams up quickly at the lunch and dinner hours for top quality sushi and well-prepared Japanese meals. Head chef Yutaka Watanabe is a former graphic designer who presents sushi with what he calls a California interpretation. With co-chef Benny they produce sushi like the Rodman roll, an albacore and cucumber roll dressed in a spicy cream sauce and with black, green and orange flying fish roes. The combination dinners are a good value at just $3 more than the single entrée prices. Taka's recently opened a Fair Oaks location that does not duplicate the intimate charm of the S Street location, but the new outlet does include a sports bar. *1730 S Street, Sacramento; 916/446-9628; 11773 Fair Oaks Boulevard, Fair Oaks; 916/961-2118; lunch Monday-Friday, dinner, Monday-Saturday; $$; www.takassushi.com*

MEXICAN

Centro Cocina Mexicana Centro meets its goal of emulating a high-end restaurant in Mexico City. Executive Chef Kurt Spataro spent months in Mexico studying regional cuisines with Diana Kennedy and came back ready to take

Sacramento beyond tacos and burritos. Consider the carne de res al chipotle, a generous hunk of beef pot roast that has been slowly braised, rubbed with chipotle salsa and served with white beans and roasted vegetables in a flavorful broth; or conchinita pibil from the Yucatan, pork slow-roasted in banana leaves. Tortilla chips fried to order and served with two fresh salsas are well worth the nominal charge. The chips go great with Centro's cocktail specialties. Try the Margarita Tradicionale, with Cuervo Tradicionale reposado, triple sec and lime juice shaken with ice and served in a martini glass. Cap the meal with one of Centro's many premium tequilas. *2730 J Street, Sacramento; 916/442-2552; lunch Monday-Friday, dinner daily; $$; www.paragarys.com/centro.html*

El Michoacano El Michoacano, which started out in a trailer, is one of Sacramento's best taquerias. In addition to the standard fillings for tacos, tostadas and burritos, El Michoacano offers cactus (nopalito) and brains (cabeza). The tender tamales make a popular dish for parties and one can put together an inexpensive dinner by ordering the prepared carnitas, carne asada and other items by the pound. *5681 Franklin Boulevard, Sacramento; 916/424-3975; lunch and dinner daily; $*

El Novillero It seems that every year or so El Novillero takes over another block on Franklin Boulevard so that the restaurant can provide enough parking for its customers. The specialty here is carnitas, served in many variations. The dish is served in a generous portions, with a deeply browned, crunchy exterior that is tender enough to cut with a fork. *4216 Franklin Boulevard, Sacramento; 916/456-4287; lunch and dinner, Monday-Saturday; $$*

Taco Loco Taqueria This Baja-style joint gets high marks for putting out tasty dishes from the grill at a reasonable price. The burritos come stuffed with your designated meat or vegetable filling, along with a mild salsa cruda, a satisfying meal for about four bucks. Kick up the calorie count for a couple additional dollars by ordering your burrito "enchilada style," which comes with red sauce, guacamole, sour cream and olives. There also is a notable veggie burrito, the Madre of all Veggies, which includes sautéed nopales, chile, corn and roasted peppers. *2326 J Street, Sacramento; 916/447-0711; 195 Blue Ravine Road, Folsom; 916/351-4303; lunch and dinner daily; $*

Texas Mexican Restaurant Downtown Sacramento's best Mexican meals are served at Griselda Barajas' Texas Mexican restaurant. Barajas' mother, Rosa Maria, formerly ran the excellent Aranda's and Tepatitlan restaurants and is now in the Texas kitchen. Virtually anything on the menu is a good bet. You'll love the fried rice and refried beans as well as the two homemade salsas. Expect a wait if you drop by during peak hours. *1114 8th Street, Sacramento; 916/443-2030; breakfast and lunch, Monday-Friday; $*

MORROCAN

Casablanca At Casablanca, the personable executive chef and owner, Mourhit

Drissi, standing in traditional Morrocan garb with slippers that curl up at the toe, will greet you and show you to your table. You will dine seated on cushions on the floor, or, if you prefer, on a low banquette. You will be eating a multi-course meal, with a delicious lentil soup, housemade anise bread, a seasonal selection of small salads (such as julienne beets in a pungent dressing and garbanzo beans dunked in a spicy sauce), a phyllo pie (finely chopped chicken, egg and almond), choice of entrée, housemade baklava, hot mint tea and a final sprinkle of flower water on your hands. No alcohol is served, though many diners bring in wine or beer for free corkage. *3516 Fair Oaks Boulevard, Sacramento; 916/979-1160; lunch Monday-Friday, dinner nightly; $$*

PIZZA

Giovanni's Sacramento has been without a good New York pizzeria since Vaccaro's shut down several years ago. The void thankfully was filled in mid-2001 when Giovanni's opened their doors. Giovanni's slides their pizza into a very hot oven, producing a crust with a nice crunchy shell. Choose among a variety of specialty toppings, including the Coney Island, topped with fresh water clams, garlic and spices. Giovanni's also offers an excellent Sicilian-style rotisserie chicken. Lunch specials include a generous personal-sized pizza and drink for under $5. The pizzeria has plenty of seating, a big screen television, and even a Pac-Man video game. *5924 South Land Park Drive, Sacramento; 916/393-7001; lunch and dinner daily; $*

Pieces This friendly Midtown joint has a Berkeley funkiness and very good pizza by the slice. One piece is almost a meal in itself, with the thin crust rolled at the outer end for a chewy finale. The dining room won't be mistaken for Wolfgang Puck's, but there is a comfortable couch, patio furniture and even a stack of childrens' books. *1309 21st Street, Sacramento; 916/441-1949; lunch and dinner daily; $*

Pizzeria Classico Pizzeria Classico not only makes good pizza, but also provides plenty of choices. First, you can choose among three types of crust (deep dish, original and stuffed). Then you can choose one of the specialties or designate your own from among the five sauces, seven meats, two types of seafood, eight vegetables, one fruit (pineapple) and one nut (macadamia). You must be patient for the deep dish and stuffed — they take a good half hour. The interior is among the classier pizza joints, with nice booths, wood paneling and clean carpeting. Decent wine is available by the glass or bottle, and there is a good selection of microbrews on draft. *702 Sutter Street, Folsom; 916/351-1430; lunch and dinner daily; $$*

Zelda's Zelda's specializes in Chicago-style, in-the-pan pizza, with a crust that has more in common with pie pastry than Italian bread. The wait here can be unforgiving during peak dinner hours. While you're waiting, enjoy a drink at the full bar or just soak up the atmosphere of Zelda's dark, gaudy interior, with its black and glittered cottage cheese ceiling and sparkling Christmas lights. Whatever your view of the crust, the pizza toppings merit high marks, particularly the robust sauce, perked up by the right touch of acidity. *1415 21st Street, Sacramento; 916/447-1400; lunch Monday-Friday; dinner nightly; $$*

SANDWICHES

Bob's Butcher Block "Glatt kosher" is the highest order of kosher supervision, and describes the products stocked by proprietors Bob and Shira Gittleman. The couple, who arrived from Scranton, Pennsylvania, in 1990, get their meats from New York, their corn rye from Los Angeles and their frozen New York pizza straight out of Broadway Jerusalem's Pizza Parlor in Manhattan. The place aims at the take–out crowd; drop by for a lean corned beef sandwich or grab some kosher chow "to go." *6436 Fair Oaks Boulevard (near Fair Oaks and Marconi), Carmichael; 916/482-6884*

Bud's Buffet Check out this popular downtown lunch spot for roast beef, roast pork and pastrami sandwiches. The meats are roasted on the premises and generously sliced to order. *1016 10th Street, Sacramento; 916/443-6905; lunch Monday-Saturday; $*

Hot Pastrami The Hot Pastrami possesses a fair amount of kitsch – a wall clock decorated with the labels of cheap beers, the 1960s Coke dispenser and the carrot cake with Cool Whip topping. In addition to the pastrami sandwiches (warm pastrami piled on a soft bun with no adornment), there are burgers and homemade chili and soup. Beer is served in an icy mug (a pitcher is under $5), and you won't find any microbrews here. *4321 Auburn Boulevard, Sacramento; 916/488-5670; lunch and early dinner, Monday-Saturday; $*

SOUTHEAST ASIAN

Hoa Viet Hoa Viet is the place to go for an inexpensive and satisfying bowl of pho (pronounced *fuh*), a hearty beef soup that the Vietnamese eat at any meal of the day. The soup comes in three sizes, a steaming bowlful of beef broth scented with star anise, with thin slices of beef, long rice noodles and yellow and green onions, served with a platter of fresh basil, bean sprouts, lime wedges, jalapeño and saw-leaf herb. Hoa Viet also handles other Vietnamese dishes with skill, such as the rice noodles with char-broiled pork and shrimp, and Chinese broccoli with just a whisper of oyster sauce. *6645 Stockton Boulevard, Sacramento; 916/399-1688; 1827 Broadway, Sacramento; 916/443-7888; 3110 Bradshaw Road, Sacramento; 916/361-3888; 305 Ist Street, Davis; 530/759-9888; late breakfast, lunch and dinner daily; $*

Lemon Grass Restaurant Lemon Grass owner Mai Pham grew up in Vietnam and Thailand. With Lemon Grass, she has brought to Sacramento the cuisine of both countries, inspired by the recipes of her mother and grandmother. Among the signature dishes are the refreshing salad rolls (shrimp, pork, mint and lettuce wrapped in rice paper and served with a black bean dipping sauce); Thai green curry, with bits of chicken, bamboo shoots, tomatoes and peas simmered in a rich coconut curry sauce; and salmon sanuk, a grilled fillet with a spicy Thai basil glaze. The setting and presentation are stylishly contemporary. *601 Munroe Street, Sacramento; 916/486-4891; lunch Monday-Friday, dinner nightly; $$*

Thai Basil Thai Basil is a sparkling, professionally run restaurant that serves delightfully fresh and satisfying Thai cuisine. The menu offers a good selection of grilled, wok, curry, noodle and rice dishes. Try gai yang takrai (grilled chicken breasts marinated with lemon grass herbs and served with a spicy lime sauce) or pad prik king (fresh green beans sauteed in spicy ginger curry sauce). The Laguna location is convenient to the nearby cinema. *8785 Center Parkway, Suite B-120, Laguna; 916/681-THAI; lunch Tuesday-Friday, dinner Tuesday-Sunday; 1613 Douglas Boulevard, Roseville; 916/782-THAI; lunch Monday-Friday, dinner nightly; $$*

Viet Ha What Viet Ha lacks in decor it makes up by delivering authentic Vietnamese dishes. You cannot go wrong with any of the charbroiled or grilled selections. All the refreshing, contrasting flavors and textures of Vietnamese food come together in Bun thit nuong: marinated char-broiled slices of pork served over cool rice noodles with cilantro, fried shallots, lettuce, cucumber, chili garlic sauce, crushed peanuts, bean sprouts and a tangy dipping sauce. The dish is served up in minutes and costs less than $5. The menu offers Chinese dishes as well, along with a host of beverages such as salted lemon and club soda, or red bean and coconut juice with young coconut meat. *6534 Florin Road (one block east of Stockton Boulevard), Sacramento; 916/424-5685; lunch and dinner daily; $*

SPANISH

Tapa the World Tapas ostensibly originated from the Spanish cafe practice of covering glasses of wine with bread slices to protect the wine from, as the menu delicately puts it, "airborne objects." Whatever the history, the appetizer-sized tapas are a great way for diners to share a variety of dishes before or after a night on the town. Check out the tortilla española, a slightly chilled potato/egg omelet served in a thick wedge. Higher up on the price scale is juicy sautéed rock shrimp with garlic, wine and parsley, or calamari with alli-oli. The menu features both authentic and creative takes on Spanish cuisine, and offers a refreshingly fruity sangria by the glass, pint or pitcher. There also is an excellent selection of Spanish wine by the glass. The restaurant often is jammed at peak hours, ringing with the sound of conversation and live Spanish guitar. *2115 J Street, Sacramento; 916/442-4353; lunch and dinner daily; $$*

STEAK/PRIME RIB

Buckhorn Steak and Roadhouse Owners John and Melanie Pickerel have taken heroic measures with their Certified Angus Beef, from dry aging 21-days for optimal flavor, to using their own butchers to select the finest cuts, to searing the steaks in a special infrared broiler that reaches temperatures of 1500 degrees

Farenheit. Try the Taylor Cut, top sirloin wrapped in apple wood smoked bacon. Adding to the restaurant's appeal is its location in a century-old hotel building at the edge of Winters' historic main street. *2 Main Street (corner of Railroad and Main), Winters; 530/795-4503; dinner nightly; $$$; www.buckhornsteakhouse.com*

Morton's of Chicago Most steakhouses are heavy on testosterone, but no other seems quite as masculine as Morton's of Chicago. The place feels like a men's club, with rich wood paneling, sports-theme prints and wooden wine lockers with brass nameplates. Morton's goes all out to provide a grand steakhouse experience, with your waiter showing you cuts of the finest quality beef and seafood before taking your order. Portions would delight an NFL linebacker (the porterhouse weighs in at close to two pounds), and, if that were not enough, many dishes are embellished with a French sauce of one sort or another. All of this comes at a price, of course, with steaks hovering around the $30 mark — baked potato costs extra. *521 L Street (at Downtown Plaza), Sacramento; 916/442-5091; dinner nightly; $$$$; www.mortons.com*

VEGETARIAN

Sunflower Drive-In Sunflower Drive-In is a viable alternative to the fast food trinity of beef, grease and salt. Here you can indulge guiltlessly in a tasty nutburger that is among the best in the region, served hot off the griddle on a soft wheat bun. Wash it down with a fresh fruit smoothie or a real milkshake. The Sunflower boasts just one indoor table and a couple of tables al fresco. *10344 Fair Oaks Boulevard, Fair Oaks; 916/967-4331; lunch daily, dinner Tuesday-Saturday, early dinner Sunday and Monday; $*

BAKERIES

Ciocolat Ciocolat's owner and pastry chef, Marylou Hedriana, used to be a researcher on small- and mid-cap stocks for Manhattan banks. Lucky for the rest of us, she now creates some of the most delectable and sensual desserts in the region. Stop by the cozy bungalow across from Davis' Central Park to grab a cup of the sublime Torrefazione Italia coffee and contemplate Ciocolat's many ways to blow your diet. The case displays eye-pleasing geometry and color, with the individual-portioned desserts shaped in pyramids, domes, cylinders and squares. Top-quality ingredients – chocolates, liqueurs, butter and fruit shine through the breakfast pastries, cakes, tarts, crème brulée and truffles. *310 B Street, Davis; 530/753-3088*

The Cookie Company The Cookie Company bakes first-rate cookies from scratch. These large and chewy cookies also make for an impressive gift. *710 Main Street, Woodland; 530/662-7920*

Ettore's Proprietor Ettore Ravazzolo produces a wide range of treats, including scones with a rich and crumbly texture, grand cinnamon rolls, impressive cakes and housemade truffles. The sparkling cafe is a popular spot on Fair Oaks Boulevard's gourmet gulch. *2376 Fair Oaks Boulevard, Sacramento; 916/482-0708*

The Farmer's Wife Nestled within the Little Prague Bohemian Restaurant in Davis, The Farmer's Wife turns out delightful pastries, cakes, muffins, breads and cookies. Check out the flaky and buttery croissants, the gratifyingly traditional sacher torte and the Czech crêpe filled with berries and melted chocolate. *330 G Street, Davis; 530/756-1107*

Freeport Bakery Bavarian native Walter Goetzeler comes from a long line of bakers, and Sacramentans are the lucky beneficiaries of all those generations of know-how. Specialties include rustic breadsticks (a crusty herb bread sprinkled with caraway seeds and salt), seasonal cakes (such as the pumpkin cheesecake for Thanksgiving and the chocolate Yule log during December) and all of the pastries. Walter's spouse, Marlene, manages the business side of the enterprise, helps refine the recipes and oversees Freeport's artistic style and courteous staff. Year in and year out, this is the top bakery in Sacramento. *2966 Freeport Boulevard, Sacramento; 916/442-4256; www.freeportbakery.com*

Il Fornaio Panetteria Il Fornaio has the benefit of a wood-fired oven, which gives its breads crunchy crusts and chewy texture. Though you can get Il Fornaio breads at many grocery stores, the freshness seems to be a notch higher at the bakery. Try the ciabatta, a long flat loaf that is good for sopping up extra-virgin olive oil. *400 Capitol Mall, Sacramento; 916/446-9694; www.ilfornaio.com*

Konditerei Konditerei is a wonderful Austrian bakery that produces cakes, cookies and pastries that are notable for their fine appearance and flavor. Try the zwetschgenfleck (plum cake), palatschinken (crêpes with seasonal fruit) or topfen strudel (strudel with European-style cottage cheese). The bakery, which moved in July 2001 to a beautiful and spacious location in East Davis, also features vegetable quiches and small pizzas. *2710 E. 5th Street, Davis; 530/738-1331*

La Mexicana This market provides an extensive selection of Mexican canned goods, spices and cheeses, as well as a great assortment of colorful piñatas. The most dominant feature, however, is the glass cases of Mexican pan dulce baked right here — pieces of cake with frosting, large cookies dusted with sugar, round sweet rolls and custard-filled pastries. As is the practice in bakeries in Mexico, just pick up a tray and a pair of tongs, grab your selections and take them to the register. You'll leave with a big bag full of treats and leave behind very little cash. *5550 Franklin Boulevard, Sacramento; 916/457-9506*

Muffins Etc. Upwards of 15 types of muffins are offered at Muffins Etc., though the bakery also excels with the cinnamon rolls with orange icing. *5635 H Street, Sacramento; 916/452-1829*

Tivoli Gardens The difference between Tivoli Garden and the hundreds of less-accomplished bakeries that make Danish-style cakes and cookies can be summed up in one word – butter. Tivoli Garden embraces butter with Northern European ardor, and the treats are assembled with Scandinavian meticulousness. *10131 Fair Oaks Boulevard, Fair Oaks; 916/863-1765*

Village Bakery Baker/owner Aziz Fattahi is dedicated to artisanal French bread-making methods. He uses organic flours, employs natural yeast, allows a slow fermentation process and bakes many items in a brick oven. His efforts are rewarded with the excellent flavor and texture of his loaves. Also worthwhile are the brick oven pizza slices served at lunch and the massive berry-cheese danish. *814 2nd Street, Davis; 530/750-2255*

COFFEEHOUSES

Boulevard Coffee Company Boulevard is an old-timer in the modern coffee roasting era, having opened its first shop in an unlikely suburban location back in 1983. Boulevard emphasizes freshness and quality, and many believe these to be the finest beans in the region. *5901 Fair Oaks Boulevard, Carmichael; 916/972-8967; 7901 Fair Oaks Boulevard, Carmichael; 916/944-0286*

Cafe Melange With its great corner location and imaginative clock tower, Cafe Melange has been a Curtis Park landmark since 1994. The cafe offers the same baked goods as New Helvetia Roasters and Bakers (the owners were former partners), as well as a good selection of salads and entrées. *2700 24th Street, Sacramento; 916/451-2312*

Capitol Garage Coffee Co. This coffeehouse actually was a garage at one time, doing smog checks and tune-ups. Now folks working near the State Capitol tune up their energy level with Capitol Garage's fine coffee and loose-leaf teas. The Capitol Garage also offers lots of beer on tap ($2 pints during happy hour, 4 p.m. - 7 p.m.). Capitol Garage attracts a cutting-edge crowd in the evening for live music. *1427 L Street, Sacramento; 916/444-3633*

Java City Java City started at the corner of 18th Street and Capitol Avenue in 1985, and now there are dozens of locations in many states. The original location is one of the best in the chain, with the shade of a huge camphor tree and a lively midtown corner. *1800 Capitol Avenue, Sacramento; 916/444-5282; www.javacity.com*

New Helvetia Roasters and Bakers New Helvetia gets big style points for locating in an 1893 firehouse, with the firehouse theme emphasized throughout (such as a dalmatian mascot, ladders and fire hats). The business has not thrived on style alone, however. The fresh-roasted coffee can compete with the best in town, and the tempting selection of baked goods (particularly the scones with devonshire cream) is many steps ahead of the competition. *1215 19th Street, Sacramento; 916/441-1106*

Peets Coffee and Tea This estimable Berkeley-based roaster, established in 1966, is known for serving a rich, high-octane cup of joe, brewed just below espresso strength. Try the dark-roasted Major Dickason's Blend, and don't ignore Peets' excellent selection of teas. *1411 W. Covell Boulevard, Davis; 530/750-7085; 2580 Fair Oaks Boulevard, Sacramento; 916/485-7887; www.peets.com*

Plantation Coffee Roasters Located in the small historic commercial area of Elk Grove, Plantation roasts a special blend of espresso beans daily, producing an outstanding cup of coffee. *9072 Elk Grove Boulevard, Elk Grove; 916/686-2633; www.plantationroasters.com*

Weatherstone Coffee and Trading Company Weatherstone's coffeehouse history goes back to the 1970s, making this the oldest coffeehouse in the city. Java City purchased the business in the late 1980s, cleaned up the old 1920s building, added a brick courtyard and transformed the disheveled coffeehouse into a neighborly place to hang out. *812 21st Street, Sacramento; 916/443-6340*

FARMERS' MARKETS

SUNDAY

State Parking Lot This popular weekly market is billed as Northern California's largest, with more than 80 vendors. There are good bargains and lots of produce, flowers, ethnic specialties, baked goods, fresh fish and poultry. *8th and W Streets (under freeway), Sacramento, 8 a.m. - noon, year-round*

TUESDAY

Country Club Plaza This well-stocked market offers convenient parking before the shops get too busy at Country Club Plaza. Convenient parking distinguishes this market. *El Camino and Watt (Butano Drive behind Macy's), 8:30 a.m. - 11:30 a.m., year-round*

Roosevelt Park This market is frequented by the state employees housed nearby. On-street parking and picnic tables are scarce. *9th and P Streets, Sacramento, 9:30 a.m. - 1:30 p.m., May - October*

Woodland County Fair Mall has an expansive farmers' market. *East Gibson Road and East Streets, Woodland, 5 p.m. - 8 p.m., May - October*

WEDNESDAY

César Chavez Plaza Popular with downtown workers and residents, this market has parking available in two garages adjacent to the park. Lots of food vendors and live music make an attractive lunchtime destination. *10th and J Streets, Sacramento, 10 a.m. - 2 p.m., May - November*

Davis This market has strong community support and best-quality goods. Organic produce, Village Bakery breads, local cheeses and Aidell's sausages are some of the regular features. Live acoustic music and tables promoting various community causes underscore the small-town atmosphere. The nearby playgrounds and foot-pedaled carousel appeal to kids. *4th and C Streets, Davis, April – September 4:30 p.m. – 8:30 p.m., October – March 2 p.m – 6 p.m.*

THURSDAY

Florin Mall Lots of Asian produce is available at this market. *Florin Road (two blocks east of Highway 99, in front of Sears) Sacramento, 8 a.m. - 11:30 a.m., year-round*

Dixon Dixon has a market right downtown. *105 E. C Street, Dixon, 4 p.m. - 8 p.m., April - November*

Garcia Bend Park This market features a breezy riverfront location, with playgrounds and picnic tables. *Sacramento River at Pocket Road (two miles from Pocket Road exit off Interstate 5), Sacramento, 4 p.m. - 8 p.m., June - September*

Downtown Lodi A farmers' market operates in Lodi's charming downtown. *School Street, between Pine and Walnut, Lodi, 5:30 p.m. - 8:30 p.m., June - October*

FRIDAY

Downtown Plaza This market is handy for shoppers of Old Sacramento and Downtown Plaza. *5th and K Streets (next to Macy's), Sacramento, 10 a.m. - 2 p.m., May - October*

SATURDAY

Davis (see listing under Wednesday). *8 a.m. - noon, year-round*

Country Club Plaza (see listing under Tuesday). *8 a.m. - noon, year-round*

Sunrise Mall This market is large, featuring a good selection of produce, seafood, flowers and baked goods. *Sunrise Boulevard (behind Sears Auto), 8 a.m. - noon, year-round*

Woodland County Fair Mall has an expansive farmers' market. *East Gibson Road and East Streets, Woodland, 9 a.m. - noon, May - October*

ICE CREAM/FREEZES

Gunther's Ice Cream Gunther's impressive neon sign has beckoned Sacramentans since the 1940s. The shop makes a wide assortment of ice cream (swiss orange chip is particularly tasty), fruit freezes, sundaes, sandwiches and novelties. Gunther's fruit freeze also is available at several locations around Sacramento. *2801 Franklin Boulevard, Sacramento; 916/457-6646*

Merlino's Orange Freeze Merlino's has been producing the quintessential Sacramento summer treat since 1946. Governor Ronald Reagan would stop by the original Stockton Boulevard location (see page 4) to grab one of the delicious freezes, made from fresh fruit juice. The standard flavors are orange, lemon, pineapple or strawberry, with seasonal flavors such as raspberry and black cherry. Ambitious expansion plans tragically led to bankruptcy for the company in 2000, and the famous freezes dried up for eight months. A local investor group has revived the enterprise, with the Merlino family running the operation. *3200 Folsom Boulevard, Sacramento; 916/731-4000*

Rainbow Fruit Bars In the rear of Los Jarritos' dining room you can peer through a big window and watch the making of *paletas*, the Mexican frozen fruit bars often sold from carts. The workers pour the mixture for each flavor into molds, allow the molds to quickly freeze in an ice-cold trough, and then poke wooden sticks into the center of each bar. Rainbow cranks out a wide array of flavors, including some less common selections such as hibiscus, tamarind/chile and walnut. You can buy by the single or by the dozen. *2509 Broadway, Sacramento; 916/455-7911*

Vic's Ice Cream Vic's has been a family-owned, Land Park institution since 1947. For some, Vic's is as much a symbol of Sacramento as the State Capitol Building. The ice cream is made on the premises (Jim Bunnell, who died in 1995, was Vic's ice cream maker for 43 years). The old-fashioned soda fountain, staffed by clean-cut young people, offers grilled sandwiches, soups and the classic ice cream concoctions. *3199 Riverside Boulevard, Sacramento; 916/448-0892*

MARKETS

Corti Brothers Corti Brothers has been the king of Sacramento's specialty grocers since 1947. Here you will find a deli counter stuffed with a vast assortment of cheeses and meats, a meat counter teaming with knowledgeable butchers, and shelves stocked with hard-to-find items such as fresh rabbit, quail, salted cod, salt-packed anchovies, truffles and an international assortment of wines and spirits. Darrell Corti, son of the founder Frank Corti, is a world-renowned food and wine expert. Corti himself, Donal Smith or others of the highly competent wine staff will patiently work with you so that you will go home with just the right bottle. Simply put, Corti Brothers is the best gourmet supermarket in Sacramento. *5810 Folsom Boulevard, Sacramento; 916/736-3800*

David Berkley Fine Wines and Deli This small shop does justice to its location in the tony Pavilions shopping center. Berkley, a former acolyte of Darrell Corti, has a keen eye for the good stuff, such as free-range eggs from Aitken Farms in Lincoln, French wines imported by Kermit Lynch, highly coveted California wines and perfect local organic produce. The deli features a great selection of cheeses, meats, salads and prepared entrées, making David Berkley a great place to put together a fancy picnic lunch or dinner-to-go. *515 Pavilions Lane, Sacramento; 916/929-4422; www.dberkley.com*

Davis Food Co-op The Davis Co-op is a well-run market with a strong following. You needn't be a member to shop here, although you will pay slightly more for the privilege. There is a strong selection of organic produce, bakery items, wines and cheeses, as well as an extensive butcher counter that features — and this is a rarity among co-ops — red meat. *620 G Street, Davis; 530/758-2667*

East West Market and Deli A very good resource for foods originating in India and the Middle East. The butcher can provide you with your choice of fresh cuts of chicken, lamb or goat. Bags of beans, legumes, rice and grains fill the shelves, along with exotic sauces, spices, condiments and candies. A number of the meat products are prepared in accordance with Islamic dietary law, and various books on Islam are available. *4411 47th Avenue, Sacramento; 916/421-4442*

Italian Importing Co. Luigi Velo operates three Italian markets. The J Street location is the most old-fashioned, a small shop packed with a good selection of Italian groceries and deli items. The roast turkey sandwich on Wednesday is worth a special trip. The Folsom Boulevard location is a full-scale grocery store, with produce, frozen foods and a good-sized deli. The Old Sacramento location is the smallest of the three stores but is handy if you happen to be in the neighborhood. *1827 J Street, Sacramento; 916/442-6678; 5030 Folsom Boulevard, Sacramento; 916/452-6974; 1100 Front Street, Old Sacramento; 916/443-6046*

Morant's Sausages Dirk Mueller passed a rigorous, five-year training course in Germany to become a certified master of the sausage-making craft. Morant's is widely acknowledged to be the best German sausage available in the metro area. The shop also stocks a variety of German food products, and gets a regular delivery of fresh German rolls and pretzels. *5001 Franklin Boulevard, Sacramento; 916/731-4377*

Nugget Market This Woodland-based market has been aiming their newer stores toward a high-end clientele. Both Davis locations, particularly the store on East Covell Boulevard, offer a great international and California wine selection. The produce also is exceptional, with lots of organic and exotic choices. *1414 E. Covell Boulevard, Davis; 530/750-3800; 409 Mace Boulevard, Davis; 530/753-6690*

Oto's Japan Food Oto's has the most complete selection of Japanese food products in the Sacramento region. Come here for an impressive variety of sake, rice and condiments. The deli offers a variety of sashimi-grade fish and pickled salads. *5770 Freeport Boulevard, Sacramento; 916/424-2398*

Sacramento Natural Foods Co-op Upon entering the SNFC, it is easy to discover why this market is one of the five largest co-ops in the United States: the store is clean, well-stocked and professionally managed. Here you find one of the best selections of organic produce in the region; a popular deli featuring plenty of organic and vegan salads; a tremendous selection of bulk foods, spices and herbs as well as a tempting array of fresh poultry and seafood. You don't need to be a member to shop here, although members get at least a five percent discount. *1900 Alhambra Boulevard, Sacramento; 916/455-2667; www.sacfoodcoop.com*

Taylor's Market Taylor's has been a corner grocery since 1962, and has emerged as the area's best gourmet market of its size. Ed Schell, the semi-retired dean of Taylor's' fine butcher shop, abandons the golf course to pitch in during busy holiday periods, when the store is jammed with shoppers looking for a free-range turkey, prime rib roast or Niman Ranch lamb. Taylor's claims to be the only Sacramento butcher shop that still breaks down beef piece-by-piece, and Sam, Jim and the other butchers will patiently take care of your needs. Ed's son Kevin manages the grocery, over-seeing a continual expansion of gourmet items on Taylor's' gleaming stainless steel shelves. Kevin has carefully select-ed a large array of wines, and he gener-ously provides a 10 percent discount on six bottles or more. The employees are all friendly and energetic, and the store still offers home delivery to the elderly. *2900 Freeport Boulevard, Sacramento; 916/443-6881; www.taylorsmarket.com*

Trader Joe's Trader Joe's is a Pasadena-based chain offering gourmet items at budget prices. European-style butter, Italian arborio rice, organic breakfast cere-als, premium vinegar and Valrhona chocolate costs nearly half of what you would pay elsewhere. Quality is high, even with frozen and canned foods. Trader Joe's sometimes finds extraordinary deals that they pass on to the cus-tomer, such as 750 ml of Johnny Walker liqueur made with 12-year-old scotch for just $5.99. *2625 Marconi Avenue (at Fulton Avenue), Sacramento; 916/481-8797; 1117 Douglas Boulevard (at Harding Avenue), Roseville; 916/784-9084; 5309 Sunrise Boulevard (at Madison Avenue), Fair Oaks; 916/863-1744; www.traderjoes.com*

Vinh Phat Market A Stockton Boulevard treasure since 1984, Vinh Phat is one of Sacramento's best stocked sources for Asian food products, particularly those originating in Vietnam, China and Thailand. The long, spotlessly clean aisles are well marked with signs in English, Vietnamese and Chinese. Shelves contain a prodigious assortment of sauces, noodles, condiments, teas, canned goods and confections. Vinh Phat also offers live frogs, turtles, sturgeon, catfish, lobsters, snails, clams and oysters. *6105 Stockton Boulevard, Sacramento; 916/424-8613*

TOBACCO

Casillas Cigars The men at Casillas patiently roll cigars in the front of the shop. Go into the large walk-in humidor to make your selection and take it to the front counter. The prices compare very favorably with those of factory-made cigars, and Casillas often throws in a free stogie with your purchase. *2201 16th Street, Sacramento; 916/442-4554; home.earthlink.net/~mhineline/casillas.html*

El Embargo Cigar Factory El Embargo sells hand-rolled cigars produced by Cuban emigres in the Garcia y Vega shop on the K Street mall. *725 K Street, Sacramento; 916/447-0804; www.elembargo.com*

Hardwick's Briar Shoppe After making a selection from Hardwick's expan-sive humidor, feel free to light up, recline in one of Hardwick's easy chairs and watch the world go by in Old Sacramento. *1115 Front Street, Sacramento; 916/498-0450*

Tower Pipes and Cigars Tower has been around since 1967, run by father and son John and Mark Just. The shop provides an extensive variety of premium cigars and pipe tobaccos at the base of the Tower Theater. *2518 Land Park Drive, Sacramento; 916/443-8466; www.towercigars.com*

WINE

Beverages & More This large chain boasts the most extensive selection of wines in the region, as well as a wide selection of beer, spirits, cigars, chocolate and specialty foods. Prices can be good but real bargains are rare. *3106 Arden Way, Sacramento; 916/481-8657; 7929 Greenback Lane, Citrus Heights; 916/728-4204; www.bevmo.com*

Capitol Cellars Capitol Cellars specializes in high-end California producers such as Ridge, Lokoya, Harlan and Opus One. The shop also carries hard-to-find magnums and splits. The fancy selection and prices reflect the upmarket Gold River location. *2220 Gold Springs Ct # 106, Gold River, 916/853-3030; www.capitolcellars.com*

Corti Brothers See listing under Markets.

Cost Plus World Market Cost Plus has been building up their wine selection and variety over the past several years, making this one of the area's best places to pick up a bottle. The pricing is attractive, although Cost Plus does not offer volume discounts. *1828 Howe Avenue, Sacramento; 916/929-0220*

David Berkeley See listing under Markets.

Nugget Market See listing under Markets.

Taylor's Market See listing under Markets.

Wine Merchant Wine Merchant provides a solid selection of wines from around the world. The Folsom shop also offers a 10 percent case discount, even on mixed cases. *307 Iron Point Road, Folsom; 916/985-9463; www.bandbwinemerchants.com*

WINE COUNTRY TOURING

Dozens of premium wineries are located in or near the Sacramento Valley, with the wines prized for their quality and value. Wine making has been an important part of the Valley's culture since miners planted the first vineyards during the Gold Rush. All of the following regions are within one hour of Sacramento.

Amador County Amador County, located in the Sierra Foothills approximately 45 miles from Sacramento, features historic Gold Rush towns and a venerable wine-making history. Most of Amador County's wineries are located in the picturesque Shenandoah Valley. The area's gentle rolling hills, gnarled oak trees and unpretentious wineries make for a perfect day trip or weekend getaway. A brochure listing wineries, lodgings and restaurants is available at the wineries or

from the **Amador County Chamber of Commerce** (*800/649-4988,
www.amadorcountychamber.com*). Amador County winemakers welcome visitors
with open arms, and even provide crayons and coloring books for the kids. **Story
Winery** (10525 Bell Road, Plymouth; 209/245-6208; www.zin.com), owned and
operated by the friendly Jan and Bruce Tichenor, features a rustic tasting room
with a picnic area overlooking the Cosumnes River Canyon. Story's Picnic Hill
Zinfandel, produced from the ancient, unirrigated hillside vines adjacent to the
picnic area, offers intense flavors of anise, chocolate and berry.
Renwood/Santino Winery (12225 Steiner Road, Plymouth; 209/245-6979;
www.renwood.com) often receives top marks in wine media for a line of deeply
extracted, single-vineyard Zinfandels that manage to combine finesse with a high
alcohol content. **Domaine de la Terre Rouge/Easton** (10801 Dickson Road,
Plymouth; 209/245-3117) is one of the state's top producers of Rhone varietals
and Zinfandel. Check out the Syrah, the Noir (a complex and spicy blend of
Grenache, Mourvedre and Syrah), the Vin Gris d' Amador (a delicious,
Provencale-style dry rose) and any of the top-notch Zinfandel bottlings. **Sobon
Estate** (14430 Shenandoah Road, Plymouth; 209/245-6554;
www.sobonwine.com) is located in one of California's oldest wineries, founded

by the Uhlinger family of Switzerland
in 1856. This historic landmark produces a range of fine Zinfandels, particularly the Lubenko Vineyard old-vine,
hillside grapes bottled unfined and unfiltered. While at Sobon, check out the
Shenandoah Valley Museum, which
chronicles the history of the region and
includes the original 1856 cellar. The
Sobon family also operates
Shenandoah Vineyards (12300 Steiner
Road. Plymouth; 209/245-4455; www.sobonwine.com), which produces a very
reliable everyday Zinfandel as well as delicious and inexpensive Muscat. In addition to wine, food lovers should seek out the following Amador County establish-
ments: **Susan's Place** (15 Eureka Street, Sutter Creek; 209/267-0945), which
features attractive cheese and fruit platters as well as dozens of Sierra Foothill
wines; **Imperial Hotel** (14202 Highway 49, Amador City; 209/267-9172,
800/242-5594), offering a fine dining experience in the hotel's 1879 dining room,
perfect for a romantic dinner; **Giannini's** (Highway 88, Pine Grove; 209/296-
7222), a popular Italian restaurant that stands out for its warm, family atmosphere
and robust cooking; **Cafe Max** (Historic Main Street, Jackson; 209/223-0174), a
Swiss bakery that uses an 1865 brick oven and produces cream pastries, fruit tarts
and hearth-baked breads; **Sutter Creek Coffee Roasting Company** (20 Eureka
Street, Sutter Creek; 209/267-5550), which produces a top-quality cup of coffee
by roasting the beans in small batches; and **Swingle's Meat Co.** (12540 Kennedy
Flat Road, Jackson; 209/223-0731), where brothers Dick, Bill and Tom Swingle
produce gourmet-quality specialties such as marinated short ribs, smoked hams
and bacons, fancy sausages, deer salami and more. *To get to Amador County wine
country from Sacramento, take U.S. 50 East to the Howe Avenue/Power Inn Road exit.
Turn right and then turn left at the first stoplight. Take Highway 16 East to Highway 49
and follow the signs to Plymouth and the Shenandoah Valley. www.amadorwine.com*

El Dorado County El Dorado County steadily has gained esteem for its mountain-grown wines. Most of the county's wineries are centered around the Apple Hill area just east of Placerville and in the Fairplay region northeast of Amador County's Shenandoah Valley. Bucolic farms, vineyards and orchards are scattered across the rolling hills and mountains of this scenic county. A brochure on El Dorado County wineries is available at the wineries or call the El Dorado Winery Association at 800/306-3956. **Boeger Winery** (1709 Carson Road, Placerville; 530/622-8094; www.boegerwinery.com) is among El Dorado County's most accomplished producers. Greg Boeger, grandson of one of Napa Valley's earliest winemakers, pioneered the modern wine boom in these foothills back in 1972.

The tasting room is located in the historic stone wine cellar of the original 1870s Fossati-Lombardo winery. Boeger focuses on red wines, providing bottlings of Cabernet, Merlot, Barbera and Zinfandel. The winery also produces blends based on Bordeaux, Rhone, Italian and Spanish varietals. **Granite Springs Winery** (5050 Granite Springs Winery Road, Somerset; 530/620-6395) planted their grapes  along a granite hillside, and the peppery, full-bodied Petite Sirah is one of the best produced in the Sierra Foothills. **Sierra Vista Winery & Vineyard** (4560 Cabernet Way, Placerville; 530/622-7221; www.sierravistawinery.com) offers an inspiring mountain view from its tasting room and picnic area at the 2,900-foot elevation. John and Barbara MacCready have been making wine here for more than 20 years and were among the first to plant Rhone varietals in the foothills. Check out Sierra Vista's high-value, distinctive Rhone blends: Fleur de Montagne, Lynelle and Belle Rose. While in El Dorado's wine country, you should take advantage of the farms and produce stands selling stone fruits, apples, pears, persimmons or whatever else may be in season, particularly **Tomary Heirloom Tomatoes** (1589 Pleasant Valley Road, 2.5 miles east of Diamond Springs; 916/622-8551). Dining choices include **Zachary Jacques** (1821 Pleasant Valley Road, Placerville; 530/626-8045), a Provencale dinner house that features roasted free-range chicken with garlic and herbs, mixed seafood in a saffron garlic broth with aioli, and roast loin of red deer with a red wine sauce; and **Lil' Mama D. Carlos** (482 Main Street, Placerville; 530/626-1612), an Italian family-style restaurant featuring hearty food and large portions. *To get to El Dorado County wineries from Sacramento, take U.S. 50 East to either the Schnell School Road or Cedar Grove exits and follow the signs to the wineries. www.eldoradowines.org*

Clarksburg Clarksburg is the center of the Delta wine industry. The largest and best-known winery is **Bogle Vineyards and Winery** (37783 Road 144, Clarksburg; 916/744-1139; www.boglewinery.com). Bogle has been growing grapes near Clarksburg since 1968, and today the winery produces 100,000 cases annually and sells in 40 states. Driving on Road 144 toward the winery you will pass by shady Delta inlets, backwoods homes and rows of vines. The winery produces several varietals, with Chenin Blanc and old vine Zinfandel among the best bets. Critics regularly praise Bogle wines for their quality and value. Visitors are welcome in Bogle's recently constructed tasting room and picnic area – pack some food and make it an outing. *To get to Bogle Vineyards and Winery from Sacramento, take Interstate 5 south to the Freeport/Pocket Road exit. Go east over the freeway and turn right on Freeport Boulevard (Highway 160). Go through the town of Freeport, turn right to cross the drawbridge, then turn*

left on South River Road. Travel four miles, then turn right onto Road 141. When the road splits, take the route on the left, which is Road 144. clarksburgwinegrowers.com

Dunnigan Hills Getting to Dunnigan Hills requires a pleasant drive through the gentle rolling hills of northern Yolo County. The appellation is dominated by **R.H. Phillips** (26836 County Road 12A, Esparto; 530/662-3215; www.rhphillips.com), a large producer of high-value wines in the $6 - $13 range. Try the Sauvignon Blanc, which is harvested during the cool hours of evening; the full-bodied Toasted Head Chardonnay; or the Rhone varietals of Syrah and Viognier. *To get to R.H. Phillips Winery from Sacramento, take Interstate 5 north to the Zamora exit, about eight miles north of Woodland. Go west from the exit, cross over Interstate 505, travel on about one mile of gravel road and turn right on Road 87. When Road 87 ends, turn left on Road 12A.*

Lodi-Woodbridge Acres of gnarled head-pruned grapevines, many dating back more than 50 years, are a common feature of the Lodi-Woodbridge area. The region produces more of the most popular varietals (Cabernet Sauvignon, Merlot, Zinfandel, Chardonnay and Sauvignon Blanc) than any other area of California. Like those from Clarksburg and Dunnigan Hills, wines from Lodi-Woodbridge provide a lot of bang for the buck. A good starting point is the new **Lodi-Woodbridge Wine and Visitor Center** (2545 W. Turner Road, Lodi; 209/365-0621), which offers interactive exhibits, wine classes, tasting bar and visitor information within an Italian-style villa. Explore **Lucas Winery** (18196 N. Davis Road, Lodi; 209/368-2006; www.lucaswinery.com), which produces one of the best unfiltered, old-vine Zinfandels in the appellation; **Spenker Winery** (17303 N. Devries Rd., Lodi; 209/367-0467, tasting by appointment only), where Chuck and Bettyann Spenker produce a gutsy, old-vine Zinfandel and employ sustainable farming methods; **Peirano Estate** (21831 N. Highway 99, Acampo; 209/369-9463; www.peirano.com) for a spicy, full-bodied Zinfandel; and **Mondavi's Woodbridge Winery** (5950 E. Woodbridge Road, Woodbridge; 209/369-5861; www.woodbridgewines.com) to sample wines under Mondavi's popular Woodbridge label that are not available anywhere else. *To get to Lodi-Woodbridge from Sacramento, take Highway 99 south to the Acampo Road or Woodbridge Road exits. www.lodiwine.com*

PART III
ACTIVITIES
ART GALLERIES

The region's galleries tend to focus on the work of significant Northern California artists. All downtown, midtown and North Sacramento galleries stay open late for receptions on Second Saturday, held on the second Saturday of each month. The downtown/midtown galleries stay open from about 6 p.m. to 9 p.m., with the North Sac galleries open from 8 p.m. to 10 p.m. Davis' ArtAbout is a similar event, with about 12 galleries open every other Friday from 6 p.m. to 10 p.m. Events in both cities often feature food, wine and music.

Art Foundry Gallery Located in a former warehouse along the R Street Corridor, Art Foundry Gallery houses a bronze foundry and an impressive gallery featuring works in a variety of media. *1021 R Street, Sacramento; 916/444-2787*

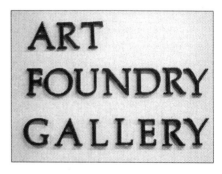

Artists Contemporary Gallery Sacramento's oldest gallery, Artists Contemporary Gallery displays the works of well-known Central Valley artists and others. *1200 K Street, #9, Sacramento; 916/444-3694*

John Natsoulas Gallery One of the premier galleries of Northern California devoted to Northern California artists, John Natsoulas focuses on the Bay Area Figurative and Abstract Expressionism traditions, as well as the Funk Movement. *521 First Street, Davis; 530/756-3938; www.natsoulas.com)*

MatrixArts Since 1978, MatrixArts has featured excellent contemporary works by artists from Northern California and around the world. *1518 Del Paso Boulevard, North Sacramento; 916/923-9118; www.sacramento.org/matrixarts/*

Pence Gallery The Pence, established in 1976 as a nonprofit, offers exhibitions, lectures, classes and musical performances. *212 D Street, Davis; 530/758-3370; www.gogh.com/pence/*

Solomon Dubnick Gallery The Solomon Dubnick Gallery is a highly professional outfit that exhibits contemporary art. *2131 Northrup Avenue, Sacramento; 916/920-4547; sdgaller.hostme.com*

CINEMA

New movie screens have proliferated in the metropolitan region in the past five years. Check listings in *The Sacramento Bee* or *Sacramento News and Review*. Sacramento possesses four movie houses that date from before the 1940s: **Tower Theater** (16th and Broadway, 916/443-1982), **Crest Theater** (1013 K Street, 916/44-CREST), **Esquire IMAX Theater**, with a six-story screen and stunning 3-D features (1211 K Street, 916/443-IMAX) and **Colonial Theater**, which features live events and occasional films (3522 Stockton Boulevard, 916/454-1700). The **Sacramento Film and Music Festival** celebrates independent filmmaking and musicianship at the Crest Theatre for a weekend in August (818/345-2201; www.sactofilmfest.com), **Sacramento Festival of Cinema** presents films written and directed by locals in October (916/456-8600, ext. 176; www.sacramento.org/film) and, also in October, the **Sacramento International Gay & Lesbian Film Festival** offers a selection of acclaimed films related to the gay/lesbian experience (916/689-3284, www.fairyflicks.com).

DANCE

Dale Scholl Dance/Art CSUS dance professor Dale Scholl's eponymous company has been a fixture in local modern dance since 1982. You can catch their exuberant performances at the CSUS campus. *916/451-3732*

Pamela Trokanski Dance Theatre In its two concerts each year, PTDT likes to examine contemporary life through postmodern dance. The Davis-based company, established in 1985, also offers dance classes for all ages. *530-756-3949, trokanski.simplependulum.com*

Sacramento Ballet Established in 1947, the Sacramento Ballet provides classical and contemporary ballet performances at the Community Center Theatre from October through April. *1631 K Street, Sacramento; 916/552-5800*

EVENTS

JANUARY
Martin Luther King, Jr. Community Celebration, Sacramento; 916/452-5052

FEBRUARY
California Duck Days, Yolo and Sacramento Counties; 530/758-1286
Mardi Gras, Old Sacramento; 916/264-7031
Sacramento Gourmet Festival, Sacramento; 916/483-9173

MARCH
Chinese New Year, Main Street, Isleton; 916/777-5880
St. Patrick's Day Parade, Old Sacramento; 916/442-7644

APRIL
Bockbierfest, Turn Verein Hall, 3349 J Street, Sacramento; 916/442-7360
Festival of the Arts, CSU Sacramento; 916/278-6156
Festival de la Familia, Old Sacramento, 916/443-6223
Whole Earth Festival, U.C. Davis; 530/752-2569
Davis Children's Fair, Davis; 530/757-5691
Picnic Day, UC Davis; 530/752-2027
Pacific Rim Festival, Old Sacramento; 916/443-6223

MAY
Cinco de Mayo Celebrations, Sacramento; 916/428-6707
Dixon May Fair, Dixon; 707/678-2650
Elk Grove Western Festival, Elk Grove Regional Park; 916/685-5218
Lodi Street Faire, Lodi; 209/367-7840
Feats of Clay Art Tour, Gladding McBean, Lincoln; 916/645-9713
Fair Oaks Fiesta, Plaza Park and Village Park, Fair Oaks Village; 916/967-2903
Sacramento Children's Festival, K Street Mall, Sacramento; 916/455-1611
Downtown Concerts in the Park (thru September), Cesar Chavez Plaza, Sacramento; 916/442-8575
Sacramento County Fair, Cal Expo, Sacramento; 916/263-2975
Strawberry Festival, Veterans Field, Galt; 209/745-2529
Spring Italian Music Festival, 3730 Auburn Boulevard, Sacramento; 916/482-5900
Sacramento Jazz Jubilee, Old Sacramento and other venues; 916/372-5277
Memorial Day Parade, State Capitol, Sacramento; 916/366-3987
Sacramento Portuguese Festa, Sacramento; 209/745-6342

JUNE
Sacramento Heritage Festival, Sacramento; 916/481-2583
Filipino Food Fair, Sacramento; 916/395-0601
Water Festival, Folsom Point, Folsom Lake; 916/985-2698
Croatian Extravaganza, 3730 Auburn Boulevard, Sacramento, 916/971-0663
Crawdad Festival, Isleton; 916/777-5880
Railfair, Old Sacramento; 916/332-8485
Father's Day Cherry Festival, Apple Hill; 916/644-7692
Taste of Fair Oaks, 7997 California Ave., Fair Oaks; 916/967-2903
Jewish Food Faire & Craft Sale, 4746 El Camino Ave, Sacramento; 916/485-4478
Renaissance Tudor Fayre, Fair Oaks Park, Fair Oaks; 916/966-1036

JULY

Folsom Championship Rodeo, Dan Russell Arena, Folsom; 916/985-2698
Eppie's Great Race, Goethe Park, Carmichael; 916/875-6640 or 444-6223
Strauss Festival, Strauss Island, Elk Grove Park, Elk Grove; 916/685-3911
Pear Fair, Courtland; 916/775-1053

AUGUST

Japanese Cultural Bazaar, 2401 Riverside Boulevard, Sacramento; 916/446-0121
Festa Italiana, 3730 Auburn Boulevard, Sacramento; 916/482-5900
Apple Hill Summer Fruit and Wine Festival, Apple Hill, U.S. 50 between Placerville and Pollack Pines; 916/644-7692
California State Fair (through Labor Day weekend), Cal Expo, Sacramento; 916/263-3000
Earthquake Street Festival, Winters; 530/795-2329
Lambtown USA, Dixon; 707/678-2650

SEPTEMBER

Greek Food Festival, Convention Center, Sacramento; 916/443-2033
Gold Rush Days, Old Sacramento; 916/264-7777
Apple Hill Harvest Festival (thru December), El Dorado County; 916/644-7692
Lodi Grape Festival and Harvest Fair, Lodi; 209/369-2771

OCTOBER

Lodi Street Faire, Lodi; 209/367-7840
Oktoberfest, Turn Verein Hall, 3349 J Street, Sacramento; 916/442-7360
Art on the River, Old Sacramento; 916/264-7031 or 916/558-3912
Salmon Festival, American River and Lake Natoma, 916/361-8700 or 264-7777
Serbian Food Festival, 7777 Sunset Avenue, Sacramento; 916/966-5438
A Taste of Folsom, Folsom; 916/985-5555
Rio Vista Bass Derby Festival, Rio Vista; 707/374-2700
Halloween Festival, Old Sacramento; 916/442-7644

NOVEMBER

Holiday Ice Rink (thru February), 7th and K Streets, Sacramento; 916/442-8575
Heritage Holidays, Old Sacramento; 916/442-7644
Santa Parade, Downtown, Sacramento; 916/558-3912

DECEMBER

Christmas in the Village, Fair Oaks Village; 916/967-2903
California International Marathon, Folsom to Sacramento; 916/983-4622
Woodland Christmas Parade, Woodland; 530/662-7327

Course data for par, yardage, rating and slope are based on the regular tees. Rates for weekends: $=less than $20, $$=$20-$40, $$$=more than $40.

Ancil Hoffman (William Francis Bell, 1965) Considered one of the most outstanding public course in Northern California, Ancil Hoffman features an American River setting, tight fairways and contoured greens. Par 72, 6434 yards, 70.9 rating, 125 slope, $$. *6700 Tarshes Drive, Carmichael; 916/482-5660, reservations 916-575-4653(GOLF); www.empiregolf.com/ah.htm*

Bing Maloney (Mac MacDonald, 1952) Mature trees border every fairway, making accurate tee shots a must at this flat course. Bing also features a 1,332-yard executive nine-hole course. Par 72, 70.1 rating, 113 slope, $$. *6801 Freeport Blvd., Sacramento; 916/428-9401; www.capitalcitygolf.com/bing/*

Cherry Island (Robert Muir Graves, 1990) Water hazards challenge play on 10 holes at this county-operated course, so you may want to bring some extra balls. Par 72, 6201 yards, 70.1 rating, 118 slope, $$. *2360 Elverta Road, Elverta; 916/991-7293; reservations 916-575-4653(GOLF); www.empiregolf.com/cigc.htm*

Lighthouse (Bert Stamps, 1990) Just a few minutes from downtown Sacramento, Lighthouse offers a well-kept course with water on 13 holes. Par 70, 5108 yards, 66.4 rating, 113 slope, $$. *500 Douglas Street, West Sacramento; 916/372-4949; www.lighthousegc.com*

Teal Bend (Brad Bell, 1997) This 250-acre course features wetlands and gently rolling hills in a scenic location by the Sacramento River. Par 72, 6201 yards, 71.6 rating, 118 slope, $$$. *7200 Garden Highway, Sacramento; 916/922-5209; www.tealbendgolf.com*

Twelve Bridges (Dick Phelps, 1996) Named one of the Best New Upscale Courses by Golf Digest in 1996, Twelve Bridges features mature oak trees, rolling hills and granite outcroppings. Par 72, 71.8 rating, 123 slope, $$$. *3070 Eight Mile Drive, Lincoln; 916/645-7200; www.twelvebridges.com*

William Land Park (1929) This easy nine-hole course offers mature landscaping, wide fairways and a challenging goal-post shot on the par-3 third hole. Par 68, 5198 yards, 63.3 rating, 101 slope, $. *1701 Sutterville Road, Sacramento; 916/455-5014; www.capitalcitygolf.com/william*

Woodcreek (Robert Muir Graves, 1995) A 210-acre course with more than 1,000 mature valley oaks, as well as wetlands, streams and lakes. Par 72, 6041 yards, 70.5 rating, 121 slope, $$. *5880 Woodcreek Oaks, Roseville, 916/771-4653*

California Governor's Mansion This 1877 mansion housed 13 govenors, ending with Ronald Reagan in 1967. The home features 14-foot ceilings, Persian carpets, Italian marble fireplaces, fancy chandeliers and French mirrors; and the informative guides relay stories about the governors and their families. *1526 H Street, Sacramento; 916/323-3047*

California Military Museum This often overlooked museum houses an impressive collection on California's military history. Exhibits focus on the Spanish/American War, Civil War, the World Wars and more recent conflicts. *1119 Second Street, Old Sacramento; 916/442-2883; www.militarymuseum.org*

California State Indian Museum Native American clothes, basketry, musical instruments, photographs, tools and other artifacts are on display at the California State Indian Museum, located just behind Sutter's Fort. The museum explores the rich culture and tragic history of Native Americans in California. *2618 K Street, Sacramento; 916/324-0971*

California State Railroad Museum At 100,000 square feet of exhibit space, this is the largest interpretive railroad museum in North America. The museum showcases 21 restored locomotives and rail cars spanning the 1860s to the 1960s, as well as 46 exhibits that includes a dining car set for dinner and a sleeper car that simulates the peaceful sway of a moving train. *125 I Street, Old Sacramento; 916/445-6645; www.csrmf.org*

Crocker Art Museum Proclaiming itself to be the "oldest museum in the West," the Crocker Art Museum is housed in the grand residence built for B.F. Hastings in 1853 (architect Seth Babson) and expanded by Judge E.B. Crocker in the 1870s. The place reeks of early California money, with an opulent ballroom, exquisite parquet floors and intricate doors and moldings. The museum collection includes Asian and European art, California art dating back to early statehood and works by contemporary artists. *216 O Street, Sacramento; 916/264-5423; www.crockerartmuseum.org*

Discovery Museum History Center Housed in a reconstruction of Sacramento's first City Hall, this modest museum focuses on Sacramento history. The exhibit on Dunlap's Dining Room, which served the city's best fried chicken dinners in Oak Park from 1930 to 1968, gives a sense for Sacramento's strong community identity. *101 I Street, Old Sacramento; 916/264-7057; www.thediscovery.org*

Explorit Science Center This Davis nonprofit center has been fascinating children with hands-on and visual science exhibits since 1982. Explorit features live animals such as an iguana, a giant cockroach and a snake. Open Tuesday - Sunday, primarily in the afternoon. *3141 Fifth Street, Davis; 530/756-0191; www.dcn.davis.ca.us/GO/EXPLORIT*

Golden State Museum The Golden State Museum uses multi-media exhibits to showcase California and its people, politics and promise. John Muir speaks about his environmental philosophy through a nifty talking hologram, a large movie screen provides an aerial tour of California's diverse landscape and oodles of artifacts from the extensive collection of the California State Archives are on

display. *1020 O Street, Sacramento; 916/653-4255; www.ss.ca.gov/museum/intro.htm*

Heidrick Ag History Center Agriculture has been a bedrock industry in the Sacramento Valley since the days of John Sutter. The Heidrick Ag History Center brings together an impressive collection of vintage agricultural equipment, from an 1890 Deering grain reaper to a large collection of Caterpillar tractors (invented by Benjamin Holt of nearby Stockton). The center also includes the **Hays' Antique Truck Museum**, featuring 123 vintage trucks dating back to 1903. The museum has one of the largest truck collections in the nation. *1962 Hays Lane, Woodland; (530) 666-9700; www.aghistory.org and www.truckmuseum.org*

McClellan Aviation Museum Inspect 10 vintage military aircraft with names like Jolly Green Giant, Voodoo and Thunderchief as well as three buildings crammed with air force history at the deactivated McClellan Air Force base. The museum is free of charge, although you must check in at the visitor's center and show proof of auto insurance, car registration and driver's license. *3204 Palm Avenue, North Highlands; 916/643-3192*

Sutter's Fort State Historic Park Sutter's Fort is an imaginative reconstruction of the original fort built in 1839 (Gold Rush vandals had destroyed all but the central two-story building by 1851). The fort was Sacramento's original central business district, with a blacksmith, physician, bakery, jail, cooper and various merchants. The knowledgeable costumed docents will give a you a sense for pioneer life in the Sacramento Valley. *2701 L Street, Sacramento; 916/445-4422*

Towe Auto Museum California's signature transportation mode is featured in this impressive collection of gleaming, restored automobiles. The museum interprets the various eras in automobile design, underscoring how important the car is to California culture. *2200 Front Street, Sacramento, 916/442-6802; www.toweautomuseum.org*

Yolo County Historical Museum Through furnishings and artifacts, this museum evokes Yolo County life from the 1850's to the 1930's. The museum is housed in the historic Gibson Mansion, dating from 1849. *512 Gibson Road, Woodland; 530-666-1045; www.yolo.net/ychm/*

MUSIC

Major concert venues include **Sacramento Valley Amphitheatre** (on Forty Mile Road 30 miles north of Sacramento, www.sacvalleyamp.com) 8,000 reserve seats, 10,500 lawn capacity; **Arco Area** (One Sports Parkway, Sacramento; 916/928-6900) 17,300-seats; **Memorial Auditorium** (15th and J Streets, Sacramento; 916/264-5181) 3,855 seats; and **Community Center Theater** (1301 L Street, Sacramento; 916/264-5181) 2,452 seats.

Sacramento Philharmonic Orchestra In 1998, the Sacramento Philharmonic rose from the ashes of the bankrupt Sacramento Symphony Orchestra. Many of the 60 musicians in the Philharmonic came from the Symphony, and under conductor Michael Morgan, the new orchestra has won raves for its performances and its ability to keep its finances in the black. The Philharmonic's season runs from October through May and performs at the

Community Center Theatre. *916/922-9200; sacramentophilharmonic.org*

Camellia Symphony The Camellia has been a community symphony for many decades. Members of the orchestra are often professional musicians but many hail from other occupations. Camellia Symphony focuses on lesser-known works of famous composers, as well as the work of underappreciate composers. The orchestra performs at the Westminster Church (1300 N Street, Sacramento) and at the Community Center Theatre. The season generally runs from October through May. *916/929-6655; www.camelliasymphony.org*

Chamber Music Society of Sacramento Founded in 1986, this ensemble features some of the finest classical musicians in the Sacramento area. The season features seven concerts from September through May, and performances are at the CSUS Recital Hall. *916/443-2908*

Sacramento Opera Founded in 1947, the Sacramento Opera features two performances from November to February. *916/264-5181; www.sacopera.org*

NIGHTLIFE

The following listings are just a sample of the dozens of clubs and bars in the region. Consult *The Sacramento Bee* (www.sacbee.com), the free weekly *Sacramento News and Review* (www.newsreview.com) or the free monthly *Alive and Kicking* for up-to-the-minute details.

Back Door Lounge The Back Door is a throwback to the days of red carpet, red candles, red and gold wallpaper and world-weary torch singers. In its dark-ended spaces are the politicians and middle-aged folk who need to find a place to slip out of sight, sip a cocktail, listen to Sinatra and find a sympathetic ear. *1112 Firehouse Alley, Old Sacramento; 916/442-5751*

Blue Cue This upscale club above Centro Cocina Mexicana attracts lots of well-dressed and attractive patrons. You pay by the hour to occupy one of the eight custom pool tables with purple felt or one of the two shuffleboards. The lounge offers a large selection of single malt scotches and champagnes. *1004 28th Street, Sacramento; 916/442-7208; www.paragarys.com/bluecue.html*

The Boardwalk The Boardwalk has been boosting the careers of up-and-coming Northern California bands since 1987. The club also features the occasional famous rock star. *9426 Greenback Lane, Orangevale; 916/988-9247; www.boardwalkrocks.com*

Bonn Lair Bonn Lair has a neighborly pub ambience. There are no crass elements — no loud jukebox, hard liquor or lounge lizards. There is a television, but it is more likely to be tuned to international soccer than the NFL. Bonn Lair offers British beers on tap, pasties from the Pasty Shack, antique couches and a fireplace. This pub also draws a great pint of  Guinness, patiently allowing the thick foam to subside before topping it off. *3651 J Street, Sacramento; 916/455-7155*

Brannan's Once upon a time, a legislator could visit any of several bars within two blocks of the Capitol — Bedell's, David's Brass Rail, El Mirador Hotel, Posey's and the Senator Hotel, to name but a few. The only survivor is located within the former Bedell's, now known as Brannan's. It is an inviting space, with mahogany walls and vintage political posters emphasizing the bar's historical pedigree. Brannan's considers itself the official headquarters of the "Third House," the legions of lobbyists who influence policy making in the old building across the street. *1117 11th Street, Sacramento; 916/444-2993*

Cantina del Cabo The Cantina is a top stop for UC Davis students and recent grads. Live music is featured most Thursday through Saturday nights, and you can work your way through the 60+ beers and ales on tap. *139 G Street, Davis; 530/756-2226;*

Centro Cocina Mexicana This upscale Mexican restaurant draws a hip and professional clientele. The lively bar stocks lots of premium and super-premium tequilas, as well as tequila infusions. Try the house margarita, Sauza Giro with triple sec and fresh lime juice, shaken and served up in a cocktail glass, or the mildly spicy sangrita with a shot of tequila on the side. *2730 J Street, Sacramento; 916/442-2552; www.paragarys.com/centro.html*

815 L Street 815 L Street took over the long-shuttered location of Sam's Hofbrau and transformed the place into one of Sacramento's top night clubs. The cavernous interior features richly grained oak booths, a fully stocked bar and large dance floor, as well as a second-floor cigar lounge. *815 L Street, Sacramento; 916/443-8155*

Faces Faces is Sacramento's premier nightclub for the gay & lesbian community. The club also is one of the top dance spots in the region, featuring dancing on two floors, with up to 10 bars at your service. *2000 K Street, Sacramento; 916/448-7798; www.facesnightclub.com*

Fox and Goose Fox and Goose, a British pub, is no phony theme bar. Co-founder Bill Dalton hails from England, and he based the establishment on a similar pub back in Blighty. The bar is housed in an old brick warehouse on R Street, which Dalton and his wife Denise transformed into a convivial meeting place back in the mid-1970s. You can hear a British accent or two around the bar, and there are plenty of beers on tap. *1001 R Street, Sacramento; 916/443-8825; www.foxandgoose.com*

Harlow's/Momo Lounge Recently renovated in the style of a 1930s supper club, Harlow's presents an eclectic roster of touring musical talent, covering blues, salsa, disco, reggae and more. Enjoy the churning action on the dance floor or head up to the swanky Momo Lounge for cigars. *2708 J Street, Sacramento; 916/441-4693; www.harlows.com*

Laughs Unlimited Jerry Seinfeld, Dana Carvey, Jay Leno and others have performed at this basement comedy club, which has been cranking out the laughs since 1980. *1207 Front Street, Old Sacramento; 916/446-5905; www.laughsunlimited.net*

Monkey Bar This outlet of Randy Paragary's 28th Street location is sized like an old-fashioned neighborhood bar but is aimed squarely at a contemporary crowd. The barstools, with their puffy, marshmallow cushions, make for a comfortable perch to check out the trendy Midtown crowd as they swill martinis and Monkey Punch. Music is provided by the 1,000-selection jukebox. *28th Street and Capitol Avenue, Sacramento; 916/442-8490; www.paragarys.com/bernardo/monkey_bar.html*

Old Ironsides Old Ironsides, the oldest bar in Sacramento, offers a venue for local talent and cutting-edge bands from around the country. *1901 10th Street, Sacramento; 916/443-9751; www.theoldironsides.com*

The Owl Club In Roseville's historic district sits the historic Owl Club, opened at the end of Prohibition in 1934. A mixed clientele drops by to enjoy the bar's art deco decor and 14 microbrews. *109 Church Street, Roseville; 916/773-1919; www.owlclub.com*

Palms Playhouse The Palms has been one of Northern California's unique spots to catch live music since 1975. Located in an ancient, rickety barn that seats just over 100 people, the Palms is a great place to catch top talent from a wide spectrum of popular music. *726 Drummond Avenue, Davis; 530/756-9901; palmsplayhouse.com*

Pine Cove One of the more endearing traits of the Pine Cove is the cheap Pabst Blue Ribbon served on draft. The bar occupies the second floor above a bottle shop along the Capitol City Freeway. The Pine Cove first achieved popularity as a stop for motorists when the bar was the first one drivers would encounter going west on the old Highway 50 between Auburn and Sacramento. These days the bar has a steady local clientele, with the youth taking over on the weekends. *502 29th Street, Sacramento; 916/446-3624*

Poor Red's Poor Red's is worth the drive into the Sierra foothill town of El Dorado, though it is advisable to have a designated driver capable of negotiating the twisting, two-lane highway. The rest of your group will want to cut loose with the rest of the crowd in Poor Red's lively, historic bar. The specialty here is the Golden Cadillac, a dessert drink with lots of cream and an Italian liqueur, Galliano. In fact, the makers of Galliano recently honored Poor Red's as the largest buyer of Galliano in the world. *6221 Pleasant Valley Road, El Dorado; 530/622-2901*

Polly Esther's and Culture Club Polly Esther's celebrates the icons of earlier generations: lava lamps, tie dye, Farrah Fawcett and Saturday Night Fever. Musically the club focuses on the 1970s and 1980s, and it instantly became one of the region's hottest nightspots when it opened in 2001. *1696 Arden Way, Sacramento; 916/922-1975; www.pollyesthers.com*

Power House Pub Power House Pub is Folsom's best blues and R&B venue. The rustic interior also is crammed with televisions for the sports fan. *614-D Sutter Street, Folsom; 916/985-3280; www.powerhousepub.com*

Punchline The San Francisco club's Sacramento outlet features the same top standup comedy talent. The club features a light menu and comedy every night of the week. *2100 Arden Way, Sacramento; 916/925-5500; www.punchlinecomedyclub.com*

Torch Club The Torch Club is Sacramento's top spot for live blues. The Torch, with its old photos of boxers and long-departed Sacramentans, was popular in a former location with administration officials during the Jerry Brown era. The Torch moved in 2000 to a roomier and sharper venue across the street from the

Memorial Auditorium. *904 15th Street, Sacramento; 916/443-2797; www.thetorchclub.com*

The Rage The Rage is among Sacramento's best dance clubs, with a state-of-the-art sound system, a chat room and multiple bar areas. *1890 Arden Way, Sacramento; 916/929-0232; members.aol.com/TheRageCA*

Simon's Bar and Cafe Simon Chan formerly tended bar at Frank Fat's, and he apparently learned a few things about keeping legislators happy. First, serve good food. Second, keep the bar well-stocked. Third, provide prompt service. Finally, know them by name. Over the past several years, Simon's has emerged as a more casual alternative to Fat's for legislators and lobbyists to unwind after hours. The bar area takes up half the restaurant, and it does a good rollicking business when legislators are in town. The Chinese food is pretty good, too. *1415 16th Street, Sacramento; 916/442-9437*

PARKS

American River Parkway Unlike other cities, Sacramento did not sacrifice its river by converting it into a concrete storm channel or relegating it to an urban sewage system. Instead, Sacramento County established the American River

Parkway, a 23-mile, 5,000-acre nature preserve that runs along the American River from Sacramento to Folsom. Where else can you hear the sound of wind rustling through ancient valley oaks, in the company of egrets and river otter, all within sight of a downtown skyline? Four million people per year visit the parkway to raft, fish, jog, bicycle, hike, rollerblade and horseback ride. The parkway features the 31-mile Jedediah Smith Bicycle Trail, which attracts 400,000 cyclists per year. One of the more enjoyable portions of the parkway is between Hazel Avenue and Folsom Lake, where the crowds are few and the scenery at its most sublime. Major parks along the parkway include **Discovery Park** (between Garden Highway and the American River), with bicycle paths, boat launch, picnic facilities, archery, horseshoe pits, equestrian trails and playground; **Glen Hall Park and Paradise Beach** (Sandburg Drive and Carlson Drive), with swimming pool, tennis courts, multi-purpose field and river access; **Goethe Park** (enter from Rod Beaudry Road from Folsom Boulevard), featuring picnic facilities, bicycle paths, equestrian trails and hiking; **Ancil Hoffman Park** (6700 Tarshes Drive, Carmichael), with an outstanding 18-hole golf course; and the **Effie Yeaw Nature Center** (a 77-acre nature area and interpretive center, 916/489-4918; www.effieyeaw.org), picnic facilities, multi-purpose sports fields, hiking, bicycle paths and equestrian trails. The best guide to the parkway is *Biking and Hiking the American River Parkway* by the American River Natural History Association, which is available at bookstores or call 916/456-7423.

Cosumnes River Preserve The Cosumnes is the Central Valley's only undammed river, and the 14,000-acre Cosumnes River Preserve provides the scarce opportunity to experience the valley's unspoiled natural environment. The three-mile Willow Slough Nature Trail Loop guides you past wetlands and marshes and a streamside valley oak forest. There is river access for kayaks and canoes and a wheel-chair accessible boardwalk. A visitor center is open 10 a.m. to 4 p.m. weekends. *Franklin Boulevard (Interstate 5 south to Twin Cities Road); 916/684-2816; www.cosumnes.org*

Davis Central Park This community gathering place is at its best during the Wednesday and Saturday farmers' markets. Children enjoy the playgrounds, fountains, music and whimsical foot-pedaled carousel. *4th and C Streets, Davis; 530/757-5626*

Elk Grove Regional Park The 125-acre Elk Grove Regional Park, site of the annual Strauss Festival and Western Festival, features ball diamonds, horseshoe pits, volleyball courts, a soccer field, a three-acre lake and a swimming pool. *9950 Elk Grove-Florin Road, Elk Grove, 916/875-6336*

Folsom Lake More than two million people per year visit Folsom Lake State Recreational Area. Folsom Lake covers 18,000 acres and has at least 75 miles of shoreline. The lake offers boat launching facilities, picnic areas, a marina, tent camping, boat camping, fishing, hiking, equestrian trails, bike paths and mountain bike trails. **Folsom Dam** (Folsom-Auburn Road at Dam Road), built in 1955, protects the Sacramento Valley from flood, generates electrical power and provides water for agriculture. **The Folsom Powerhouse**, located below the dam, meets about 10 percent of regional electricity needs. Tours of both facilities are held Tuesday through Saturday from 10 a.m. to 1 p.m. Call 916/989-7275 for information. At Lake Natoma, **Negro Bar** offers picnic facilities, multi-use fields, sand volleyball courts, campgrounds and a boat launching ramp. Equestrian trails follow the route of the Pony Express. *Park headquarters is at 7806 Folsom Auburn Road between Greenback Lane and Douglas Boulevard, Folsom; 916/988-0205; cal-parks.ca.gov*

Gibson Ranch Park This 325-acre park also is a working ranch. Gibson Ranch features barns, bunkhouses, farm animals, a historic blacksmith's shop, a fishing lake, a carriage house, a swimming hole, picnic facilities, horseshoe pits and equestrian trails. **Gibson Ranch Equestrian Services** (916/991-7592) provides hayrides, horse rentals and lessons. Guided tours of the park are by reservation only. *Elverta Road, west of Watt Avenue, Elverta; 916/875-6961; www.gibson-ranch.com*

McKinley Park Indicative of the strong community spirit surrounding McKinley Park, hundreds of neighbors pitched in to buy and build the park's exceedingly popular playground equipment back in the mid-1990s. The playground is just one of many amenities (swimming pool, basketball court, tennis courts, library branch, jogging trail, rose garden, picnic facilities and horseshoe pits) featured in this jewel of the city park system. *Alhambra Boulevard and H Street, Sacramento; 916/277-6060; www.cityofsacramento.org/parks*

Sacramento River Parkway The Sacramento River extends from Mount Shasta to the Delta. The City of Sacramento has developed a parkway (with bike path) that runs along the river from Miller Park (located at the west end of Broadway) south to 25th Avenue (with the unfortunate roar of Interstate 5 accompanying the route). You can also tour the Sacramento River via either the Garden Highway or River Road. **Garden Highway**, on the Sacramento County side of the river, is accessible from northbound Interstate 5 (Garden Highway Exit). The highway sits atop a levee, affording elevated views of the river and fancy homes. The highway again hooks up with Interstate 5 near Sacramento International Airport. **River Road** runs along the Yolo County side of the river and is accessible either from Interstate 80 (Harbor Boulevard Exit in West Sacramento; take Harbor Boulevard north and turn left onto River Road) or by crossing the I Street Bridge from Sacramento. River Road offers views of the homes and boat docks along the other side of the river. There are few homes on the Yolo side of the river, just a scenic, agricultural setting. The road meets up with Interstate 5 near the airport.

Stone Lakes National Wildlife Refuge A free permit is required and monthly tours are available to this massive wildlife sanctuary in South Sacramento county. *West end of Elk Grove Boulevard, west side of Interstate 5; 916/979-2085*

William Land Park This 236-acre park is Sacramento's most popular outdoor destination. The park features small amusement parks, lakes, playgrounds, swimming pools, a nine-hole golf course, picnic areas, five ball diamonds, multi-use sports fields and jogging trails. **The Sacramento Zoo** (3930 Sutterville Road, Sacramento; 916/264-5885; www.saczoo.com)

contains 15 acres and more than 340 species, including many exotic and endangered animals. *Between 11th Avenue and Sutterville Road and Riverside Boulevard and Freeport Boulevard, Sacramento; 916/277-6060; www.cityofsacramento.org/parks*

PROFESSIONAL SPORTS

Sacramento Capitals World Team Tennis was created by Billie Jean King in the 1970s. A match consists of five sets: one set each of men's and women's singles, men's and women's doubles, and mixed doubles. The Capitals feature five players who have years of competing at the highest levels of the sport. The short season (during the month of July) features about seven home matches.

Gold River Racquet Club, 2201 Gold Rush Drive (at Coloma Road, East of Sunrise), Gold River; 916/638-4001; www.saccapitals.com

Sacramento Kings Under the guidance of coach Rick Adelman, owners Joe and Gavin Maloof and executive Geoff Petrie, the Kings have emerged as one of the hottest teams in the National Basketball Association. Led by the lethal scoring duo of all star forward Chris Webber and shooting guard Peja Stojakavic, the team should be a championship contender for years to come. Keep that cowbell handy. *Arco Arena, One Sports Parkway, Sacramento; One Sports Parkway, Sacramento; 916/928-6900 (box office), 916/928-3650 (season tickets), 1-800-4NBA-TIXS (single tickets); www.nba.com/kings*

Sacramento Monarchs The WNBA Sacramento Monarchs take the floor at Arco Arena from June through August. The Monarchs have had a strong team since arriving in Sacramento when the league debuted a few years ago. The tickets are relatively affordable, the exciting play hews strongly to the fundamentals and the fans are loud. *Arco Arena, One Sports Parkway, Sacramento; 916/928-6900 (box office), 916/928-3650 (season tickets),916/419-WNBA (single tickets); www.wnba.com/monarchs*

Sacramento River Cats After a long hiatus, the Pacific Coast League returned to the Sacramento region in the 2000 season with the Sacramento River Cats. The Triple-A affiliate of the Oakland A's plays at the beautiful new Raley Field near the Tower Bridge in West Sacramento. Those who might scoff at minor league ball need  to experience the pure baseball pleasure of a River Cats game at Raley Field. Tickets start at just $5 for the lawn. The 14,000 capacity ballpark offers great sight lines from almost everywhere. The ushers treat the fans with uncommon courtesy. The food, particularly the fries and the barbecue platter, are top-notch. The quality of the ball is good, as scrappy up-and-comers and major league veterans vie for their chance to go to "the show." The weather is often perfect. *400 Ballpark Drive (just west of Old Sacramento and the Sacramento River), West Sacramento; 916/766-2277, 530/766-2277 or (800) 225-2277; www.rivercats.com*

Sacramento Knights Indoor soccer is a fast-paced sport distinguished from regular soccer by a smaller field and playable wall surfaces. The Sacramento Knights are in their ninth season, and in 1999 were the champions of the World Indoor Soccer League. The Knights play from August through December at Arco Arena. *Arco Arena, One Sports Parkway, Sacramento; 916/928-3697; www.wislindoor.com/sacramento.html*

RECREATION

Amusement Parks Children love the 11 amusement park rides and pony rides at **Funderland** (Sutterville Road and Land Park Drive, Sacramento; 916/456-0115). **Fairy Tale Town** (Sutterville Road and Land Park Drive,

Sacramento; 916/264-5233) is a park with features based on classic fairy tales. When at Fairy Tale Town, don't miss the puppet shows by **Puppet Art Theatre** (916/443-2556, puppetarts.com). Puppeteer Art Gruenberger creates the puppets, writes the scripts and performs all the roles. He has performed at schools, fairs and festivals throughout the world; and kids love him. **Paradise Island** (Gate 10, Exposition Boulevard, Sacramento; 916/924-0757) features miniature golf, rides, go-karts, bumper boats, a maze and an arcade. **Waterworld USA** (1600 Exposition Boulevard, Sacramento; 916/924-0556; www.sixflags.com/parks/waterworldsacramento/home.asp) has the highest slides in the West, such as the six-story Cobra.

Bicycling Bike paths line the American and Sacramento Rivers, the Yolo Causeway and downtown Sacramento streets. The City of Davis has gone to great lengths to accommodates bicyclists. See Visitor Essentials for places to rent bicycles.

Billiards Family-oriented billiard halls include **Scratch Billiards and Deli** (120 I Street, Old Sacramento; 916/441-7442) and **Rack-Em Family Billiards** (7811 Lichen Road, Citrus Heights; 916/721-3597).

Boating The Sacramento and American Rivers, the Delta and Folsom Lake are particularly popular with boaters. For boat and personal watercraft rentals, check out **Performance Jet Ski and Boat Rentals** (2788 Primo Way, Sacramento; 916/927-4606) and **Just Add Water** (916/386-8463). For houseboat rentals try **Herman and Helen's Marina** (Venice Island Ferry, Stockton; 209/951-4634, 800/676-4841; www.houseboats.com/hermanandhelens) or **Seven Crown Resorts** (800/752-9669; www.sevencrown.com).

Bowling For 1950s space-age architecture, check out the 48-lane **Country Club Lanes** (2600 Watt Avenue, Sacramento; 916/483-5105). Country Club offers all the latest bowling gimmicks, including automatic scoring and glow bowling.

Excursions Paddlewheel cruises on the Sacramento River are offered by the **Spirit of Sacramento** and **Matthew McKinley** (110 L Street, Old Sacramento; 916/552-2933 or 800/433-0263; spiritofsacramento.com). **River Otter Taxi Company** (L and Front Streets, Old Sacramento; 916/552-6808, ext. 226; www.riverotter.com) offers fun and inexpensive roundtrips from Old Sacramento to the Virgin Sturgeon and other restaurants along the Sacramento River. **The California State Railroad Museum** operates a steam-driven excursion train on a three-mile run from the Central Pacific Freight Depot (Front Street between J and K Streets, Old Sacramento; 916/445-6645) on weekends from April through September. **Yolo Shortline Railroad** (E. Main and Thomas Streets, Woodland; 530/666-9698 or 800/942-6387; www.ysrr.com) provides scenic trips through the countryside between West Sacramento and Woodland on weekends, May - October.

Fishing Discovery Park, Goethe Park and Nimbus Dam are popular fishing spots along the American River Parkway (see additional information under Parks). In addition, ponds in Land Park, Southside Park, Elk Grove Regional Park and Gibson Ranch Park are regularly stocked for fishing in the city.

Gaming Live harness racing and satellite wagering are featured at **Cal Expo** (1600 Exposition Boulevard, Sacramento; 916/263-7893;

www.capitolracing.com). Indian bingo and casino gaming are available at **Cache Creek** in northwest Yolo County (14455 Highway 16, Brooks; 530/796-3118; www.cachecreek.com). Sacramento's largest card room is the **Capital Casino Cafe** (411 N. 16th Street, Sacramento; 916/446-0700).

Ice Skating In North Sacramento since 1940, **Iceland** (1430 Del Paso Boulevard, Sacramento; 916/925-3121) has a 140 x 70 foot rink. In Roseville, **Skatetown** (1009 Orlando Avenue, Roseville; 916/783-8550; www.skatetown-roseville.com) features two NHL surfaces. Ice skating is available at St. Rose of Lima Park from November to February (7th & K Streets, Sacramento).

Rafting Those who enjoy shooting white-water rapids will want to try the South, Middle or North Forks of the American River. These are Class III-V rapids that require a life jacket and experienced guide. For beginners, there are a few things to be aware of from the start: paddling is physically demanding, you will get wet, you may fall into a rushing river and you may find some of the rapids (with names like Troublemaker, Triple Threat and Satan's Cesspool) to be a bit frightening. Also realize, however, that tens of thousands

of people safely navigate the waters each year and that you will be in good hands with an experienced guide. The South Fork is the most popular raft trip west of the Mississippi and is the best place for a beginner. The South Fork passes by the site of James Marshall's gold discovery in 1848. For guided tours, food included, check out **A Whitewater Connection** (530/622-6446 or 800/336-7238; www.whitewaterconnection.com), **American River Recreation** (530/622-6802 or 800/333-7238; www.arrafting.com) or **O.A.R.S.** (800/346-6277). For those who wish to avoid the rapids and enjoy a more leisurely float, check out some of the rental agencies located near the popular Sunrise Bridge access: **American River Raft Rentals** (11257 South Bridge Street, Rancho Cordova; 916/635-6400 or 888/338-RAFT; www.raftrentals.com) or **River Rat** (9840 Fair Oaks Boulevard, Fair Oaks; 916/966-6777; www.river-rat.com).

Softball Sacramento has more organized softball teams than any other city in the nation. **Del Paso Park** features a city softball complex for league and tournament play (3450 Longview Drive, Sacramento; 916/277-6087).

Trapshooting The City of Sacramento has operated a trapshooting club since the 1920s at **Del Paso Park** (3701 Fulton Avenue, Sacramento; 916/484-9889; www.commercemarketplace.com/shops/sactrap). Membership is not required, and you can fire away at clay disks to your heart's content.

SHOPPING

Old Sacramento There are some nice shops in Old Sacramento amidst the tourist schlock, including **Solar Syndicate** (114 K Street, 916/447-6419 or 800/701-4449; www.thesolarsyndicate.com), with a fine selection of wood stoves, solar gadgets and kitchen items; **Sacramento Sweets** (1035 Front Street, 916/446-0590 or 800/496-0590; www.sacsweets.com), selling handmade fudge, chocolates and brittles since 1964; **Laszlo's Gourmet Smoked Fish** (1100 Front Street, 916/331-4836), providing a variety of house-smoked seafood and **Evangeline** (113 K Street, 916/443-2181), a great shop for gag gifts and cards. *Bordered by the Sacramento River and 2nd, I and L Streets, Sacramento; www.oldsacramento.com*

Downtown Plaza Sacramento's Downtown Plaza provides a lively, open-air shopping experience. Anchored by **Macy's** (916/444-3333, www.macys.com), the mall has 115 businesses, including **Banana Republic** (916/442-0406, www.bananarepublic.com), **Doubleday Books** (916/442-7609, www.doubleday.com) and **Z Gallerie** (916/442-2299, www.zgallerie.com). *Bordered by 4th and 7th, J and L Streets, Sacramento; downtownplaza.shoppingtown.com*

K Street Mall Sacramento's K Street Mall, first developed in 1969, offers a bit of local color with noontime preachers and street musicians. Shops to look for in and around this outdoor pedestrian mall include **Records** (710 K Street, 916/446-3973), cluttered with thousands of used records, cassettes, compact discs and videos; **Longshore's Luggage** (714 J Street, 916/443-8757), a 1920s downtown veteran; **Davis & Company** (1015 8th Street, 916/443-1741), offering art, antiques and home accessories; **Avid Reader** (1003 L Street, 916/443-7323), a friendly, service-oriented bookshop; **Newsbeat** (1005 L Street, 916/448-2874), providing downtown's best selection of periodicals and newspapers; **Capitol Books and Gifts** (State Capitol Basement, 916/444-0317; www.capitolbooksandgifts.com/), featuring books on California and souvenirs of the State Capitol; **The Crate** (1200 K Street #9, 916/441-4136), with artful, handcrafted goods and **Beer's Books** (1431 L Street, 916/442-9475), a longtime downtown presence providing new and used books. *Bordered by 7th, 13th, J and L Streets, Sacramento*

Midtown Sacramento's Midtown has dozens of fine independent boutiques, gift shops, bookstores, cafes, restaurants and other businesses, though they are haphazardly scattered across a 78-square block area. Some of note include **The Beat** (1700 J Street, 916/446-402), with a great selection of new and used recordings; **How Tacky** (2425 J Street, 916/443-1379), featuring gifts that push the boundaries of good taste; **Reality Boutique** (2314 J Street, 916/492-0211), with contemporary women's clothing, shoes and gifts; **Tasha's** (1005 22nd Street, 916/444-5159), with an international selection of clothing, jewelry and gifts; **Mixed Bag** (2405 K Street, 916/447-6123), with a huge assortment of cards and gifts; **Time-Tested Books** (1114 21st Street, 916/447-5696; sl.net/~ttbooks), with old and rare books and a nice cat; **Gifted Gardener** (2122 J Street, 916/447-5956), with quality accessories for the yard; and **Postcards, Etc.** (1115 21st Street, 916/446-8049), featuring a large selection of postcards, greeting cards and gifts. *Most shops located between 16th Street and 28th Street and I Street and Capitol Avenue, Sacramento*

Arden Fair Mall Anchored by **Nordstrom** (916/646-2400, www.nordstrom.com), **Sears** (916/924-6100, www.sears.com), **Macy's** (916/925-2845 (www.macys.com) and **J.C. Penney** (916/564-0315, jcpenney.com), Arden Fair is among the most popular malls in the region. The mall also features a **Scribner's** bookstore (916/923-5278), **Barnes and Noble Booksellers** (916/565-0644, www.bn.com) and **Virgin Megastore** (916/564-0414, www.virginmega.com). *1689 Arden Way, Sacramento; 916/920-4809; www.ardenfair.com*

Pavilions Pavilions draws a well-heeled crowd to its collection of fine shops, boutiques, cafes and restaurants. It is an elegant outdoor mall that is easy to get around. The mall features **Julius Clothing** (916/929-0500) for men and women, **Borders Books and Music** (916/564-0168, www.borders.com) and **David Berkley Fine Wines and Deli** (916/929-4422, www.dberkley.com). *Fair Oaks Boulevard between Howe Avenue and Fulton Avenue, Sacramento*

Sunrise Mall Sunrise was the heavyweight mall in the region when it opened in 1972, and, despite time's having diminished some of the glow, it still draws a healthy market share. The mall is anchored by **Sears** (916/536-5300), **Macy's** (916/962-3333) and **J.C. Penney**. *Sunrise Boulevard at Greenback Lane, Citrus Heights; 916/961-7150; www.sunrise-mall.com*

Downtown Davis Davis offers a walkable downtown shopping district with lots of independent merchants. **Avid Reader** (617 Second Street, 530/758-4040; avidreader.booksense.com) and the nearby **Avid Reader for Young Readers** (232 E Street, 530/758-7700; avidreader.booksense.com) are known for their strong service and civic activism; **The Artery** (207 G Street, 530/758-8330, www.arteryart.com) features stylish crafts and art by more than 50 Northern California artists; **Bogey's Books** (223 E Street, 530/757-6127) sells new, used and out of print titles; and **Newsbeat** (514 Third Street, 530/756-6247) provides a comprehensive selection of magazines, newspapers and cards. Downtown also features Davis Commons, a smartly designed outdoor mall with parking located behind the mall and a big lawn facing toward the rest of the downtown shopping district. Davis Commons features major national retailers such as **The Gap** (530/750-2706, www.gap.com) and **Borders Books and Music** (530/750-3723, www.borders.com). *Most shops in area bordered by First, Fifth, A and G Streets, Davis*

Galleria at Roseville The Galleria opened in 2000 on former ranchland, and, as is usually the case with the newest malls, the Galleria is bigger than all that have come before. The mall features 1.1 million square feet of fine shops and restaurants and is anchored by **Nordstrom** (916/780-7300), **Macy's** (916/771-3333), **Sears** (916/787-7400) and **J.C. Penney** (916/772-8800). Located adjacent to the mall is just about every big-box retailer and chain restaurant known to humankind. *Harding Boulevard and Roseville Parkway, Roseville; www.galleriaroseville.com*

Folsom Premium Outlets Folsom Premium Outlets is the largest outlet mall in Sacramento County, with more than 70 stores offering big discounts. *13000 Folsom Boulevard, Folsom; 916/985-0312; www.premiumoutlets.com*

Historic Old Town Folsom Sutter Street is the main drag through Folsom's historic downtown district, a two-lane affair with a median dotted with the granite pillars from the old State Capitol fence. The street has the feel of the Old West, with shops featuring antiques, galleries and gifts. Check out **Snook's Candies** (702 Sutter Street, Suite G, 916/985-0620, www.snookscandies.com) a family-run enterprise since 1963, and **Milepost 1 Railroad Books** (198 Wool Street, 916/985-4777, www.mp1.com), operated by the Railway and Locomotive Historical Society. *Sutter Street, Folsom; www.web-images.com/folsom*

THEATRE

B Street Theatre In a town where the main celebrities are politicians, B Street Theatre stands out for having a bonafide Hollywood star. Timothy Busfield, formerly of the weekly television series *Thirtysomething* and a Sacramento native, has been the artistic director of this small, 178-seat theatre since co-founding the company in the early 1990s. The other co-founder, brother Buck Busfield, is the talented producing director. B Street Theatre has put on scores of outstanding productions, with Timothy occasionally starring and directing. *2711 B Street, Sacramento; 916/443-5300*

California Musical Theatre

Established in 1951, California Musical Theatre is the largest nonprofit musical theatre company in the state. Under the sure hand of New York theatre veteran Leland Ball, the theatre offers Music Circus and The Broadway Series. Music Circus

attracts 100,000 patrons annually for top-quality summer stock. Producing Director Ball brings in directors, choreographers, designers and actors from New York and Los Angeles to work with local actors, artisans and students. With the help of hundreds of volunteers, Music Circus produces seven shows in seven weeks. The seasonal circus-tent arena at 14th and H Streets that has been summer landmark soon will give way to a permanent structure for this beloved Sacramento institution. The Broadway Series, established by Ball in 1989, brings Broadway-style theatre to the Community Center Theatre during the non-summer months. The Broadway Series has staged scores of glittering productions, some still running on the Great White Way, attracting stars like Carol Channing, Tommy Tune and Christopher Plummer to the local stage. *1419 H Street, Sacramento; 916/557-1999; www.californiamusicaltheatre.com*

Sacramento Theatre Company

Sacramento Theatre Company Established in 1942, the Sacramento Theatre Company is the region's premier theatre organization. Artistic Director Peggy Shannon leads the company through classical and modern plays at the 300-seat McClatchy Mainstage Theatre, with more experimental works performed at the 90-seat Stage Two Theatre. The company seeks out top-quality actors, directors and designers and offers about 17 productions from September through June. *1419 H Street, Sacramento; 916/443-6722, www.sactheatre.org*

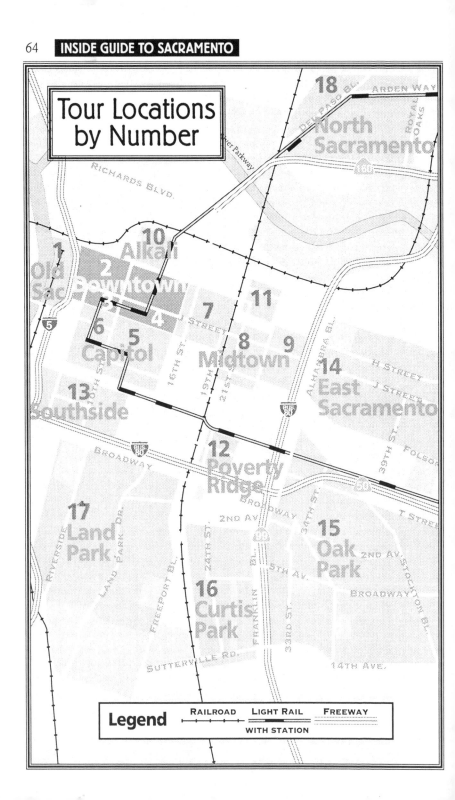

PART IV
SACRAMENTO
OLD SACRAMENTO

A common misconception is that Sacramento residents never go to Old Sacramento, except perhaps when Aunt Martha and Uncle Ned roll into town. The thought is that Old Sacramento is too tourist-oriented, too reliant on the sales of candied apples and T-shirts, to be of much interest to locals.

The conventional wisdom does not provide an accurate picture, however. About half of Old Sacramento's five million annual visitors are Sacramento residents. And, despite the cotton candy reputation, Old Sacramento contains real history. A National Registered Landmark and State Historic Park, Old Sacramento's 28 acres contain the greatest concentration of historic buildings in the state. Top that off with some fine restaurants, unique shops and a choice location and you have one of California's most interesting areas.

OLD SACRAMENTO'S BEGINNINGS

To appreciate Old Sacramento's origins, one must first know the story of Sacramento's founder, John Augustus Sutter. Ironically, the Old Sacramento area never would have been developed if Sutter had gotten his way.

Sutter was born in Germany in 1803 and reared in Switzerland. He was of average build, with blond hair and blue eyes.  Women were drawn to the handsome young man with the charming demeanor, and Sutter was not shy about flirting. Eventually, he got one of his girl-friends pregnant. Sutter married in 1826, just one day before his first child, John Sutter, Jr., was born.

Possessed by a fierce desire to succeed, Sutter convinced his new mother-in-law to finance his entry into the dry goods business. The benefactor soon tired of Sutter's penchant for living beyond his means, however; and within four years she cut off his funding. With creditors clamoring for his arrest, Sutter plundered the remaining equity in his business and fled to New York in 1834. He left his family behind, promising them that they would reunite once he got his financial affairs in order.

After several years of traveling, drinking, gambling and womanizing, Sutter came upon the California coastal city of Monterey. He requested the Mexican government to allow him to establish a colony in California's interior. The government agreed, having previously avoided settling in what they considered hostile Indian country. Sutter set sail from Monterey with a crew of 15 and landed in the Sacramento area, two miles above the mouth of American River, in 1839.

Sutter established a friendly relationship with the Native Americans of the area, finding them to be a ready source of cheap labor. To guard against attack from hostile Indians, Sutter built an adobe fortress about two miles east of the Old Sacramento area. The stronghold was called Sutter's Fort, and it became the commercial center of the new settlement.

Sutter traveled back to Monterey and became a Mexican citizen. He was commissioned a captain in the Mexican army and received a land grant from Mexico of approximately 115 square miles. Captain Sutter was now the ruler of a fertile empire he called "New Helvetia" — New Switzerland — the world's last undeveloped alluvial valley.

The rich valley soil produced astounding yields for his crops, orchards and vineyards. Never a careful businessman, Sutter invested haphazardly in real estate and business ventures. One of his investments, a sawmill near the town of Coloma, would lead to his financial doom.

On a chilly January morning in 1848, Sutter's business partner, James Marshall, spotted gold in the sawmill's tailrace. Marshall rode the 45 miles to Sacramento to show Sutter the glimmering find. Sutter did not share Marshall's excitement, however. Believing that the discovery would cause his workers to desert him to seek their fortune in the mines, Sutter urged Marshall to keep the matter a secret.

Word got out, however, and the news spread fast. It was estimated that 75 percent of San Francisco's adult males abandoned their homes -- and why not? Miners were earning up to $150 per day during the initial rush.

Prospectors would come through Sacramento on their way to the mines. Merchants at Sutter's Fort, who had more business than they could keep up with, began finding the fort's location to be cramped and inconvenient. They believed it would be much handier to peddle their goods by the Sacramento River, where Old Sacramento sits today. Sutter disagreed, knowing that the area

was prone to flooding.

Ignoring Sutter's concern, merchants abandoned the fort for the Embarcadero on the river. The Old Sacramento area quickly grew into a bustling, raucous city, fueled by quick fortune and pioneer energy. Many of the merchants became more wealthy than the miners themselves.

Then, as Sutter had anticipated, disaster struck. A devastating flood hit in 1850, the same year Sacramento incorporated as a city. A cholera epidemic broke out months later, killing more than 600 and forcing 80 percent of residents to flee. Fires struck in 1850, 1852 and 1854, destroying much of the city each time. More floods came in 1861 and 1862.

Yet, with all the disasters, residents adapted. After the 1852 fire, citizens banned wooden buildings and rebuilt with brick and cast iron. Sacramentans also raised the streets 12 feet between 1864 and 1873 to defeat the persistent flooding. This remarkable desire to weather adversity helped build Sacramento into California's state capital, the western terminus for the Pony Express and the birthplace of the Central Pacific (which later became the Southern Pacific and today the Union Pacific) Railroad.

The gold rush was a boon for many, but not for John Sutter. As he had predicted, his workers abandoned him for the mines. Development of the Old Sacramento area led to his fort's losing its position as the center of area commerce. Hordes of miners trampled his crops and stole his livestock. Trusted subordinates cheated him, traders took advantage of him and squatters stole his land.

Creditors were threatening foreclosure when his son, John Sutter, Jr., arrived from Switzerland in August, 1848. To protect the remaining assets, the elder Sutter deeded his Sacramento land to his son. The younger Sutter settled his father's debts, allowing Sacramento's founder to retire to his Hock Farm, located on the Feather River, about 25 miles from Sacramento. John Sutter, Sr., finally reunited with his family and later moved to the East Coast. His financial difficulties continued, however, until his death in 1880.

DECLINE & RESURRECTION OF OLD SACRAMENTO

Old Sacramento was a vital commercial and residential center in the decades after the gold rush. The area began sliding in the 1920s, however, when Sacramento's commercial center moved eastward. Cheap lunch counters, run-down hotels and boozy honky tonks gradually took over the old buildings of Sacramento's historic district. By the 1950s the area was considered the worst slum west of Chicago.

City leaders were delighted, then, when the state Division of Highways announced plans in the early 1960s to wipe out Old Sacramento with the construction of the Interstate 5 freeway. The way the city saw it, the freeway would provide highway access to downtown businesses and get rid of an embarrassing slum at the same time. On top of that, the state and federal governments would pick up most of the tab.

Others did not see the project in the same light. Opponents decried the city's willingness to sacrifice a precious historical district. *The Sacramento Bee*, whose original newspaper building was slated for demolition by the project, condemned the proposed freeway alignment. The "city's native beauty," editorialized the *Bee*, would be violated by an "undulating, eight lane, stilted monstrosity." In the end, highway planners agreed to shift the alignment two blocks to the east, thereby saving the portion of Old Sacramento that exists today. Nevertheless, Interstate 5 claimed a number of historic buildings, including the *Sacramento Bee's*, and cut off downtown Sacramento from the river.

The movement to save Old Sacramento heightened civic interest in the historic district's potential as a tourist attraction. The Sacramento Housing and Redevelopment Agency hatched a scheme to recapture the area's pioneer ambiance through the restoration and reconstruction of buildings in the historic district. Work on the project began in 1969 and now, $100 million later, just one existing building remains to be restored in Old Sacramento.

TOUR 1 – HISTORIC OLD SACRAMENTO

This tour focuses primarily on historic structures that have been restored. There also are many other structures in Old Sacramento that were reconstructed based

on photos or drawings of the original buildings. Restoration occured in the 1970s unless otherwise noted.

1 Delta King

Sacramento River at K Street *1926*
Renovated *1984*

This paddlewheeler transported passengers between Sacramento and San Francisco from 1927 to 1940. Built in Stockton, the boat was particularly popular during Prohibition — gambling and drinking were legal on board during the overnight excursions. The vessel's popularity dwindled with the growth of highway travel, and, after an undignified period of decay, the Delta King was renovated in 1984 as a hotel, restaurant, bar and theatre. A sister ship, the Delta Queen, today carries passengers on the Mississippi River in the New Orleans vicinity.

2 Tower Bridge

Sacramento River at Capitol Mall, George Pollock *1935*

The dock of the Delta King is a good place to view the Tower Bridge, which links Sacramento and West Sacramento. The span's middle section, which weighs 2.3 million pounds, mechanically lifts at the rate of 1 foot per second. It is one of the highest lift span bridges in the world. The bridge was the formal gateway to Sacramento in the pre-freeway years, and a notorious traffic bottleneck. Nationally known engineers called the span "one of the most beautiful in America" when the bridge was completed in 1935.

3 Cavert Building

1207 Front Street *ca. 1856*

The original owner of this building was reputed to be M.L. Cavert, a produce dealer. An early tenant was William S. Jewett, a New York artist who earned a comfortable living painting portraits of John Sutter (see Sutter portrait on page 65) and other famous persons of the era. The Cavert Building became a storage facility for the Central Pacific Railroad in the 1870s.

4 Stanford Brothers Store

1203-07 Front Street, Seth Babson probable architect *1856*
Raised one story after the *1861-62* flood

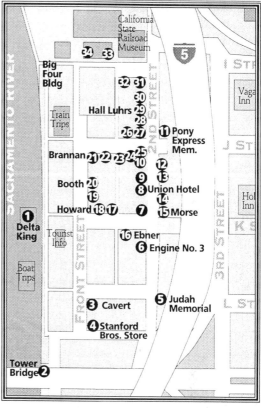

Stanford Brothers store was headed by Leland Stanford, a railroad baron, governor, U.S. senator and university founder. This building served as warehouse for the import and wholesale business, which supplied groceries, wine, liquor, cigars, mining supplies and other essentials of early Sacramento.

5 Theodore Judah Monument

SE Corner, 2nd and L Streets, J. MacQuarrie *1930*

California might not have grown to be the most populous state in the union were it not for Theodore Judah. Judah was an engineer who had the ambitious dream of building a transcontinental railroad to California. Others had the idea before him, but "Crazy" Judah was the first person to discover a feasible route through the treacherous Sierra Nevada mountains. In 1861 he convinced four prominent men (Collis Huntington, Mark Hopkins, Leland Stanford and Charles Crocker, who became known as the Big Four) to invest in the project. Eventually Judah became disenchanted with the Big Four's handling of the venture and journeyed east to find funds to buy them out. Judah contracted yellow fever while crossing the Isthmus of Panama, dying in New York within one week of his arrival. The Big Four went ahead and built the Central Pacific Railroad, using the route that Judah had mapped out. The railroad, which eventually became the mighty Southern Pacific, ended California's isolation from the rest of the nation and facilitated tremendous growth. This monument was erected by Southern Pacific employees in 1930. At the time, it was the only public recognition of Theodore Judah.

6 Sacramento Engine No. 3
1112 2nd Street *1853*
Restored *1960*

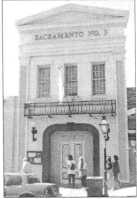

Sacramento Engine No. 3 is the oldest firehouse building in California. The City of Sacramento abandoned the structure in 1921. In 1960, Newton Cope decided to restore the firehouse and open a fancy restaurant, a questionable venture given the decaying, skid-row atmosphere of the area at the time. Lo and behold, Cope's gamble paid off. The Firehouse restaurant is popular with legislators, lobbyists and the city's elite. The iron balcony on the front of the building is from the Ebner Hotel (see #16). The tree-shaded courtyard on the alley side of the building is a splendid dining and reception area.

7 Bank Exchange Building
1030 2nd Street *ca. 1853*

A bank was located in this building only until 1856. Thereafter, the building served as the Bank Exchange Saloon for more than a century.

8 Union Hotel
1024-28 2nd Street *1855*

In 1859 the Union Hotel won a contract to providing lodging for stage coach travelers. The contract was quite a coup for the Union, besting the offer of its arch-competitor, the Orleans Hotel, which at one time was located next door. The Union became the "in" place among the politically powerful and the site of the governor's inaugural ball.

As you continue on the sidewalk heading north on 2nd Street, note the photos of the redevelopment of Old Sacramento, posted at the site of the Orleans Hotel.

9 Adams & Co. Building
1014 2nd Street *1853*

With a construction cost of $85,000, this building was once among the fanciest in town. The Adams & Co. Express and Banking House was the first to represent a large eastern banking firm on the west coast. The business failed in 1855 due to stiff competition from Wells Fargo & Co. Wells Fargo operated banking and express services in the building from 1861 to 1882.

10 B.F. Hastings Bank Building
1002 2nd Street, Alexander Boyd and Jacob Z. Davis, probable architects *1852-53*
Restored, Bob McCabe *1970s*

The B.F. Hastings Bank Building is one of the most historically significant buildings in Old Sacramento. In addition to housing B.F. Hastings Bank (1853-71),

Wells Fargo & Co. (1853-57), the California Supreme Court (1854-57) and the Pony Express (1860-61), the building also is where Theodore Judah mapped out the western route of the transcontinental railroad. The modest Supreme Court chambers and offices on the second floor suggest an unpretentious state government in California's early years.

11 Pony Express Monument
SE Corner, 2nd and J Streets, Thomas Holland *1976*

Covering a 1,966-mile route that began in St. Joseph, Missouri, and ended in Sacramento, the Pony Express featured 190 stations, 121 riders and 500 horses. The service was able to slash the time needed to send a transcontinental message, which had previously taken as long as four months, to just ten days. During its brief, 79-week existence, the Pony Express' riders covered 650,000 miles, lost just one rider to an Indian attack, completed every schedule except one and had just one incidence of lost mail. The service collapsed in 1861 with the completion of the transcontinental telegraph.

12 Heywood Building
1001-09 2nd Street *1857*

Built by Joseph Heywood, the city's first butcher, the Heywood Building later was acquired by Darius Ogden (D.O.) Mills, a prominent early banker. Tenants have included a saloon, opticians, gunsmiths, jewelers, an insurance company and a restaurant.

13 Smith Building
1009-13 2nd Street, First story *ca. 1853*
Second story *ca. 1865*

Tenants of this building have included a tailor shop, saloon, restaurant and bank.

14 Pioneer Telegraph Building
1015 2nd Street *ca. 1853*

The California State Telegraph Service had lines extending to many cities, including San Francisco, Stockton and San Jose. By 1861, the same year the Pony Express expired, the California State Telegraph Service had a monopoly on California telecommunications. The company was incorporated into Western Union in 1868, which maintained offices in this building until 1915. The building also served as the headquarters of Sacramento's first telephone exchange, beginning in 1882.

15 Morse Building
1033-39 2nd Street *1853*
Upper story *1864*, restored *1969*

This building is named for Dr. John Frederick Morse, a Sacramento pioneer and one of the first directors of the Central Pacific Railroad. The Sacramento Post

Office shared the building with Morse in the 1850s. In 1851, Morse became the first editor of the *Sacramento Union* newspaper. Mark Twain became one of the *Union's* correspondents in 1866, writing 25 letters to the newspaper on his travels to Hawaii. For more than 140 years, the *Sacramento Union* was the "oldest daily in the West." The historic newspaper finally folded in 1994.

16 Ebner Hotel
116 K Street *1856*

The last original building in Old Sacramento awaiting restoration. The dilapidated Ebner Hotel is a reminder of Old Sacramento's down-and-out condition before redevelopment in the 1960s and 1970s. Charles and Francis Xavier Ebner built the hotel in 1856, where they entertained their good friend John Sutter on many occasions. The brothers sold the building in 1863 to pursue a more profitable career in wholesale liquor. The building continued as a hotel into the 1950s, when it was converted to a warehouse. The hotel originally was decorated with French Renaissance Revival ornamentation, including small busts of George Washington along the cornice.

17 Lady Adams Building
119 K Street, Lewis Fielder *1852*
Restored, Bob McCabe *1970s*

The Lady Adams Building was the only structure to emerge from the great 1852 fire unscathed, making this the oldest structure in Old Sacramento. The building takes its name from the *Lady Adams* brig, which sailed into Sacramento in 1849. On board were the ship's owners, a group of German immigrants. The new arrivals quickly converted the vessel into a floating store at the foot of K Street, where they sold quality European merchandise. Profits from the enterprise allowed the immigrants to construct this building three years later, reportedly using the German brick that had been used as ballast on the vessel. The partners operated their wholesale merchant and banking business in this building until retiring in the 1870s.

18 Howard House
109-111 K Street *1865*
Restored, Bob McCabe *1970s*

One of the more elaborate buildings in Old Sacramento, with a central projecting bay, arched windows and handsome railings. Ground-floor tenants have included a clothing store, a wholesale grocery and an insurance company. The upper floors were rented out to lodgers.

19 Leggett's Ale House
1025 Front Street *1852*
Restored, Bob McCabe *1970s*

Leggett was a Scotsman who loved to spin a yarn with customers over pints of English ales and porters. He ran the popular drinking establishment for 10 years, then moved to Amador County in the Sierra foothills.

20 Booth Building
1017-23 Front Street
North building *1866,* South building *1879*
Restored, Bob McCabe *1970s*

Newton Booth was one of Sacramento's most powerful figures, serving as state senator (1862-63), governor (1871-75) and U.S. senator (1875-81). Booth ran a wholesale grocery business from this structure. Reportedly, Booth and Company conspired with captains of merchant ships to control the price of goods coming into Sacramento. When the ships were about five miles south of K Street, Booth and Company would flag signal the ship from the platform on the roof of the building. The ship would signal back the worth of the cargo, giving Booth and Company the information needed to outbid competitors. When Booth was governor the building contained a ballroom with a capacity for 1,500 people.

21 Brannan Building
Southeast corner, Front and J Streets *1853*

This building housed Sam Brannan's general store, which served the needs of gold rush miners. Brannan's life of ambition, opportunism and tragedy make him one of early California's most remarkable figures. He racked up a number of state "firsts," including first leader of the Mormon Church, first founder of a newspaper and first owner of a flour mill. He also was California's first millionaire, reaping gold rush profits faster than anyone else.

Shortly after James Marshall's gold discovery at Sutter's Mill, two members of Brannan's church found gold at Mormon Island (now beneath Folsom Lake). Brannan immediately made sure that the citizens of San Francisco knew about the discovery, thereby ensuring that hordes of gold seekers would stop by Brannan's Sacramento store for provisions and equipment. Brannan also announced that the church controlled Mormon Island and therefore should receive a tithe from any Mormons who extracted gold there. Church founder Brigham Young excommunicated Brannan when the Sacramento businessman refused to turn over the tithe. Brannan said he would pay only when Young brought a receipt signed by the Lord! Brannan was charged with embezzlement of church funds, making him the defendant in California's first jury trial (the jury hung and Brannan was released).

Brannan eventually moved to the Napa Valley, where he discovered hot springs on his property and opened a popular summer resort that he called "Calistoga," a combination of "California" and "Saratoga." The later part of Brannan's life saw an unhappy chain of events; heavy drinking led to a divorce, which led to a huge cash settlement for his wife and liquidation of his assets. His problems worsened with a series of bad investments. Brannan died a forgotten and ruined man in Escondido (San Diego County) in 1889.

22 Vernon-Brannon House
112-114 J Street *1853*
Restored, Bob McCabe *1970s*

This structure was built for Sacramento's first postmaster, H.E. Robinson. The building served as a hotel under a variety of owners until 1918. The Sacramento Society of California Pioneers was organized by Sam Brannan here in 1854 for

Sacramentans who arrived in California before 1849. Sacramento's first modern brewpub, The Hogshead, opened in the basement in 1986.

23 Pioneer Hall and Bakery
120-124 J Street *1854*

The Sacramento Society for California Pioneers held their meetings and events on the second floor of this building. George Schroth ran the bakery on the ground level and lived in the building until 1892. The bakery did not close until 1924.

24 Gregory-Barnes Store
126 J Street *ca. 1853*

The California State Library occupied the second story of this building in the 1850s. Julius Gregory operated a wholesale market beginning in 1860, which expanded to 128 J Street in 1870. The market offered wholesale produce and dairy products. Gregory's two sons took over the business by 1883, and one of the sons, Eugene, became Sacramento's mayor in 1888.

25 I. & S. Wormser Building
128 J Street *1853*

This structure was built by B.F. Hastings and rented to I. & S. Wormser, two clothing merchants from Germany.

26 Haines Building
127 J Street *1856*
Restored, Bob McCabe *1970s*

This building housed Collicott's Apothecary as well as Sam Colville, publisher of the Sacramento Directory, a book as essential in pioneer days as the phone book is today.

27 Sazerac Building
131 J Street *ca. 1853*
Restored, Bob McCabe *1970s*

This structure was built on the site of the Gem Saloon, a popular gambling spot. The Sazerac Building housed subsequent saloons such as the Sazerac, the Adriatic and the Blue Wing. In the 1870s a coffee and spice mill occupied the building, followed by a wholesale grocery business.

28 Our House Saloon
926 2nd Street *early 1850s*

This building housed one of many saloons that popped up in the 1850s to slake the thirst of pioneers and miners.

29 Hall, Luhrs & Co.
912-16 2nd Street, Nathaniel Goodell *1883*

The largest brick building in Old Sacramento, this structure housed Halls, Luhrs & Co. Wholesale Grocers. The company shipped fresh California fruit across the country by having ice quarried in the Sierra, hauled to Sacramento and packed with the fruit onto rail cars. One of the owners, Thomas Hall, became the president of Orangevale Colonization Company, laying out the 10-acre tracts and town site of Orangevale. *The Daily Record–Union* remarked in 1884 that the building "commanded the attention of the eye of every passer in the street."

30 Eureka Swimming Baths
908-10 2nd Street *1854*

Patronized by guests of nearby hotels, the public baths featured 14 rooms. Water was heated by the sun in a tank behind the building and was changed for patrons after every 10 baths.

31 Original Street Level
900 2nd Street

Persistent flooding of Old Sacramento inspired a movement to raise the streets above the flood level. The painstakingly slow process, which required hauling dirt wagonload-by-wagonload, was carried out between 1864 and 1873. The original street level, 12 feet below the existing grade, can be seen in the courtyard at the corner.

32 Mechanics Exchange Hotel
116-22 I Street *1860*

The two-story building to the east was constructed in 1860, with the larger structure to the west built at some point thereafter. The hotel was frequented by those connected with the iron works, flour mills and railroad activities in the industrial area north of I Street.

33 Dingley Spice and Coffee Mill
115 I Street *1853*

This building was constructed for Nathaniel Dingley, a miserly '49er from Maine. Dingley lived in the second floor residence and reportedly powered the mill by tapping steam that was generated by boilers from the nearby city waterworks.

34 Big Four Buildings
111-113 I Street *ca. 1852*
Relocated *1970*

These buildings originally were located on the south side of K Street between 2nd and 3rd Streets. The central buildings are the Huntington and Hopkins Hardware Store. A replica of a 19th Century hardware store is located on the ground floor. Leland Stanford's store is located right next door. Stanford operated a wholesale merchandise store on the ground floor and rented the second story to the Masonic Lodge. A small room above the hardware store is where Theodore Judah first pitched to the Big Four his dream of building a transcontinental railroad. The Big Four invested in Judah's scheme, and Stanford enlarged the second floor to house the first office of the Central Pacific Railroad in 1862.

DOWNTOWN

In the early 20th Century, a bitter debate broke out in Sacramento over whether to replace the county courthouse located downtown. The structure had served as California's State Capitol Building from 1855-69 and many in the community believed that the historic structure should be saved. Critics argued that the county needed a larger courthouse to serve its growing population. Verdict: the old courthouse was razed, replaced by a new facility.

The conflict between past and future still exists in Sacramento's burgeoning downtown. Historic buildings and affordable housing are still falling to the wrecking ball to make way for the kind of shiny new development that befits an emerging metropolis. The city is trying to come to grips with its transition to big-city status, like an adolescent experiencing growing pains.

THE DOWNTOWN BUILT FROM CLAY

Brick and terra cotta are Sacramento's indigenous building materials, formed out of the rich alluvial soil of the Sacramento Valley. The materials were an obvious choice for the city's pre-World War II commercial structures.

THE ART OF TERRA COTTA

Terra cotta, which means "burnt earth," is clay that has been shaped into a desired form and then fired in a kiln at extremely high temperatures. The malleable substance can be crafted into intricate ornamentation such as gargoyles and cartouches, or transformed into sleek, colorful tile, or sprayed as a veneer that looks just like expensive granite, limestone or marble.

Responsible for much of the city's fine terra cotta work is Gladding, McBean & Co., located about 30 miles northeast of Sacramento in the town of Lincoln. Founded in 1875 and still in business today, Gladding, McBean & Co. employed skillful artisans who left their mark in many cities around the world. Notable California examples include City Hall and the Biltmore Hotel in Los Angeles, City Hall and the Hearst Building in San Francisco and the Paramount Theatre and Tribune Building in Oakland.

THE MAKING OF K STREET MALL

K Street once was downtown Sacramento's major retail street. Prior to World War II, department stores, movie theatres, restaurants and shops provided K Street with an energetic, central city bustle.

Suburbanization in the post-war era eroded the downtown's retail base, however; and many of the old stores fell to competition from outlying shopping malls. In an attempt to revive the ailing corridor, the city converted K Street to a pedestrian mall in 1969. A Bay Area architect convinced the city to erect along the mall monstrous concrete structures with cascading fountains and pools of water. The project was supposed to represent the Sierra Nevada mountain range and its tributaries. Apparently the architect had never experienced a Sacramento summer — the concrete Sierras radiated the punishing heat and made the nearly deserted mall an even more forbidding place.

K STREET IN THE 1920s

With the arrival of light rail in 1986, the mall entered a new phase — brick paving replaced the ugly mountain range, newly planted sycamores softened the landscape and electric trolley cars brought patrons and workers directly to the mall. A popular draw is the ice-skating rink at St. Rose of Lima Park during the winter.

TOUR 2 – CIVIC CENTER

1 City Hall

915 I Street, Rudolph Herold *1911*

Sacramento City Hall, with its ornate terra cotta decoration, is dramatically sited across the street from César E. Chavez Plaza. The building's Beaux Arts style reflects the City Beautiful sentiments of the early 20th century. The City Beautiful movement called for dignified civic buildings that were carefully positioned to provide striking vistas. The movement expressed the idealism of municipal government reformers during the progressive era. City Hall's copper-domed clock tower looms into view between the tall trees of César Chavez Plaza. The exterior of the building was featured in the movie *All the King's Men*. Two annexes were built in the 1930s to house the city's fire department. The interior has been remodeled and little original detail remains. The city is contemplating the construction of a new annex behind City Hall and a restoration of the council chambers.

2 César E. Chavez Plaza

I and J Streets, 9th and 10th Streets *1849*
Renovated *2000*

California's State Capitol was supposed to be located in this park. Sacramento had donated the block to the state in 1856, just one of the incentives that had collectively convinced the Legislature

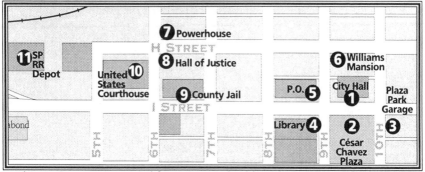

to choose Sacramento as California's capital. Although the Legislature approved bonds for the building's construction, the California Supreme Court stopped the project cold by ruling that the bonds would exceed the state's debt limit. The state returned the property to the city, which developed the property into a public park. In 1915, when the City Beautiful movement was in full flower, Harvard architect John Nolen envisioned the park (then known as City Plaza) to be the center of a beautiful civic center, surrounded by city hall, a post office, an auditorium, art gallery, library, hotel and offices. The city made a half-hearted effort to implement the plan but soon forgot about Nolen's drawings and sold off the land. Today, the park serves as a major community gathering place, hosting a weekly farmers' market and summer concerts. Located in the center of the park is the socialist realist *Coleman Memorial Fountain* (Ralph Stackpole, 1926), funded by Frances Coleman for the enjoyment of thirsty animals and birds. The three female figures depicted in the fountain represent the Sacramento, American and Feather Rivers. The 1889 statue on the south end of the park was built by Central Pacific employees in honor of Andrew Jackson Stevens, an innovator in locomotive construction and design. The statue is the oldest outdoor sculpture in

the city. On the opposite side of the park, directly in front of City Hall, is a much more recent sculpture honoring a contemporary hero, César Chavez (Lisa Reinertson, 2001) . The work shows a determined Chavez leading a group of farmworkers marching for better wages and working conditions. The city named the plaza in honor of Chavez in 1998.

3 Plaza Park Garage
SE Corner, 10th and I Streets, Niiya, Calpo, Hom and Dong *1992*

At $26 million, this is the most expensive city garage in Sacramento history. Regardless of whether one thinks that this was a wise expenditure, or even an appropriate use of the site, one cannot help admiring the handsome, classical styling of the 1000-car structure. It is a postmodern expression of City Beautiful sentiments, this time exalting the auto rather than civic government. The waterfall by Roger Berry that magically runs down the garage's tapered corner column is an engaging surprise. Pedestrians cannot resist poking a finger into the shimmering layer of water.

4 Sacramento Public Library
828 I Street, Loring P. Rixford *1918*
Annex and galleria Kaplan, McLaughlin, Diaz *1991*

The original library was donated by industrialist Andrew Carnegie and was
designed by San Francisco City Architect Loring Rixford in a Florentine
Renaissance style. Gladding, McBean & Co. provided the terra cotta sheathing
and ornamentation, such as the 12 lion heads on the first
floor and the bear paws at the foot of the ornate lamp
standards. With the construction of a galleria and annex in
1991, the original library is now used for conference
rooms and special events. The four-story galleria provides
an impressive setting for receptions and the annex offers a
smartly appointed interior for the city's central library.

5 Federal Building/Post Office
801 I Street, Starks and Flanders *1933*

This building's blend of Neo-Classical and Renaissance
architecture, suggesting governmental strength and stabili-
ty, must have been a reassuring sight in a city wracked by
the Great Depression. Gladding, McBean & Co. provided
the terra cotta ornamentation, as well as the simulated
granite veneer above the first floor. The exterior lion heads appear to be roaring
at the lion heads facing from the library across the street. The long lobby features shiny terrazzo floors and a gilded, coffered ceiling.

6 Llewelyn Williams Mansion
900 H Street, Seth Babson and James Seadler *1885*

This Victorian home was converted into a mortuary in 1907. Mory Holmes later
purchased the residence and used it as a reception hall until the 1980s, when it
was purchased by local developers. Faced with demolition unless a new site was
found, the home was moved to the City Hall parking lot from across the street in
1994 to serve as Sacramento's first youth hostel.

7 Old Folsom Powerhouse, Sacramento Station A
6th and I Streets *1895*

This Classical Revival powerhouse was the first distribution point of electricity for a major city. The station
received power generated from Folsom Powerhouse,
located 22 miles away, on what was then the world's
longest transmission line. The power network distrib-
uted electricity from Station A to all homes and businesses in Sacramento and helped make electric trolleys
possible in the Central Valley. Station A also allowed
Sacramento to celebrate Admission Day in 1895 with
an extraordinary Carnival of Lights festival. Twenty-
five thousand red, green and orange lights illuminated
buildings, flag poles and bunting in the city, attracting

60,000 people from throughout the valley. The building is now owned by the Sacramento Municipal Utility District and still serves as a power distribution station.

8 Hall of Justice
813 6th Street, Frank Shea and John Lofquist *1916*

Remodeled, *2000*

This Neo-Classical building was constructed for Sacramento's police department and included a 32-cell jail. The city's awarding of the design contract to the San Francisco firm Shea and Lofquist caused an uproar among local architects, who believed that such a prominent public building should be designed by Sacramentans. A compet-

CARNIVAL OF LIGHTS, 1895

ing design by city hall architect Rudolph Herold was rejected by the city as being too expensive. The windows of the building were covered over with patterned brick to avoid breakage during the civil unrest of the 1960s. The building's original brick and stone came from quarries near Folsom and were prepared by inmates at the state prison there. The police department moved out in 1997, and the building was converted to the county law library and law offices.

9 Sacramento County Jail
651 I Street *1989*

The jail occupies the site where the original county courthouse served as the State Capitol Building from 1855-69. The old courthouse was demolished to make way for a Neo-Classical structure designed by city hall architect Rudolph Herold. Herold's courthouse was an impressive addition to I Street, a monumental structure in the City Beautiful tradition. Eventually, however, the county outgrew the building and in 1965 constructed a larger facility two blocks away. The board of supervisors rejected a costly rehabilitation of Herold's courthouse, believing the structure to be not as architecturally significant as buildings from earlier Sacramento history. A wrecking ball brought down Herold's creation in 1970, replaced by a parking lot that remained until the jail was constructed in the late 1980s.

10 United States Courthouse
601 I Street, Nacht and Lewis/HLM *1999*

The 16-story courthouse appears to be worth every cent of its $130 million price tag. The design by one of Sacramento's oldest firms (Nacht and Lewis is the successor of Starks and Flanders, which was established in 1921) recalls the high standards once common to government buildings. The courthouse reveals distinctly different personalities on each of its four sides. Clad in the same warm, Indiana limestone that covers the Empire State Building, this modern structure fits in quite well with the older downtown structures. The plaza features pavers inscribed with *Truisms and Survival Texts* (Jenney Holzer), and a long black fountain decorated with comical figures representing early periods of California history (Tom Otterness). The four-story elliptical rotunda is decorated with a mammoth *Scales of Justice* (Larry Kirkland). Anegre wood veneer from Ghana covers the Biedermeyerish, McIntosh-inspired chambers and courtrooms. The building's most generous feature is the panoramic city view afforded from windows located just outside the elevators on each floor. The amenity is available to anyone who cares to wander into the building, perhaps underscoring the ideal that, in America, the people rule.

11 Southern Pacific Railroad Depot
501 I Street, Walter Bliss and William Faville *1926*

This Mediterranean/Renaissance Revival building quickly became the seventh-busiest freight and passenger depot in the nation upon opening in 1926, averaging 86 trains and 4500 passengers daily. The depot's well-known architects also designed San Francisco's St. Francis Hotel and Flood Mansion. The depot has

Italian marble floors and fine-grained oak benches, with a ceiling that rises 44 feet above the floor. The mural on the east wall is by San Francisco artist J. MacQuarrie and depicts the 1863 Sacramento ground-breaking ceremonies for the Central Pacific Railroad. The Big Four can be seen in the mural: Leland Stanford holding a shovel, Charles Crocker gesturing on the speaker's platform and Mark Hopkins and Collis Huntington standing in front of the platform.

The Central Pacific evolved into the mighty Southern Pacific Railroad empire. The Southern Pacific monopolized transportation in California for decades, allowing the company to establish high freight rates, buy judges, dominate regulators and control the Legislature. Hiram Johnson was elected governor in 1910 on a platform of ending the Southern Pacific's grip on California politics. Johnson went on to enact the most sweeping progressive reforms of the era, including the initiative, referendum and recall; workers' compensation system; civil service system; and women's suffrage. Johnson was Theodore Roosevelt's vice presidential running mate on the 1912 Bull Moose Party ticket and served as United States Senator from 1917-45. The Southern Pacific was

absorbed by the Union Pacific Railroad in 1996, ending a major chapter in California history.

The 240-acre rail yards to the north of the depot are slated for redevelopment over the coming decades, which will increase the size of the central city significantly. A lot of history could be lost. The rail yards, the first spot in California with heavy industrialization, contain several historic

OLD SP SHOPS DATE FROM THE 1860s.

brick shops once used for locomotive fabrication and maintenance. These shops are among the oldest masonry buildings in the city.

TOUR 3 – WEST DOWNTOWN

1 Downtown Plaza
Bordered by 4th, 7th, J and L Streets, John S. Bowles, Associates *1971-72* Renovation, Jon Jerde *1993*

Originally constructed in the 1970s, Downtown Plaza was a key component of the city's efforts to redevelop its slum-ridden "West End." The mall threw a life preserver to downtown retail, although the shopping center's clunky concrete design quickly became as fashionable as a polyester leisure suit. While the architects of the 1993 renovation restrained themselves from wiping away all of the original mall (recognizing that even 1970s architecture will one day be appreciated), their efforts gave the mall a new verve. The once-expansive pedestrian street, which had made the previous mall seem more lifeless than it really was, has been squeezed into intimate walkways; and the three-block complex is now divided into four distinct urban "rooms": The Piazza, featuring a stadium style roof, which is a center for live entertainment; the 5th Street Market, with a decorative steel lattice on the upper-level that evokes the city's industrial past; the

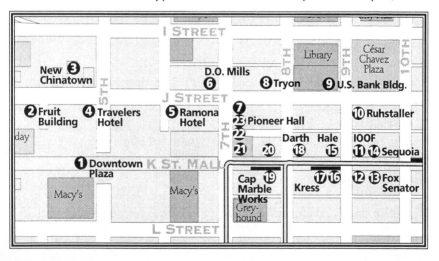

Rotunda, a circular courtyard that is capped by a stunning 85-foot tall dome; and the Garden Court, appointed with wood furniture, gurgling tile fountains and tree-sized planters.

2 California Fruit Building
1006 4th Street, Charles Kaiser *1914*

This early Sacramento high rise was designed in the Chicago School style. Note the Gladding, McBean & Co. terra cotta floral decoration at the base and top of the structure. The California Fruit Growers Association was an agricultural cooperative that made fruit available to retail consumers through contracts with growers. The association vacated the building in 1967 and the structure currently provides office space primarily for lawyers.

3 New Chinatown
Bordered by 3rd, 5th, I and J Streets *1959 - 1973*

Persons of Chinese descent were an integral part of Sacramento history, having endured the backbreaking labor of mining in the Sierra foothills, constructing the transcontinental railroad and building the Sacramento River levee system. Located between I and J Streets and 2nd to 6th Streets, Sacramento's old Chinatown was the largest in California after San Francisco's. The area was once crowded with small shops offering glazed ducks, herbal medicines, groceries and household items. Redevelopment in the 1950s-70s cleared out the old-fashioned shops in favor of this complex of boxy modern buildings. In a nod to the site's history, all the structures — even the telephone booth — feature a pagoda cap. This feckless architectural afterthought fails to evoke with any vibrance the soul of the old Chinatown, but the central pedestrian mall does provide a shady refuge from the outside traffic. The 18-foot statue of Dr. Sun Yat-sen located in the courtyard faces in the direction of China. The noted statesman wrote China's first constitution during a visit to Sacramento in the early 20th century. One of the redevelopment buildings also houses Sacramento's oldest restaurant, Royal Hong King Lum, which dates from 1906.

4 Traveler's Hotel
428 J Street, Clarence Cuff and Maury Diggs *1914*

Sacramento's premier hotel when it opened in 1914, the Traveler's featured such modern innovations as dust chutes, a central vacuum and an ice-water circulating system. The building features an eclectic design with Classical and Prairie School influences. After a period of decline, the hotel was rehabilitated for office use in the early 1980s. Even so, the fine lobby, with its tile floors, central fountain and gold leaf railing, now appears eerily vacant.

5 Ramona Hotel
600 J Street *1930*

Long since converted to offices, this attractive Spanish Colonial Revival hotel building adds some pizazz to an otherwise undistinguished block.

6 National Gold Bank of D.O. Mills & Co.
631 J Street, Willis Polk *1912, annex 1925*

The heavy granite columns of this Neo-Classical bank building establish an authoritative presence at its corner location, as if to assure depositors that their money was in good hands. Operated as a bank under various owners until 1990, the building was purchased by developer Gregg Lukenbill, who preserved or restored much of the exquisite interior while transforming the building into a private reception hall. The soaring, 45-foot-high lobby may be viewed by entering the annex to the left of the building on J Street, walking to the end of the hall and peering through the glass doors on the right. The bank's founder, Darius Ogden Mills, had died by the time this structure was built. Mills had come to California in 1848 after a successful career as a banker in New York City. He established the Bank of D.O. Mills in Sacramento in 1859 and later became a regent of the University of California. Mills subsequently moved back to New York and constructed a number of low-cost residences for the poor. He left an estate then valued at $60 million when he died in 1910.

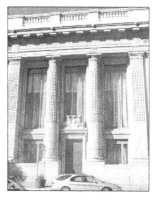

7 Capitol National Bank
700 J Street, Rudolph Herold *1915*

This Renaissance Revival building is distinguished by the terra cotta figures perched seven stories above the sidewalk. At the time of its opening, *The Sacramento Bee* praised the $250,000 structure for its "modern, monumental style of architecture, having a Gothic feeling." Unfortunately, no detail remains of the original impressive lobby.

8 Sylvester Tryon Building
727 J Street *1861*

This building is one of the oldest in the downtown area. The structure was remodeled in 1917 to its current appearance, a blend of Mission Revival and Chicago School design. The structure originally served as a hay and grain shop. Later uses included a salesroom for Capital Woolen Mills and a small market. The original entry, built before the streets were raised 12 feet between 1864-73, is located in the basement.

9 U.S. Bank Building
980 9th Street, Kaplan, McLaughlin, Diaz *1991*

A standout among Sacramento's new breed of skyscrapers, the U.S. Bank Building's understated Art Deco style recalls the great New York City high rises

of the 1930s. The clay-colored tile sheathing compliments the traditional brick and terra cotta of the older downtown structures. Sleek bronze cougars (Gwynn Murrill, 1991) stretch out by the front entry, and the lobby's marble floor is punctuated by distinctive geometric patterns. Colorful lobby murals by Richard Piccolo, entitled *Aer and Terra* and *Aqua and Ignis*, as well as the building's Plaza Park location, create a dramatic environment for the harried professionals who daily climb into the tower's shiny chrome elevators.

10 Ruhstaller Building
900 J Street *1898*

Frank J. Ruhstaller was the owner of the Ruhstaller Brewery, located at 12th and H

Streets until it was demolished in the 1930s. The first floor of the Ruhstaller Building was a tap room for the brewery, with upper floors serving as office space for doctors, dentists and Ruhstaller himself. The building embodies an eclectic combination of styles, combining Queen Anne with Classical and Italianate elements. It boasted the first structural air cooling system in California, which must have seemed a wonderful innovation to tenants who had long suffered through Sacramento's simmering summers.

11 I.O.O.F. Temple
1017-31 9th Street, A.A. Bennett *1870*
Remodeled, Charles Dean *1936*

Originally this building, constructed for the local chapter of the International Order of the Odd Fellows, featured an ornate, Second Empire design, with a Mansard roof, classical columns and arched windows (the original shape of the windows may be observed on the alley side of the building). A Depression-era remodel stripped away the ornamentation and substituted sleek, aqua-colored terra cotta tile from Gladding, McBean & Co. The halls on the third floor, known as Capitol Plaza Halls today, are available for events and are often open for viewing. These remarkable rooms retain the original 19th-Century decor, with hand-painted ceilings, crystal chandeliers and intricate moldings.

12 Forum Building
1107 9th Street, Rudolph Herold *1911*
Remodeled, *ca. 1930s*

The building originally was half as tall, and with more exterior embellishment. Remodeling provided the structure an Art Deco appearance that relates well to the I.O.O.F. Temple directly across the mall. The lobby is small but inviting.

13 Fox Senator Theatre
912 K Street, Leonard Starks *1925*

Only the modified facade remains of this theatre, the first of many Sacramento projects for Architect Leonard Starks.

14 Sequoia Hotel
909 K Street *1911*

This otherwise unexceptional building at one time was the residence of future California Governor and later U.S. Supreme Court Chief Justice Earl Warren. Warren stayed here in 1919 as a young staff attorney for the Assembly Judiciary Committee.

15 Hale Bros. & Co.
825 K Street, A.A. Cook *1881*
Remodeled *1909*

This structure comprises several buildings that were combined and remodeled over the course of a century. Hale Brothers and Company was a dry and fancy goods merchandiser that first opened in San Jose in 1876. The first Sacramento location for this store opened across the street in 1880. In the 1950s the exterior was given a stark, windowless remodel, but was later restored to its 1909 appearance.

16 Montgomery Ward and Co.
830 K Street *1936*

Company officials considered this branch the finest and most modern of the chain's 500 stores at the time of its opening. The building has what *The Sacramento Bee* described as a Colonial architecture theme, and the original fixtures and furniture were made of walnut.

17 Kress
818 K Street, John Fleming *1931*

This building features an impressive Zig Zag Moderne facade. Kress was a chain of 5-and-25-cent stores headquartered in New York City. The chain occupied the building until 1980. The structure is now used for offices.

18 Renaissance Tower
801 K Street, Anthony Lumsden *1989*

Landing like an alien in the late 1980s, the Renaissance Tower was the tallest structure in Sacramento history when built. It quickly was dubbed "The Darth Vader Building" by unimpressed observers. The brown granite and dark glass exterior appears perpetually dusty, and the building already looks dated, like an avocado refridgerator. Sharp angles and impenetrable windows make the building seem anti-social, as if it does not want to get along with its older neighbors. The Renaissance Tower dominated the skyline for a couple years, bumtiously announcing Sacramento's emergence into the urban big leagues. Subsequent construction of additional high rises has allowed this sore thumb to recede somewhat into the background.

19 Capitol Marble Works
722 K Street *1872*
Remodeled, F.A. Cunnius *1930s*

The marble works were here for the building's first 20 years. Later the building was the first Sacramento location of the W.T. Grant variety store chain.

20 Oschner Building
717 K Street *1904*

Original owner John Oschner was a cask and barrel manufacturer. The building has housed doctors, lawyers and dentists and is one of the few remaining office buildings in Sacramento that date from its period.

21 St. Rose of Lima Park
7th and K Streets

This small park was formerly the site of St. Rose of Lima Church, a pioneer parish and the founder of St. Joseph's Cemetery at 21st and Broadway. The site was later occupied by a Richardsonian Romanesque post office, dedicated in 1894 and constructed of rusticated Arizona red sandstone. The park was established when the post office was demolished in the 1960s and is now the site of a popular winter ice-skating rink.

22 Merchants National Bank
1015 7th Street, H.H. Winner *1921*

This bank has been in business, under its original name and in the same building, longer than any other bank in Sacramento. The building features lavish use of Napoleon Grey, San Saba and Tennessee marble in its lobby. The classical entry is distinguished by a clock with a marble dial flanked by two sculptural figures. At its grand opening the bank announced that, in addition to the promotion of private enterprise, "a homelike atmosphere will be pursued in attending to and inviting the accounts of children, who will be encouraged to follow a program of thrift."

23 Pioneer Hall
1009 7th Street, Nathaniel Goodell *1868*

Pioneer Hall was constructed by the Sacramento Pioneer Association, a group established in 1854 in Old Sacramento's Vernon-Brannon house by 70 people who had arrived in California before 1850. Architect Nathaniel Goodell, who also designed the Governor's Mansion and the Heilbron House, was president of the Pioneer Society in 1876-77 and had an office in the hall's basement. The building is one of the best surviving examples of Goodell's commercial work. The Sacramento Housing and Redevelopment Agency restored the building in the late 1980s and is now a tenant on the second floor.

TOUR 4 – EAST DOWNTOWN

1 California-Western States Life Insurance Building
926 J Street, George Sellon *1925*

A French Renaissance Revival building with a Chateauesque copper mansard roof, the Cal-Western Building was the tallest structure between Oakland and Portland when it opened in 1925. The 14-story tower was a prestigious showpiece for Gladding, McBean & Co. terra cotta and was once considered a top-notch business address. The building's architect, George Sellon, served as California's first state architect.

2 American Trust Company
1015 10th Street, Harry Devine, Sr. *1938*

This Streamline Moderne building features a colorful interior mural by artist Millard Sheets, depicting California industries such as gold mining, logging, agriculture, ranching and government.

3 Hart's Cafeteria
1016 10th Street, Dean and Dean *1925*

Exterior terra cotta shields, imprinted with an "H," hint at this building's former glory. The Hart brothers, who owned two other Sacramento cafeterias, spent $150,000 to outfit the building in opulent Spanish style. The upstairs dining room was particularly grand: seating for 300, mahogany paneling and furniture, pricey chandeliers, an orchestra and waiters in Spanish costumes. The cafeteria had the capacity to serve 3,000 meals per day.

César Chavez Park

⑲ Graf House

⑱ Elks ⑰ Masonic

Cal Western Life Building ❶

Mayes Clock

J STREET

⑳

❷ Mohr &

Fuller

Public ⑮ Market

⑯

⑬ Sacramento Community Convention Center

St. Paul's Episcopal Church ⑭

Hart's ❸

Yoerk

Cathedral ❾

Ban Esquire ⑪ ⑫

Empress ❹ ❺

K ST. MALL

Regis ❻

❽ PG&E

⑩ Weinstocks

Howe ❼

Hyatt Regency

L STREET

4 Empress Theatre
1013 K Street, Lee De Camp *1912*
Remodeled *1949*

The Empress Theatre was a vaudeville house that was converted in 1918 to a silent movie theatre, the Hippodrome. In 1949, the theatre was remodeled again as The Crest, and dressed in a swirling late Art Deco style. The Crest shut down for a few years in the 1980s, then reopened in 1986 as a venue for concerts and movies. The theatre survived an arson fire in 1993, saved by its thick masonry walls. Two additional basement theatres were added in the late 1990s.

5 Mohr and Yoerk Building
1031 K Street *1910*
Remodeled, George Sellon *1933*

Originally this building held a market, a realty business and apartments. In 1933 the building was remodeled in a Prairie School and Art Deco style to accommodate the Bon Marche women's store. Ransohoff's, a San Francisco women's apparel shop, took over the Bon Marche in 1956, staying in business about 35 years.

6 Hotel Regis
1106 11th Street *1911*

The building is smartly appointed with terra cotta rams' heads. Espresso Metropolitan has been the most successful of a series of tenants in bringing the public back into the building, which is listed on the National Register of Historic Places.

7 Howe Apartments
1110 11th Street *1914*

Now known as the El Cortez Apartments, this building is distinguished by its protruding cornice. Although now looking tattered, the building used to count among its tenants many legislators and lobbyists.

8 PG&E Headquarters
1100 K Street, Edward C. Hemming *1912*

The Pacific Gas and Electric Company had its headquarters in this building 1912-66. PG&E is one of the nation's largest utility companies, formed by a series of mergers dating back to the earliest years of statehood. This handsome structure combines Prairie School and Chicago styles and relates well to other buildings in the vicinity.

9 Cathedral of the Blessed Sacrament
1017 11th Street, Brian Clinch *1887*

Modeled after a Paris cathedral (L'Eglise de la Trinite), Sacramento's Cathedral of the Blessed Sacrament was the largest west of the Mississippi until the 1960s — not bad for a city of about 24,000, which was Sacramento's population when the

cathedral was built. The building features a 216-foot belfry tower, two 120-foot towers and a three-story octagonal sanctuary. The cathedral is the headquarters of the Sacramento Diocese of the Catholic Church, which covers an area from Vallejo to the Oregon border. To celebrate its centennial in 1987, the building received a new copper roof, a paint job and new stained glass windows. The diocese plans a complete restoration of the cathedral in the next few years.

10 Weinstock, Lubin & Co.
1111 12th Street, Powers and Ahnden *1924*

Modeled after the Printemps department store in Paris, this building was the flagship for the Weinstock-Lubin department store chain. The impressive, three-story arched entry, as well as the other terra cotta ornament and sheathing, is the work of Gladding, McBean & Co. Weinstock's moved its store to Downtown Plaza in 1980 and the old building was converted to office use. In 1995, the Weinstock's chain was bought out by the parent company of Macy's, Bloomingdale's and Bullock's.

11 1201 K Street
1201 K Street, Hellmuth, Obata and Kassabaum *1990*

This structure is locally known as the "Ban Roll-on Building" for its distinctive round tower that extends from the lobby to the roof. The building's copper dome seems to take its inspiration from the State Capitol and the Cathedral of the Blessed Sacrament. Large lobby windows extend an invitation to passersby to walk inside.

12 Esquire Theatre
1211 K Street, William David *1940*
Rehabilitated, *1999*

The tall, Streamline Moderne marquee stands out as the only pre-1974 feature on the block. Its architect, William David, also designed the Tower Theatre on Broadway. After enduring a dreary period as an office building, the Esquire was reborn in 1999 as a state-of-the-art IMAX Theatre.

13 Sacramento Community Convention Center
J between 13th and 15th Streets, Vitiello and Niiya *1974*
Expansion, Vitiello and Associates *1995*

The 1974 initial construction and subsequent expansion of the convention center was a civic battle royal. Preservationists decried the demolition of historic structures, the center's bulky design and the accuracy of rosy revenue projections.

Proponents contended that the center would be a financial boon and was essential for Sacramento to compete with other cities. The City Council gave final approval to an expansion at the tail end of the economic boom of the 1980s and time will tell as to whether the $80 million investment will pay off. Check out the fountain sculpture *A time to cast away stones* (Stephen Kaltenbach, 1999) in front of the west entrance of the convention center, a provocative piece that features a bust of the late artist Robert Arneson.

14 St. Paul's Episcopal Church
15th and J Streets, D.H. Burnham, *1903-09*

St. Paul's Episcopal is Sacramento's first church, established August 16, 1849. The rusticated white granite structure was designed in an Olde English style by the famous Daniel Burnham firm of Chicago. On the east side of the church is the *Stanford Memorial Window*, which was made by the famous Louis Comfort Tiffany of New York. Jane Stanford commissioned the window in 1890, six years after the death of her only son, Leland Stanford, Jr. The window is consistent with the Victorian penchant for emotionally wrenching memorials. The central panel depicts a true likeness of the boy being carried into heaven by a guardian angel. The left panel illustrates a grieving angel, her face prematurely aged, while the right panel shows an angel in her teens. In each case the angels have the face of Jane Stanford (the church program notes that "it might be said that the artist was a little generous in his representation of that lady.") Experts consider the window to be among the most beautiful and highly valued in the world. A 1993 evaluation estimated the window to be worth up to $7 million. The window underwent an 18-month restoration beginning in 1992 by local craftsman Richard Graf. Facing the Stanford window is the *St. Cecelia Window* (John Mallon, 1889). St. Paul's also features a tracker organ built in 1877 by Johnson & Son of Westfield, Massachusetts. The church often is locked, in which case one should ring the bell on the south side of the building to request access.

15 Public Market
1230 J Street, Julia Morgan *1923*
Remodeled, Hellmuth, Obata and Kassabaum *2001*

The Public Market is the only commercial project in Sacramento by Julia Morgan, designer of Hearst Castle and America's most famous female architect. The Classical Revival building was hailed at its opening for providing a central location for produce, groceries, pharmaceuticals, lunch counters and restaurants. The building was converted to office use in the late 1970s, and began the 21st Century as the lobby of the Sheraton Grand Hotel.

16 W.P. Fuller & Co.
1011 12th Street, Rudolph Herold *1924*

Founded in Sacramento in 1849, W.P. Fuller & Co. evolved into a large corporation, Fuller-O'Brien Paint. Gladding, McBean & Co. terra cotta is found in the Roman capitals, medallions, urns and other features decorating the building, but the colorful glazed brick of the exterior has been painted over.

17 Masonic Temple
1123 J Street, Rudolph Herold *1920*

The building features glazed terra cotta with a skillful blend of green, rust and brown hues. Two sentries, eyes shut, flank the entrance. Terra cotta cupids perform the function of keystones above the ground level shop archways. For decades the temple hosted ballroom dancing in its upper level ballroom.

18 Elks Building
921 11th Street, Edward Hemming and Leonard Starks *1926*

This 226-foot high rise, along with the Cal-Western Life Insurance Building and the State Capitol, dominated the city skyline for more than a half century. The building features Classical and Renaissance styles. Gladding, McBean & Co. terra cotta is used extensively and the building is topped by a 30 foot copper lantern. The top floor was once occupied by a restaurant called "Top of the Town." The Benevolent and Protective Order of Elks occupied the building from 1926 to 1977, when the organization moved to a new lodge. The basement still contains a health club and swimming pool.

19 Graf House
915 11th Street, Markus Graf *1878*

A well-preserved Italianate residence that somehow managed to survive in the downtown business district. Originally built for billiard manufacturer Markus Graf, the house has been owned since 1964 by the Teichert family.

20 Fred Mayes Clock
1008 J Street *1925*
Restored *1993*

This novelty was one of the first neon signs in Sacramento. Originally owned by former Sacramento Mayor and jeweler Tom B. Monk, the timepiece was purchased in the 1950s by Fred Mayes. The diamond ring design provided an appropriate symbol for Mayes' jewelry store.

CAPITOL AREA

Sacramento's political scene is the most vibrant outside of the Washington beltway. Recent California governors are a Who's Who of late 20th century American politics: President Ronald Reagan liked to eat at Posey's and grab an orange freeze at Merlino's, U.S. Supreme Court Chief Justice Earl Warren once lived in the Sequoia Hotel on K Street and perennial presidential candidate Jerry Brown would wander into Capitol watering holes to shoot the breeze with reporters.

California's status as the nation's most populous state, the world's fifth largest economy and the most diverse population in world history all contribute to the supercharged atmosphere of Sacramento politics. Sacramento's Capitol Area features the people and places that make California tick.

GEN. AND MAMIE EISENHOWER WITH GOV. EARL WARREN IN SACRAMENTO, 1952 CAMPAIGN

HOW SACRAMENTO SNARED THE CAPITOL

The Legislature had a difficult time finding a suitable city in which to establish California's capital in the mid-19th century. In the first years of statehood, lawmakers held sessions in Monterey, San Jose, Vallejo, Sacramento and Benicia. Although Sacramento impressed legislators with its hotels, saloons, restaurants and theatres, it was in no shape to host the Legislature following the floods and fires of 1852. The city was back on its feet by 1854, however; and when lawmakers convened session in Benicia, Sacramento launched a hardball recruitment campaign.

Hundreds of Sacramentans traveled to Benicia and intentionally booked all

the hotel rooms, leaving frustrated legislators to find lodging in saloons and stables. The City of Sacramento dangled numerous incentives in front of the lawmakers, including use of the courthouse as a temporary capitol building, a site to build a permanent capitol and a fireproof vault to house the state archives. Even the private sector got into the act, with local newspapers offering to print legislative files and other documents free. Sacramento legislators made a deal with the San Francisco delegation — Sacramento would support a San Franciscan for the U.S. Senate if the San Francisco legislators would vote to designate Sacramento as the state capital. The tactics worked and, within two months, lawmakers boarded a waiting steamboat (chartered by the City of Sacramento, of course) to travel to California's newly designated capital city.

THE MAKING OF CAPITOL MALL

Running from the Sacramento River to 10th Street, Capitol Mall (originally known as M Street) today provides dramatic views of the State Capitol. Perhaps John Sutter, Jr., foresaw a special function for this street when he laid out Sacramento's grid in 1849 — Sutter made M Street 20 feet wider than any other road in town.

For years, however, views of the Capitol from M Street were obscured by trees and buildings. The first to suggest development of a mall was German city planner Werner Hegemann, who visited Sacramento in 1913. Echoing the City Beautiful sentiments of the era, Hegemann suggested that development of a mall on M Street would open up views of the State Capitol and transform the area into a majestic civic center. A mall plan was drafted in 1929 but the city never adopted it. A 1935 plan, drafted by fruit rancher Frank Snook, proposed that a

mall extend from L to N Streets and from 10th Street to the Sacramento River, which would have made the mall even larger than Capitol Park. Although Snook's idea was greeted with civic enthusiasm, the plan died for lack of federal funding.

By this point M Street was marred by unsightly telephone poles, flophouses, gas stations, billboards and night clubs. The Oak Park Merchants Association expressed their dismay in a 1940 resolution: "M Street is the main entrance to the city and ... an eyesore to our beautiful state buildings. The first impression is the lasting one."

Embarrassed, the city aggressively pursued a mall after World War II — establishing a committee, adopting zoning requirements and acquiring redevelopment powers. The city, state and federal governments, in partnership with the private sector, agreed to develop office buildings on M Street if the existing

MALL DURING REDEVELOPMENT, 1962

buildings were cleared away. By the 1950s, the redevelopment agency was wiping out whole blocks to make way for new, modern office buildings.

While the redevelopment of Capitol Mall succeeded in injecting new investment into the area, slum clearance also claimed dozens of historic early residences, eliminated affordable housing and left the street deserted in the evening. By the 1980s city planners took steps to make sure that the mall's next generation of development would enliven the area. The Wells Fargo Building (400 Capitol Mall, 1991), which features an Il Fornaio restaurant and cafe seating, is a first step in generating more activity on the mall.

TOUR 5 – EAST CAPITOL AREA

1 California State Capitol

10th, 12th, L and N Streets,
Miner F. Butler *1861-74*
Restored and reconstructed,
John Worsely, Welton Becket
and Associates
Historical consultant,
Raymond Girvigian *1975-82*

STATE CAPITOL UNDER CONSTRUCTION, 1868

California's State Capitol is designed in the Renaissance Revival style, reminiscent of the U.S. Capitol in Washington, D.C. Construction was hindered by delays, floods and lack of money. Problems got so bad that Reuben Clark, the original supervising architect, went mad. Clark checked into the Stockton Insane Asylum in February 1866 and died several months later.

The Capitol's granite base has color variations because the stone initially used, excavated from a quarry near Folsom, was found to be too coarse. A new quarry was selected in nearby Rocklin, though the granite was several shades lighter. The building finally was completed in 1874 at a cost of $2.4 million. The bronze state seal in front of the west entrance was fashioned by San Quentin State Prison inmates.

Over the years the building endured a number of remodelings, many of them insensitive to the building's architectural character. When a powerful earthquake struck Southern California in 1971, lawmakers began questioning whether the State Capitol could withstand a major temblor. An investigation found that the old brick walls were bearing loads far exceeding their structural capacity. Some legis-

CAPITOL ROOF STATUARY

lators favored demolishing the old building in favor of a modern Capitol with twin skyscrapers, first suggested by Senator Randolph Collier back in 1964.

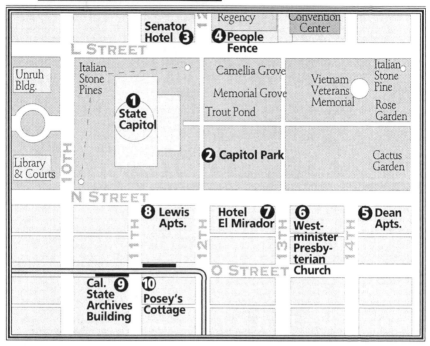

Senate President Pro Tem James R. Mills demurred, announcing that he supported restoring the old Capitol. Governor Ronald Reagan agreed, and soon lawmakers were planning one of the greatest reconstruction projects in American history.

The State Capitol reconstruction took six years and cost $67.8 million. The Capitol was gutted, with only the exterior walls and dome left standing, and the walls were structurally reinforced. Dozens of workers, employing old-world craftsmanship, painstakingly restored the building to its 1900-1910 appearance. Today the California Department of Parks and Recreation manages the historic rooms of the State Capitol, the most significant public building in the state.

CAPITOL RECONSTRUCTION, 1980

Tour Office. (Room B-27, 324-0333). Free guided tours of the State Capitol are available every hour from 9 a.m. to 4 p.m. on a first-come, first-served basis. Advance reservations are needed for parties of more than 10. Tickets may be obtained at the tour office one-half hour before the tour. The standard tour examines the legislative chambers, Capitol restoration, historic offices, governors' portraits and legislative process. Also offered is the Historical Tour, which takes visitors into the historic offices on the ground floor, allowing an up close look at the furnishings and operations of state government in the first years of the 20th century. Self-guided tour brochures are also available from the tour office.

Rotunda. The most dramatic public interior in Sacramento, the rotunda rises 120 feet above the marble tile floor. Natural light fills the dome interior, showing off pastel colors and intricate design work. The central statue of *Columbus' Last Appeal to Queen Isabella* was carved of Carrara marble by Larkin Mead, an American sculptor living in Italy. The statue was given to the state by banker D.O. Mills in 1883. Ronald Reagan was sworn in as governor in 1967, at midnight, in front of the statue. Some contend that the unorthodox timing of the ceremony may have been suggested by Reagan's astrologer, although Nancy Reagan insists that the real reason was to prevent outgoing Governor Pat Brown from making last minute judicial appointments.

Historic offices. The ground floor state constitutional offices are preserved to their appearance circa 1900-10. The old Governor's Office depicts the appearance of the office on the day of the great 1906 San Francisco earthquake. Former Governor and U.S. Supreme Court Chief Justice Earl Warren was the last governor to occupy the old office before moving to the State Capitol Annex in 1952.

Legislative chambers. The beautifully restored Senate and Assembly chambers may be viewed from their respective third floor galleries. Colors used for the two chambers were based on the British Parliament's: red for the upper house and green for the lower house. Eagle figures are embed-

GOV. JERRY BROWN (RIGHT), 1976

ded in the capitals of the columns surrounding the chambers. The portrait of George Washington that hangs behind the President Pro Tempore's chair in the Senate Chambers was painted by Jane Stuart. Stuart made her living duplicating the famous portraits of her father, Gilbert Stuart. In 1854 fire struck the temporary Capitol Building in Sacramento's original county courthouse. Governor John Bigler reportedly shouted at fire fighters tackling the blaze, "There is the portrait of the father of your country! Will you permit it to be destroyed?" The portrait was saved.

Legislative hearings. The two houses of the legislature markedly differ in their membership and style. The Assembly, with 80 members elected to two-year terms, is inclined to have younger legislators who engage in partisan, combative hearings. Floor votes are registered electronically, and it is not uncommon (though officially forbidden) for a member to push the voting button of an absent member.

The Senate, with 40 members elected to four-year terms, tends to be older, less partisan and more tradition-bound. Floor votes are cast in a time-consuming roll call, and the unwritten dress code demands that every male wear a jacket and tie to the floor.

Legislative hearings reveal representative democracy in all its beauty, diversity and sometimes pettiness. The public is welcome to view floor hearings, which are usually on Mondays and Thursdays when the Legislature is in session, from the gallery. The public also is welcome to observe committees in various rooms throughout the Capitol. Ask the tour office for details.

Jerry Brown Portrait. (Don Bachardy, 1984). Located in the third-floor hallway between the Assembly and Senate chambers is the controversial portrait of former Governor (now Oakland Mayor) Jerry Brown. In contrast to the somber, formal paintings of other governors, Brown's portrait shocks the observer with colorful expressionism. Critics disagree about the quality of the work, but there is little doubt that the picture is as bold, infuriating, wry and enigmatic as the governor himself. Brown's abstract portrait was the top tourist attraction in the building when the painting was unveiled in 1984.

State Capitol Museum. (State Capitol Basement). The museum provides modest exhibits that outline the history of the State Capitol. A 10-minute film that examines the historical development of the State Capitol, *A Legacy Restored*, is shown every quarter hour in a small theatre next door to the museum. The basement rotunda features murals depicting eras in California history, painted in 1913 by Arthur F. Mathews and originally installed on the first floor.

State Capitol Annex. (Arthur Dudman, 1952). The annex houses legislative offices and hearing rooms. The stairwells that connect the two buildings can be somewhat confusing given that the annex building has six stories while the original Capitol, with its higher ceilings, has four stories. Little-known to the general public is the cafeteria located on the sixth floor of the annex, where one is likely to spot legislators, lobbyists and staff. The most distinguished interior feature of the annex are the murals in Room 4203 by Lucille Lloyd. Painted in

1937 for the California State Building in Los Angeles, the WPA murals are based on the theme of California's Name. Lloyd committed suicide in 1941.

2 Capitol Park
Bordered by 10th, 15th, L and N Streets *1870*

Filled with fertile silt from the Sacramento River, Capitol Park contains mature trees, shrubs and vines from throughout the world. Tours of the park are provided by the Capitol Tour Office (Room B-27, 324-0333) at 10:30 a.m. daily from mid-June through Labor Day, or by appointment at other times of the year. The Tour Office also has brochures for self-guided tours.

The 40-acre park originally ended at 12th Street, but later was extended to 15th Street. A number of original plantings from 1870-71 survive on the 10th Street side of the park. Much of the landscaping was performed under the direction of William O'Brien, who became the park's head gardener in 1878. The park is bordered by tall California Fan Palms, an enduring symbol of the Golden State's temperate climate.

On the Capitol's east side, near 12th Street, are the scenic Trout Pond and adjacent Memorial Grove. The grove was planted in memory of those who lost their

CAPITOL PARK TROUT POND

lives in the Civil War. Toward L Street is the statue of Father Junipero Serra (Maurice Loriaux, 1965), founder of the California Missions, and a Camellia Grove, where one can observe Sacramento's official flower in full bloom during February and March.

Near 15th Street stands the poignant *Vietnam Veterans' Memorial* (Michael Larson and Thomas Chytrowski, 1988). The memorial features panels of India black granite, etched with the names of 5,615 Californians who died in the war. Bronze panels and life-size statues powerfully depict wartime scenes. The nearby Rose Garden, with more than 800 rose bushes, graces the site of the original Governor's Mansion. The mansion was built for Governor Newton Booth in 1870 but was never occupied by any governor; it later housed the State Printing Plant. Near 15th and N Streets is the Cactus Garden, repre-

VIETNAM VETERANS' MEMORIAL

senting the California desert. The garden is on the site of the original State Fairgrounds Pavilion, home of the State Fair from 1884 to 1905. Many of the plants for the cactus garden were sent by schoolchildren to Governor Hiram Johnson in 1914.

3 Senator Hotel
1121 L Street, Kenneth MacDonald and G. Albert Lansburgh *1924*

The Senator Hotel was a center for lobbyists and legislators during the Artie Samish era of California politics. Samish was California's dominating lobbyist from the 1920s to the 1950s; his clients included liquor, horse racing, oil, trucking and railroad interests. During legislative sessions, the self-described "Governor of the Legislature" made his home in Room 428 of the Senator, his icebox always filled with steaks and beer. He would go down to the lobby around noon and be available until 4 a.m. to meet with legislators, judges, reporters, cops and anybody else who needed a favor or wanted his opinion. Samish eventually served time in the federal pen for income tax evasion.

The Senator Hotel also was the site of a presidential assassination attempt. On September 5, 1975, President Gerald R. Ford had just left the hotel when Charles Manson disciple Lynette "Squeaky" Fromme attempted to fire a .45 caliber pistol at him. Luckily, the gun failed to go off. The building was converted to offices in the early 1980s and is still a prestigious address for the Capitol's most powerful lobbyists. The 165-foot portico once served as a shady veranda for hotel guests. The glazed terra cotta is from Gladding, McBean & Co. and relates well to the Weinstock building to the north, which was built at about the same time. Small lion heads decorate the hotel's roof line.

4 People Fence
Northeast corner, 12th and L Streets, Ed Haag *1990*

This small landscaped plot is the site of the Francesca Apartments, a 1924 apartment house that was demolished in 1988 as part of the city's deal to lure the Hyatt Hotel downtown. The apartment building had a bar on the street level, David's Brass Rail, which was a popular hangout for Governor Jerry Brown and his staff. The plot is surrounded by a topiary fence with human figures in a variety of poses, intended by its designer to represent the humanity that once existed in the Francesca Apartments. Interestingly, landscape architect Ed Haag did not discover until after the project was finished that his own mother and father had once lived in the Francesca Apartments. The topiary fence was constructed by a Davis High School shop class based on Haag's design.

5 Dean Apartments
1400 N Street, Dean and Dean *1930*

During his 1974 campaign for governor, Jerry Brown vowed not to move into the suburban Governor's Mansion built by outgoing Governor Ronald Reagan, declaring it to be a "Taj Mahal." Upon his election, Brown moved into Apartment #10 on the top floor of this Tudor style apartment house, remaining a resident during his eight years as governor. The unconventional Brown kept odd hours and would sometimes stroll over to the Capitol to get some work done in the middle of the night. Ed Meese, attorney general while Ronald Reagan was president, also lived in this building when he served in Governor Reagan's administration. The building's original owner, architect James S. Dean of the local firm Dean and Dean, served as city manager at the time the apartment house was built.

6 Westminster Presbyterian Church
1300 N Street, Dean and Dean, Earl Barnett *1927*

This fine Romanesque Revival church has a campanile that stands like a sentry guarding Capitol Park. The church was modeled after the church of St. Sophia of Constantinople. The interior may be viewed by entering the 13th Street entrance. A pleasant shady courtyard is visible through the gate on N Street.

7 Hotel El Mirador
1230 N Street *1958*

Now a senior citizens home and office building, this building, then a hotel, was the site of the annual "Moose Milk" bash in the years prior to voter passage of the Political Reform Act in 1974. Moose Milk is the name of a cocktail with a base of rum and milk. For some reason the name was tagged onto a lavish party, paid for by lobbyists for returning lawmakers, that was held at the beginning of each legislative session. The Hotel El Mirador's other claim to fame was that it contributed to legendary Assembly Speaker Jesse Unruh's downfall. Unruh got angry at Assembly Republicans for not voting for the state budget in July 1963. The Speaker locked the legislators in the chambers and stormed over to the hotel for a steak dinner. As Unruh drank Beefeaters-on-the-rocks at the hotel bar, his Democratic colleagues tried in vain to convince him to end the embarrassing stalemate. Many observers believe the negative publicity resulting from the incident forever doomed Unruh's dream of occupying the governor's chair.

8 Lewis Apartments

1100 N Street *ca. 1925*

This Romanesque Revival apartment house that still has trash chutes and old-fashioned phone systems in each room. The apartments are conveniently located for lobbyists and legislators, and the rooms provide a stunning view of the State Capitol.

9 Secretary of State / California State Archives Building

Bordered by 10th, 11th, O and P Streets, Esherick, Homsey, Dodge and Davis *1995*

This complex, occupying a full square block, contains two separate but integrated buildings. The Secretary of State Building addresses the corner of 11th and O Streets, curving toward the corner to allow the Secretary of State a nice view of the Capitol. The rotunda was designed to resemble a wine barrel, in tribute to

California's wine heritage. The floor and base of the rotunda feature black and white granite quarried near Yosemite, as well as walnut staircases that circle toward the second floor viewing area. The courtyard is dominated by the *Constitution Wall* (Mike Mandel, Larry Sultan, Paul Cos), a six-story sculpture depicting 36 words from the California Constitution. The words protrude from, or are inset into, the wall, with their prominence changing as the daylight shifts. The word "RIGHTS" covers nearly the entire wall surface, yet at certain times of the day is nearly invisible. Metal oxides in the cement plaster finish contribute to an ever-changing patina of earth tones representing California's diverse natural landscape. *Constitution Wall* creatively conveys that the state constitution is

not a rigid edict, but a document permitting alteration and reinterpretation. Next door, the State Archives Building houses the snazzy Golden State Museum. The public is welcome to use the plush fourth-floor Research Room to explore the past.

10 Posey's Cottage

1100 O Street, *ca. 1930s*

Posey's was an old fashioned steak-and-potato restaurant that was a favorite of Governor Ronald Reagan. Before closing down in the mid-1990s, the restaurant was the site of the Derby Club, the only remaining legislative lunch club. Established in 1953, the Derby Club is for legislators and lobbyists, who may join by invitation only. The bipartisan club forbids lobbying, candidates and reporters. The purpose of the club is to provide legislators and lobbyists with the opportunity to socialize outside of the rancorous and hectic world of the Capitol. Posey's' closure led to the Derby Club's moving into Vallejo's Mexican Restaurant, which now occupies much of Posey's' former quarters.

TOUR 6 – WEST CAPITOL AREA

1 Library and Courts Building

914 Capitol Mall,
Weeks and Day *1928*

This Neo-Classical building, along with the Jesse Unruh Building across the street, beautifully frame the view of the State Capitol Building up Capitol Mall. The figures which flank the entrance, *Floral Wealth* and *Romantic Wealth,* are by Edward Field Sanford, Jr. Sanford also designed the pediment located above the entrance, which depicts *California's Gift to the World.* The female figure, representing California, holds the sword of justice in her right hand and the owl of wisdom in her left. The exterior is composed of granite on the first level and simulated granite terra cotta from Gladding, McBean & Co. on the upper levels.

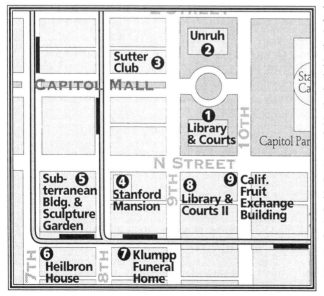

Architects Weeks and Day were unhappy with the terra cotta company's work, calling the color match of the granite-finished terra cotta to the real granite "disastrous." *The California Peace Officer Memorial* (Vic Riesau, 1987), near the front entrance, honors the men and women killed in the line of duty.

One enters the

building through a small vestibule lined with Indiana limestone and proceeds into the larger Memorial Vestibule. Dimly lit and somber, the Memorial Vestibule is a silent, dramatic tribute to those who gave their lives in World War I. Thick columns of black and gold Italian marble support light fixtures designed as Greek tripods. The fixtures illuminate 12 mural panels depicting warriors from the dawn of time up until World War I, painted by San Francisco artist Frank Van Sloun. The California Supreme Court holds session in a ground-floor hearing room twice a year (other sessions are held in San Francisco). The third floor Reading Room features a mural of California's evolution by Maynard Dixon, while the Public Catalogue Room houses two other Sanford statues, *Wisdom* and *Inspiration*, in green bronze.

2 Jesse M. Unruh State Office Building
915 Capitol Mall, Weeks and Day *1925*

The entry statues of *Climatic Wealth* and *Mineral Wealth* are the work of Edward Sanford, Jr., as is the pediment symbolizing *The Gift of the World to California*. The central female figure, representing California, has her arms outstretched to welcome the world. The Unruh Building's lobby features a forest of thick columns. Named for former Assembly Speaker Jesse Unruh (who died in 1987 while serving as State Treasurer), the building houses the State Treasurer's offices, other state offices and a post office. A statue honoring American Serviceman of Hispanic Descent (1975) is on the 10th Street side near the front entrance.

3 Sutter Club
1220 9th Street, Dean & Dean, Starks & Flanders *1930*

This Spanish Colonial Revival building houses one of the state's oldest social clubs, formed in 1889 to promote "social and business intercourse among its members." Former Governor and U.S. Senator Newton Booth was the Sutter Club's first president. Earl Warren lived in the building temporarily when he was elected governor in 1942 while the Governor's Mansion was being remodeled. The Sutter Club did not admit a female member until 1989.

4 Stanford Mansion
800 N Street *1857*
Addition, Seth Babson *1872*

This exceptional Second Empire home belonged to railroad baron, California Governor and Stanford University founder Leland Stanford and his wife Jane. Originally the home was two stories high, but Stanford had the home remodeled to its current appearance in 1872. The remodel included jacking up the

home one full story and adding another full story and Mansard roof. In 1869, when their son, Leland, Jr., was about one month old, the Stanfords held a large dinner party. A servant entered the dining room bearing a covered silver platter. Everyone in the room, including Mrs. Stanford, was shocked when the cover was removed to reveal the baby Stanford, nestled in a bed of blossoms. "My friends, I wish now to introduce my son to you," said Leland, Sr. The baby smiled as he was shown to each guest. Tragically, the son died at age 15, and the grieving parents decided to found Stanford University in his memory. The 38-room mansion later was donated by Mrs. Stanford to the Catholic Church for use as a children's home. The home now belongs to the state and is being restored as a formal reception hall for visiting dignitaries.

5 Subterranean Building and Sculpture Garden
701 N Street, Bennem Blair *1983*

One of the more unusual architectural features of the city, this state office building was developed during Governor Jerry Brown's energy-conscious administration. Banks of ivy are the main visual feature at the street level, but ascend the stairs to see that a sculptural garden has been plopped right on top of a subterranean state office building. Heating and cooling for the well-insulated building are supplied by the solar panels of the state office structure on the north side of N Street. While unique, the project has a number of design limitations: the underground office workers do not have much of a view, most pedestrians do not know that the elevated garden exists, the garden's potted trees provide little shade and the banks of ivy do nothing to enliven the street. The building's days appear limited, because the state plans a new building for the site.

6 Heilbron House
704 O Street, Nathaniel Goodell *1881*

The Heilbrons, merchants and butchers, commissioned this Second Empire design from architect Nathaniel Goodell, who also designed the Governor's Mansion at 16th and H Streets. The building served as Antonina's, a fancy Italian restaurant, in the 1950s. Wells Fargo later purchased the building and in 1992 donated the structure to La Raza Galeria Posada, an art gallery and gift shop dedicated to the work of Latino and Native American artists. La Raza has recently sold the historic structure to an owner that can afford to pay for the expensive restoration that the building requires.

7 Klumpp Funeral Home
808 O Street *1931*
Reconstructed *1985*

Now serving as the weight room for the Capitol Athletic Club, this building features an attractive Spanish Colonial Revival design. Klumpp Funeral Home relocated to Riverside Boulevard in 1972, and this building served as state offices until the Capitol Athletic Club purchased it in the mid-1980s.

8 Library and Courts II
900 N Street, The Architects Collaborative *1994*

The $25 million annex to the Library and Courts Building features a circular terrazzo floor with an alphabetical design. The first floor contains the Braille and Talking Book Library Reading Room, with an adjoining fragrance garden. The structure also has the Rare Materials Reading Room, which is accessible to the public, and the California History Room, which features rotating exhibits, a huge photograph collection and, on microfilm, many of the newspapers published in the state.

9 California Fruit Exchange Building
1400 10th Street, Starks and Flanders *1932*

This charming Spanish Colonial Revival structure housed the California Fruit Exchange cooperative until 1966. At one time the building contained a large, opulent board room, but that was removed when the structure was converted to state offices. The Governor's Office of Planning and Research now occupies the building.

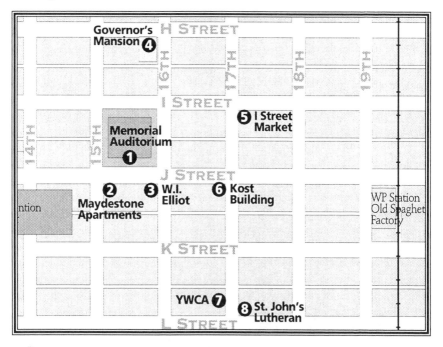

MIDTOWN

Vibrant coffeehouses, unique shops, good bookstores, distinctive homes, tree-lined streets, great restaurants and short commutes — Midtown has all of the qualities that make central city living attractive. Much of Midtown retail concentrates around J Street, although you will find additional shops scattered throughout the area. You will also find a rich variety of the city's most distinctive buildings.

TOUR 7 – WEST MIDTOWN

1 Sacramento Memorial Auditorium

J Street, between 15th and 16th Streets, James S. Dean, G.A. Lansburgh and Arthur Brown *1927*

Featuring what has been described as a Byzantine motif, the monumental Memorial Auditorium is an architectural masterpiece inside and out. Gladding, McBean & Co. was responsible for the ornate terra cotta work, from the medallions over the doors to the

elaborate capitals topping the columns. For decades, the Memorial has been Sacramento's great public gathering place, hosting graduations, circuses, dances, concerts, boxing matches and inaugural galas. Will Rogers, Jack Benny, The Beach Boys, Jimi Hendrix and Eleanor Roosevelt are some of the attractions that have graced the Memorial's stage. At one famously abbreviated event,

the Rolling Stones' Keith Richards was knocked unconscious by an improperly grounded microphone during a 1965 performance. The city shuttered the building in 1986, citing safety concerns. A controversial plan to remodel the building into a concert hall was narrowly rejected by voters in 1992. The city subsequently agreed to restore the building and the spiffed-up auditorium reopened in 1996.

2 Maydestone Apartments
1001-5 15th Street *1915*

This four-story Mission Revival apartment house is one-of-a-kind in the city. The curvilinear parapet recalls the California missions, a popular style of the period.

3 W.I. Elliott Company
1530 J Street, Starks and Flanders *1922*

A fine brick structure, this building has been an auto garage and showroom for close to 80 years. The structure embellishes its industrial form with classical features such as pilasters and capitals.

4 Governor's Mansion
1524 H Street, Nathaniel Goodell *1877*

This 30-room French Second Empire and Italianate mansion was built originally for Albert Gallatin, manager-partner of Huntington-Hopkins and Co. The home was sold in 1888 to Joseph Steffans, whose son, Lincoln, went on to become a famous muckraker and gubernatorial candidate. In 1903 Steffans sold the house to the State of California, after which it served as the home of 12 governors. Governor Pat Brown, decked out in swimming trunks, would wander across the street to use the swimming pool and socialize with guests of the Mansion Inn (now the Clarion Hotel). A group of Governor Brown's supporters later had a pool built on the mansion grounds. The Reagans did not care for the home. Nancy Reagan considered the "so-called mansion" to be "depressing" — it reminded her of a funeral parlor and she complained about a rope ladder "fire escape." After three months, the Reagans moved to the Fabulous Forties in East Sacramento, and the state converted the home into a museum.

5 I Street Market
1700 I Street *1888*

John Clauss and brother-in-law Frank Kraus opened a meat market on the ground floor of this building in 1888. By 1934 the business had evolved into a wholesale operation, and Clauss and Kraus, Inc., went on to become one of the valley's largest meat processing and packaging plants until going out of business in 1981. The building is a unique blend of Queen Anne and Colonial Revival styles, featuring a polygonal corner tower, decorative frieze, patterned stained glass and metal balcony.

6 Kost Building
1624-30 J Street *1910*

This edifice is actually two buildings, with the corner structure housing a saloon and cafe from 1911-49. Sam's Hofbrau took over the location in 1955. Sam's established an international reputation as a blues venue during the hofbrau's last seven years of business. Nationally and locally known blues talent took the stage in the presence of Sam's hedonistic mural of a Bavarian hofbrau. The eclectic clientele, fueled by freshly-sliced meats and the emphatic beat, would coagulate in a sweaty mass on the tiny dance floor. Apparently, the scene was too much

out of the mainstream for Sam's owner, Denny's Restaurants, who pulled the plug on Sam's flashing corner sign in 1993. Hamburger Mary's opened in 1994 with the hofbrau mural painted over.

7 Young Women's Christian Association
1122 17th Street, Dean and Dean *1932*
Addition, Dean and Dean *1942*

This attractive Mediterranean Revival building continues to serve its mission of providing safe and inexpensive accommodations, in addition to social gatherings and educational classes, for girls and young working women.

8 St. John's Lutheran Church
1701 L Street, L.B. Valk *1911*

A dramatic Neo-Gothic church building with Medieval German influences, St. John's is constructed of concrete block on a rusticated brownstone foundation. Services at the church were conducted in German until 1918, when the church voluntarily converted to English as a patriotic gesture during World War I.

TOUR 8 – CENTRAL MIDTOWN

1 Western Pacific Railroad Passenger Station
1910 J Street, Willis Polk *1909*

Mission Revival architecture, evoking early California history, was favored by railroad companies in the early 20th Century. This station is the finest represen-

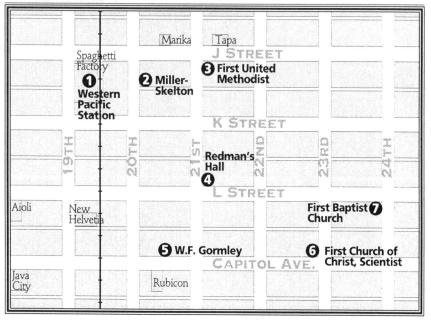

tative of the style in Sacramento. The Western Pacific line, stretching from Oakland to Salt Lake City, was part of the last transcontinental railroad built in the United States. President Harry S Truman stopped here on his 1948 whistle-stop campaign. The station closed in 1970 and later was taken over by the Old Spaghetti Factory restaurant.

2 Miller-Skelton Funeral Chapel
1015 20th Street *1921-22*

Rehabilitation, Mogavero-Notestine and Associates, *1994*

This Colonial Revival building now houses *Sacramento News & Review*. The style of the building suggests that the architect attempted to have the business fit in with the nearby residential structures.

3 First United Methodist Church
2100 J Street, Woolett and Lamb *1925*

This church resulted from a 1918 merger of two churches from Sacramento's pioneer days, the Baltimore-California Chapel, established in 1849, and the H Street Methodist Episcopal Church, established in 1855. The Romanesque Revival architecture was patterned after the St. Ambrose Church in Milan, Italy.

4 Redman's Hall
2101 L Street *1926*

The Improved Order of Red Men is a fraternal organization, introduced into California in 1850, that looks to Native American culture for lessons on friendship and helpfulness. The organization's lodge rooms are on the second floor. Terra cotta Indian heads are mounted between the arched windows.

5 W.F. Gormley and Son

2015 Capitol Avenue, Harry Devine, Sr. *1924*

This Spanish Colonial Revival/Mediterranean Revival funeral home is an attrac-

tive Capitol Avenue feature. The mortuary has been in continuous operation by the Gormley family since 1897. W.F. Gormley was the sheriff of Sacramento County early in the century.

6 First Church of Christ, Scientist

2231 Capitol Avenue, Henry Gutterson *1939*

This building is the only local work of Henry Gutterson, a Bay Area architect and protege of famed Berkeley architect Bernard Maybeck. The church combines Mediterranean and Romanesque Revival architecture in a striking, simplified style. Particularly dramatic is the tall arched entry, supported by a pair of smooth columns.

7 First Baptist Church of Sacramento

2324 L Street, Ivan Satterlee *1929*

Clinker brick is interspersed with red brick on this Gothic-influenced Period Revival church, providing an interesting texture. The church got its start in Sacramento in 1850 by the Rev. O.C. Wheeler, who owned a number of homes in the Alkali Flat neighborhood. Ivan Satterlee, the local architect who designed the church, also did the interior carving.

TOUR 9 – EAST MIDTOWN

1 St. Francis of Assisi Catholic Church

1112 26th Street, Brother Adrian Wewer *1908-10*
Restoration *1992-93*

Although the 112-foot towers, modeled after Mission Santa Barbara, recall California's early Spanish heritage, the interior of St. Francis has a distinctly German flavor. Constructed at a time when the State Capitol was being remodeled, the church and its thrifty German parishioners gladly accepted the Capitol's handsome carved rosewood for the church's stair and organ loft railings. Constructed of more than one million bricks covered by concrete plaster (and later by stucco), the unreinforced structure required seismic strength-

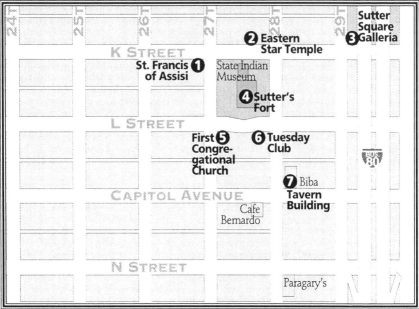

ening and restoration in the early 1990s. Frescoes that had sustained water damage from a severely leaking roof were restored to their original vivid colors, and the grime that had dulled the Tyrolean stained glass was cleaned away. For decades an artesian well provided water for the church and the adjoining school

and rectory, as well as for anyone else who wanted to fill up a jug at the fountain located on the K Street side of the building. The fountain went dry when water levels dropped in 1959.

2 Eastern Star Hall
2719 K Street, Coffman, Sahlberg, and Stafford *1925*

Like many of the downtown commercial buildings, the Eastern Star Hall features a striking combination of brick and terra cotta. The Romanesque Revival hall is owned by the Eastern Star Order, an affiliate of the Masons, which welcomes both men and women. The order advocates conducting one's life according to biblical example.

3 Sutter Square Galleria
2929 K Street, Stan Felderman *1987*

Californians spend a good percentage of their lives on the freeway, so it seems fitting that a freeway has evolved into a commercial destination. The Sutter Square Galleria is the only commercial center in the state that sprouts from a freeway right-of-way. The postmodern structure, with its gabled roof, salmon-colored stucco exterior and piercing corner columns, appears to be split in half by Business 80. It is a fun piece of design, created appropriately enough by a Los Angeles architect.

4 Sutter's Fort
2701 L Street, John Sutter *1839-44*
Restored *1893*

Sacramento founder John Sutter chose this site to put down roots when he arrived in Sacramento in 1839. Sutter built a fort to defend his new empire against hostile Indians. The fort hosted California's first great wave of immigration. Trappers, traders and immigrants bought groceries, rented equipment and obtained horses from the businesses within the rectangular complex. Sutter sold the property in 1849 and the complex was abandoned shortly thereafter. By 1851 vandals had destroyed all but the two-story central living quarters. The state restored the fort in 1893, making it one of California's earliest historic preservation projects. A tour of Sutter's Fort provides interesting insights into the lives of California pioneers. The grounds outside the fort were landscaped under the supervision of John McClaren, architect of Golden Gate Park in San Francisco.

5 First Congregational Church
2700 L Street, Hemmings and Stark *1926*

A fine Gothic-Revival complex, the First Congregational Church is a dramatic presence on L Street. The tower features a bell cast in New York in 1854. The bell originally hung in an earlier church building located on 6th Street.

6 Tuesday Club
2722 L Street

Tuesday Club was established in 1896 as a civic improvement organization that was "officered and directed by some of the most intellectual women in the city," according to one account. One of the club's first acts was to urge the city to establish McKinley Park in East Sacramento. The modern stucco exterior of this building belies the terrific 1920s ballroom inside, with a spring-suspended dance floor. The Tuesday Club moved out of the building in the late 1990s.

7 Tavern Building
2801 Capitol Avenue *1849*
Remodeled *1922*

Originally this building was the brick, one-story Sacramento Brewery, a favorite hitching post for travelers coming through town. The building was remodeled to its current English Period Revival style in 1922 and today houses one of Sacramento's best restaurants, Biba.

CENTRAL CITY NEIGHBORHOODS

ALKALI FLAT

Dating back to the 1850s, Alkali Flat is Sacramento's oldest neighborhood. The neighborhood is named after the chalky white powder that covered this flat section of the city prior to its development in the 1850s. Alkali Flat accommodated not only the city's most elite residents, but working class households as well. The area declined after World War II and, through redevelopment and gentrification, has more recently been struggling to regain some of its polish.

TOUR 10 – ALKALI FLAT

1 The Sentry House
700 E Street *ca. 1850s*

Listed in the National Register of Historic Places, this structure may have been used as a sentry house during the Civil War. The building now serves as office space.

2 Mesick House
517 8th Street, Nathaniel Goodell *1881*

The Mansard roof and Second Empire design were Architect Goodell's hallmarks, giving the Mesick House similarities to his designs for the Governor's Mansion

and the Heilbron House. Mary Mesick, the home's original owner, probably first rented the home to widower Owen Pendergast, a foreman for Southern Pacific. The building is on the National Register of Historic Places.

3 Zapata Park
9th and E Streets

This park was named for Emiliano Zapata, Mexican revolutionist and agrarian reformer who died in 1919. The bust of Zapata was a 1982 gift from Mexico City.

4 A.C. Huelsman Property
930 E Street *ca. 1905-15*

The building offers commercial space on the first floor and a distinctive blend of Mission Revival and Moorish design on the upper levels.

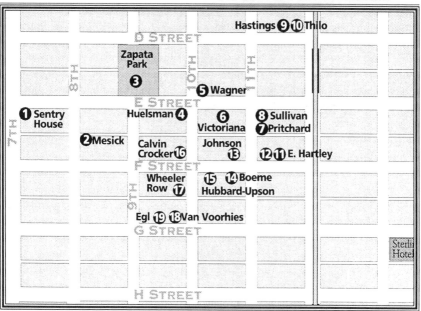

5 Anton Wagner, Grocer
1001 E Street *1868*

Now the Tru-Value Market, this building has been continually used as a corner grocery since 1868, making it Sacramento's oldest grocery. Originally of Italianate design, the store has been altered on several occasions.

6 The Victoriana
E Street, between 10th and 11th Streets

A redevelopment project that demonstrates the importance of good affordable housing design. The simple Victorian-style structures fit in well with their aged neighbors.

7 Pritchard House
511 11th Street *ca. 1890-95*

This Italianate/Eastlake home has been restored to pristine condition. The home is distinguished by its bracketed eaves, scrollwork around the windows and angled bay window overlooking J. Neely Johnson Park.

8 Sullivan Home
1100 E Street *1894*

Sullivan was a foreman for the Southern Pacific. This Eastlake home makes lavish use of decorative moldings and trim.

9 Maria Hastings House
1119 D Street *1860*

Hastings owned the Orleans Hotel, once one of the fanciest in Old Sacramento. She lost this Greek Revival home in 1863 as the pay-off of a debt, and eventually the house passed into the ownership of Robert K. Wick, who founded the first funeral home in California in 1849. The residence was rehabilitated in the early 1990s and today serves as a Montessori day care center. It is listed on the National Register of Historic Places.

10 Thilo House

1129 D Street *ca. 1877-78*

Thilo was an instrument maker for the Central Pacific Supply Depot. The Eastlake style residence is distinguished by its portico with both Greek temple and Gothic design elements.

11 E. Hartley House

1115 F Street *ca. 1893*

The owner of this home may have been a relative of Judge H.H. Hartley (see #12). The Queen Anne and Colonial Revival residence is striking for its 'witch's hat' turret and asymmetrical design.

12 Judge H.H. Hartley House

1107 F Street *ca. 1865*

Hartley was an attorney from England who was appointed judge of Yolo County by the first State Legislature in 1850. The Hartley family lived in this Greek Revival home until the turn of the century.

13 J. Neely Johnson House

1029 F Street *1854*

This structure is the oldest house remaining in Sacramento. J. Neely Johnson resided here when he was elected California's fourth governor in 1856. Supreme Court Justice David Terry lived here at the time of his 1859 duel with David Broderick, a former U.S. Senator who became the namesake of the town of Broderick (now part of the City of West Sacramento). Broderick was killed in the duel. Justice Terry later became a general in the Confederate Army. The Greek Revival home is listed on the National Register of Historic Places.

14 Boehme House

1024 F Street *1869*

George Boehme lived in this splendid example of the Italianate style from 1869-1871. He was a tinsmith who carried out the contract for the copper roofing of the State Capitol dome. Apparently Boehme did not carry out the work very well — the dome leaked for 100 years. The leaks finally were fixed in the 1975-82 restoration. Boehme also lived for some time in the Stanford Mansion. He later moved to Southern California and became a founder of Santa Monica.

15 Hubbard-Upson House

1010 F Street *1856*

This home was built for I.M. Hubbard, a Wells Fargo agent who assisted in building the first transcontinental telegraph and supervised pumping out the city during floods. The Italianate and Gothic residence is unusual for its crenelated roof line, giving the house a castle-like appearance. Subsequently converted to office use, the structure is on the National Register of Historic Places.

16 Calvin Crocker House
530 10th Street *1902*

Crocker was a relative of Big Four member Charles Crocker. The home is a combination of Queen Anne and Colonial styles and is in excellent condition.

17 Wheeler Row
608-14 10th Street *1872*

These wooden row houses are the only ones of their kind in the city. The homes were owned and possibly built by Rev. O.C. Wheeler, a pioneer Baptist minister. The flamboyant Wheeler preached the first Protestant sermon and taught the first Sunday School in California, back in 1849. Wheeler Row is listed on the National Register of Historic Places.

18 Van Voorhies Residence
925 G Street *1868*

A.A. Van Voorhies, who had seen his Placerville leather store prosper during the Comstock Rush of 1859, moved into this home in 1869. Known as "The Prince," Van Voorhies went on to establish several businesses in Sacramento, including a harness factory, a horse collar factory and an investment company. The stuccoed brick home is a combination of Italianate and Georgian architecture and is on the National Register of Historic Places.

19 The Egl Residence
917 G Street *1860*

Anthony Egl was an immigrant who fled Hungary in 1848 and arrived in Sacramento in 1855. He established a wholesale fruit, nut and confectionery business on J Street and built this two-story home the same year that Abraham Lincoln was elected president. Borrowing a design trick he observed in humid Tennessee, Egl had a detached kitchen built behind the home, so that his wife's cooking and canning would not overheat the residence. The Federal design suggests the type of home one might find on the East Coast.

BOULEVARD PARK

Flush with mining wealth, residents of early Sacramento had a penchant for gambling and fast horses. Soon the city had two racetracks, with one of them, the Union Racetrack, located in what is now known as the Boulevard Park neighborhood.

The Union Racetrack was developed in 1861 by the Sacramento Park Association. With a brick wall around the complex, the track was the site of California State Fair horse races for 40 years. The track would bring in thousands of people, including racehorse owner Governor Leland Stanford. The track was just outside the city limits, and it functioned as a city development boundary for many years.

As Sacramento's population grew, however, the city decided to move the State Fairgrounds to Stockton Boulevard. The Union Racetrack was subdivided and sold for residential devel-
opment. With its large lots and well-built Colonial Revival and Craftsman homes, the neighborhood was marketed to the well-to-do. Two requirements for building within the subdivision were that the home cost at least $3,950 and that the owners keep no livestock. To establish a distinctive identity for the area, the developers built grassy medians on 21st and 22nd Streets, roughly parallel to the Union Track back-stretch.

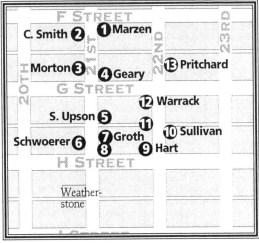

After World War II, the neighborhood went into decline, with many of the homes used as boarding houses. Young professionals rediscovered the area beginning in the 1970s, and today Boulevard Park, with its tree-lined medians, ranks among the central city's most distinctive neighborhoods.

TOUR 11 – BOULEVARD PARK

1 Joseph Marzen House
2100 F Street, possibly Rudolph Herold *1911*

Art Nouveau styling on the pilaster and column capitals distinguishes this beautiful Colonial Revival home. Converted to a rooming house in the 1940s, the residence was restored by down-town realtor Bonnie Fitzpatrick between 1979-86.

2 Clarence Smith House
608-10 21st Street *ca. 1905-10*

This Cube-Type Mission Revival apartment house is similar to the home at 1104-6 E Street in Alkali Flat. It was originally owned by Clarence Smith, who was employed by the State Controller's office.

3 Charles W. Morton House
626 21st Street *1905-10*

This Cube-Type Craftsman/Colonial Revival home has upper-story front win-dows that feature diamond-shaped leaded glass. Morton was a clerk for Weinstock-Lubin department store.

4 Cranston-Geary House
2101 G Street, George Sellon *1909*

The Cranston-Geary House is one of the city's finest Craftsman homes, with extensive use of brick on the porch and terrace, exposed and pointed rafters, and leaded glass windows. The architect, George Sellon, was California's first state architect and had studied under Frank Lloyd Wright. Original owners Robert and Mary Cranston received the home as a wedding gift ($11,000 value) from the bride's father, who was a wealthy copper miner from Michigan. Robert Cranston was the director of the Marysville Dredging Company, a company that caused considerable environmental damage along the American River during the

20th Century. The Cranstons lived in the home for only three years. The subsequent owner, William Geary, was vice-president of a wholesale drug business. Geary and his family resided in the home for 30 years. The home is listed on the National Register of Historic Places

5 Stuart Upson House
715 21st Street *1905-10*

This Cube-Type Craftsman house has Colonial Revival and Prairie Style influences. Note the sunburst decoration on the front gable. Upson was one of the fastest bicyclists in the nation on the high-wheeled cycles. He set speed records that were never broken.

6 Louis Schwoerer House
724 21st Street *1905-10*

This Cube-Type dwelling is in the Colonial Revival style. Schwoerer worked for a packing company. The house was later owned by Elbert Rulison, a physician.

7 Louise Groth House
725 21st Street *1913*

This Cube-Type Craftsman house is typical of other Boulevard Park residences, with a box-like shape, overhanging eaves and notched rafters. Groth was a widow who lived here through 1920.

8 J.L. Mayden House
2101 H Street *1909*

This Colonial Revival home has Craftsman influences. Particularly interesting is the second-floor pavilion. Mayden was a department store manager.

9 Aden C. Hart House

2131 H Street *1907*

The lion heads over the front porch gives this home a rather brooding countenance. The home is a combination of Colonial Revival and Craftsman styles. Features include a porch of artificial stone, stained glass windows and arched windows. Physician Aden C. Hart was the founder of Sutter Hospital, one of the largest hospitals in the Sacramento region.

10 John Sullivan House

717 22nd Street *ca. 1910-1915*

This house is in the Colonial Revival and Craftsman styles. Sullivan was a real estate broker.

11 Shared yards

Note on the west side of 22nd street between G and H Streets the walkway leading to the private yard shared by the surrounding homes. The developers of Boulevard Park put three such yards in the neighborhood as an additional enticement to prospective buyers.

12 Hartley House

700 22nd Street, *1906*

This house, combining Cube-Type Craftsman and Colonial Revival styles, was built for Carter Blair Hartley, a Welshman who worked for the Southern Pacific Railroad. The second owner, Faith Murphy, converted the residence to a boarding house during the 1950s. The house returned to the original family owners when Randall Hartley purchased the home in 1987 to operate Hartley House Bed and Breakfast Inn.

13 William Pritchard House

627 22nd Street *1905-10*

This Craftsman house has a pedimented front, a clinker-brick porch on the ground level and an open porch on the second level. Pritchard was a manager of a wholesale produce business.

Sacramento's persistent flooding in the 19th Century would send suddenly impoverished citizens scurrying for higher ground — hence, the name of this neighborhood, which sits on a modest plateau and offered flood refugees a place to wait for the waters to recede.

Developers began building lavish homes in the district in the late 19th and early 20th Centuries. They tried to buff up the area's image by naming the neighborhood "Sutter's Terrace." The marketing ploy did not stick — Poverty Ridge is the name that survives.

The fine variety of homes, with their ample dimensions and high elevations, made Poverty Ridge one of Sacramento's fanciest neighborhoods. The Business 80 Freeway slashed along the edge of the neighborhood in the mid-1960s, over the protests of Poverty Ridge residents, including *The Sacramento Bee*'s Eleanor McClatchy. Though damaging to the neighborhood's fabric, the freeway did not kill Poverty Ridge, a neighborhood that still exudes elegance.

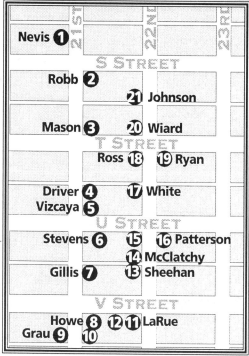

TOUR 12 – POVERTY RIDGE

1 Manuel Nevis House

1822 21st Street *1898*

Nevis immigrated from the Portuguese islands of the Azores. He started one of California's first wineries in Shingle Springs and later owned wineries in Sacramento. This Queen Anne/Eastlake house is almost identical to the house two blocks away at 1930 22nd Street. In tribute to his profession, Nevis had representations of grapes carved into the newel posts of the oak staircases as well as imprinted in the wainscoting of the dining room. Converted to offices, the home today is physically isolated from its residential neighbors.

2 Charles S. Robb House

1903 21st Street *ca. 1898*

Charles Robb, a retired Southern Pacific conductor, deeded this house in 1902 to his daughter, Myrtle, and her spouse, Daniel W. Carmichael. Carmichael later parlayed his real estate and oil interests into development of the unincorporated area of Sacramento County known as Carmichael. A staunch Democrat who served as mayor, city treasurer, county treasurer and president of the Chamber of Commerce, Carmichael counted William Jennings Bryan among his friends and was a delegate for Bryan at the 1900 Democratic National Convention. The house features a pyramidal corner tower.

3 Fred Mason House
1931 21st Street *1900*

Mason owned a haberdashery and a steam laundry. This Shingle/Queen Anne house is in splendid condition and is distinguished by its round tower and turret, with an open-air balcony on the third floor. Also impressive is the semi-circular front porch supported by Doric columns.

4 Philip S. Driver House
2019 21st Street *ca. 1899*

Driver was a noted attorney who was active in civic affairs. Now a bed and breakfast known as Vizcaya, the home is a blend of Colonial Revival, Shingle and Craftsman styles.

5 Vizcaya Pavilion
21st and U Streets, Daryl Chinn, Mark Rusconi and Steve Goldstein *1993*

A reception/meeting hall extension of the bed and breakfast next door that aspires to harmonize with the Colonial Revival and Italianate styles of its neighbors. The large fountain is a smart design feature that obscures the traffic noise coming from the nearby freeway.

6 John Stevens House
2110 U Street *1883*

"Honest" John Stevens arrived in California in 1856 and quickly established a reputation for integrity and hard work. He became president of the Pioneer Box Company and vice president of a lumber company. He had such a good reputation that Mayor George Clark campaigned on the promise that Stevens would be his first appointment. Stevens' Italianate home was nearly destroyed by fire in the 1950s, but the residence later was carefully restored by Dr. Audley Hale. Urns that flank the front walk are filled with concrete fruit, and large trees and shrubs shelter the home from 21st Street.

7 James Louis Gillis House
2121 21st Street *1911*

Gillis served as California State Librarian from 1899 until his death in 1917. He was the father of California's library system. Prior to Gillis' tenure as state librarian, use of the State Library was restricted to state officials, legislators, clergy and the press. Believing that a library owned by the public should be accessible to the public, Gillis pushed the Legislature to open up the State Library to everybody. He also headed an effort to build a new state library building, the fine Neo-Classical Library and Courts Building near the State Capitol. Gillis also led the movement to establish California's county library system, which allowed for pooling of state, county, city and school resources under the supervision of county librarians. This county system served as a model for many states and nations. Gillis' daughter, Mabel, followed in her father's footsteps as State Librarian. Mr. Gillis' home is an exceptional example of the Craftsman Bungalow style, with a stone base and chimney, notched rafter ends and exposed timber rafters.

8 Edward P. Howe House
2201 21st Street *1888*

This Semi-Italianate home is set back far from 21st Street. Professor Howe became a high school principal at age 20. In 1873 he established Howe's High School and Normal Institute, considered to be one of the best learning institutions in the area.

9 Herman Grau House
2214 21st Street *ca. 1902*

This Cube-Type house is in the Colonial Revival/Gothic Revival style. Grau was an employee of a wholesale grocery firm. Located close to the freeway, the house bears the brunt of traffic noise and has been converted to offices.

10 Edward P. Howe House
2215 21st Street *1903*

A variation on the style also found in the Philip S. Driver house, the Howe residence is a combination of Shingle and Colonial Revival styles. The house has a grand porch entry and is distinguished by the steep pitch of its shingled twin dormers.

11 John LaRue House
2128 V Street *1915*

This house is a striking combination of Colonial Revival and Prairie Style, as are several of its neighbors near 22nd Street that were built between 1910 and 1915. The stucco structure features pedimented dormers and small-pane leaded glass windows. LaRue was secretary-treasurer for the Sacramento Abstract and Title Company.

12 George Jackson House
2120 V Street *1915*

This house is in a simplified Mediterranean style. Window and door niches feature columns with fancy capitals.

13 Timothy W. Sheehan House

2122 22nd Street *ca. 1905-10*

This Delta-Type Colonial Revival house sits far back on a huge lot. Sheehan was the manager of the *Record-Union*, an early Sacramento newspaper.

14 Charles K. McClatchy House

2112 22nd Street, Rudolph Herold *ca. 1910*

McClatchy was vice-president of the James McClatchy Company, publishers of *The Sacramento Bee*. The Beaux Arts style house now provides a dignified setting for a branch of the Sacramento Public Library.

15 Rudolph A. Herold House

2100 22nd Street, Rudolph Herold *1911*

Herold was one of the city's most accomplished architects, the designer of Sacramento's City Hall, Masonic Temple, Capitol National Bank and Forum Building. Herold's own Prairie Style house is one of the city's most dramatic, with its horizontal profile, projecting cornice with painted soffits, facial decoration, and Egyptian columns.

16 James G. Patterson House

2101 22nd Street *ca. 1900-05*

Patterson came to California in 1851 and worked on the construction of railroads. His Shingle Style and Queen Anne house has a beautiful curving front porch and a rounded bay.

17 Nicholas E. White House

2014 22nd Street *ca. 1905-10*

White was a journalist. The house is a combination of Cube-Type Colonial Revival and Craftsman styles.

18 Mary E. Ross House

2000 22nd Street, architect possibly Rudolph Herold *1911*

One of the city's most beautiful, this house is a blend of Colonial Revival and Prairie Styles. The huge L-shaped porch is supported by classical columns. The structure is in fine condition.

19 Frank D. Ryan House
2200 T Street *1910*

The most exceptional of the Colonial Revival/Prairie Style dwellings in the neighborhood, this house features an expansive front porch lined with Ionic columns and cathedral glass windows. Ryan was an assistant cashier at Capitol Banking and Trust Company.

20 William Wiard House
2131 T Street *ca. 1900*

This Queen Anne is particularly imposing as a result of its size and corner location. Wiard was a physician.

21 Howard K. Johnson House
1914 22nd Street *ca. 1912*

Johnson was an agent of the Sacramento Transportation Company. The house is a formidably sized Craftsman Bungalow with a clinker brick and pedimented porch.

SOUTHSIDE

Southside is a melting pot of Asians, Latinos, Caucasians and African-Americans. It is among the city's older neighborhoods, with residences dating back to the 1880s.

Post-war changes hit Southside particularly hard. Blows came from all directions: The Business 80 freeway severed the neighborhood's south end, Interstate 5 chopped off its western sector, one-way traffic lacerates the east end and high-rise office development encroaches from the north.

Despite these challenges, the neighborhood survives and in some ways flourishes: Neighbors organized to drive out prostitution in the 1980s, a huge farmers' market convenes under the freeway near 5th Street on Sundays, popular community festivals are held in Southside Park and an innovative residential development recently located in the heart of the neighborhood.

TOUR 13 – SOUTHSIDE

1 Southside Park
bordered by 6th, 8th, T and W Streets

This area was home to a small lake, peach orchard, Chinese vegetable garden, refuse dump and sewage canal during the 19th century. The city purchased the property in 1906, after some pressure from the Southside Improvement

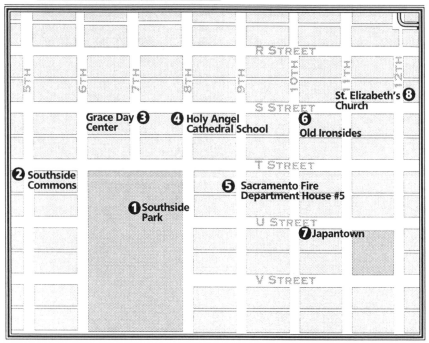

Grace Day **3** Center

4 Holy Angel Cathedral School

St. Elizabeth's **8** Church

6 Old Ironsides

2 Southside Commons

5 Sacramento Fire Department House #5

1 Southside Park

7 Japantown

Association. The city hired Rudolph Herold, George Randle and John McClaren (who was the landscape architect for San Francisco's Golden Gate Park) to land-scape the area. Dredging equipment expanded the lake and increased the depth to 50 feet, the sewage canal was filled and a public swimming pool was installed. The park once featured a reproduction of an early California gold mining town. Bleachers were set up along the lake for fireworks displays on Independence

Day. The near-by freeway eliminated two square blocks of the park during the 1960s. Southside Park remains an important community gathering place, hosting festivals, con-certs and jog-gers.

2 Southside Commons

T Street, between 4th and 5th Streets, Mogavero-Notestine and Associates *1993*

Co-housing is a Danish affordable housing innovation that combines private home ownership with facilities owned in common. The gabled roofs, front porches and lap siding of the units fit in well with the older residences in the neighborhood. Deteriorated residences originally on the site were restored and integrated with the project rather than demolished. Residents of Southside Commons have the option of eating in their own units, or taking part in communal dining held in the large common house. The common house also has child care facilities, a kitchen, library, craft shop, tools and guest rooms. Instead of private yards, there is a large common yard that all residents share. The development has a mix of residents of various incomes, ages and household sizes; and the cost of the dwellings is significantly less than conventional single family housing. Southside Commons demonstrates that inner city development does not have to be in conflict with sensitive design, housing affordability or strong communities.

3 Grace Day Center

1909 7th Street, Dean and Dean *1920*
Addition *1923*

This institution is the oldest day care center in Sacramento. Today the center cares for as many as 150 children. The Franciscan sisters began caring for children as early as 1915 to allow mothers to work in local canneries. The opening of the Del Monte Cannery in 1916 led to a need for a large facility and planning for the Grace Day Center began. Cost per child up until 1940 was 25 cents for six days.

4 Holy Angel Cathedral School

730 S Street *1924*

A Catholic elementary school for 50 years, this building now serves as a Catholic service center. The building's design is eclectic, blending Romanesque, Spanish and English Revival styles.

5 Sacramento Fire Department House #5

2014 9th Street *1911*

This old firehouse was remodeled in 1957 to serve as the Ben Ali Temple. Although some of the original architectural features have disappeared, the building remains an unusual feature in this residential area.

6 Old Ironsides
1901 10th Street *ca. 1865-70*
Remodel, Comstock Johnson
Architects *1994*

This bar is the oldest in town,
with the first drinks served in
this building in 1895. Thomas
Ryan, who lived at 1913 10th
Street, operated a grocery and
saloon out of the building
beginning about 1895. A saloon
existed in the building until
Prohibition in 1918. After a
period of vacancy, a soft drink
bar opened up. In 1934,
William Bordisso opened Old Ironsides immediately after Prohibition; and the
business has remained in the family ever since.

7 Japantown
Between 10th, 12th, T and V Streets

The redevelopment of Sacramento's West End in the 1950s uprooted hundreds
of Japanese homes and businesses. Many of the dislocated citizens settled in
Southside. Although the number of Japanese in the area has dwindled to a few
hundred (while the number of Chinese has grown into the thousands), there are
still a few longtime Japanese
businesses, particularly along
10th Street.

8 St. Elizabeth's Church
1201 S Street, Frank Shea and
John Lofquist *1910*

Portuguese immigrants, who
established small family farms
when they came to Sacramento
in the 19th Century, had established themselves in a neighborhood bound by S, U, 3rd and 5th
Streets by the turn of the century. They went on to build this
compact, Mission Revival
Catholic church in 1910.

EARLY SUBURBS
EAST SACRAMENTO

Two U.S. Presidents are most associated with East Sacramento: William McKinley, namesake of a popular neighborhood park, and Ronald Reagan, who lived in the neighborhood during his eight years as governor of California. Developed primarily in the 1920s - 1940s, East Sacramento is one of Sacramento's most coveted neighborhoods.

ALL THAT REMAINS OF THE ALHAMBRA THEATRE

Perhaps the biggest controversy to hit East Sacramento was the 1973 demolition of the Alhambra Theatre, which once stood on Alhambra Boulevard between J and L Streets. Leonard Starks and Edward Flanders designed the grand, Moorish-style structure in 1927. Moviegoers entered the theatre through a vest-pocket garden to the sound of water fountains. The city renamed 31st Street "Alhambra Boulevard" in honor of the theatre, and commercial buildings along the boulevard were constructed in a complementary Spanish Colonial Revival style.

The Alhambra Theatre was demolished to make way for a nondescript Safeway after city voters failed to approve a bond measure to save the building. The only remnant of the theatre is a one-story tiled fountain on the south side of Safeway's parking lot, which Safeway restored in 1997. Alhambra Boulevard subsequently lost a great deal of its former charm, with many of the old buildings replaced by medical centers and parking garages. Like New York City's 1963 demolition of its historic Penn Station, the demise of the Alhambra Theatre catalyzed a local historic preservation movement responsible for saving other vulnerable structures from the wrecking ball.

TOUR 14 – EAST SACRAMENTO
1 McKinley Park
Bordered by Alhambra Boulevard, 35th, E and H Streets *1901*

The area now known as McKinley Park was first purchased in 1871 by the Sacramento City Railway Company. The company named the area East Park and, to attract streetcar ridership to the area, put in lavish amounts of landscap-

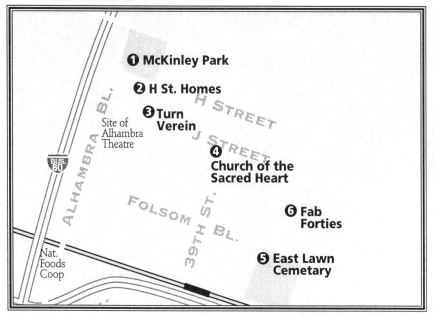

❶ **McKinley Park**

❷ **H St. Homes**

❸ **Turn Verein**

Site of Alhambra Theatre

❹ **Church of the Sacred Heart**

❻ **Fab Forties**

Nat. Foods Coop

❺ **East Lawn Cemetary**

ing, built a bandstand for concerts and dancing and provided refreshment stands that offered wine, beer and cigars. After 30 years the railway found that the investment was not paying off and decided to sell. Sacramento's Tuesday Club urged the city to purchase East Park for a playground for children and other city residents. The city initially was reluctant to make the expenditure, but the club's persistence finally convinced local officials to shell out $12,500 for the property. The park was renamed McKinley Park, in honor of President William McKinley, who had been assassinated in 1901. With a paved jogging track, municipal pool, art and garden center, tennis courts, playground, Clunie Memorial Clubhouse (Harry Devine, Sr., 1936), library branch and duck pond, the park is one of Sacramento's busiest and most family-oriented. The park's Rose Garden is a popular wedding site.

2 H Street Homes

H Street, between Alhambra Boulevard and 33rd Streets

Facing the park on H Street are a collection of Sacramento's finest homes, including the John T. Greene House (3200 H Street, 1915), designed by the influential Craftsman architects Charles and Henry Greene. The home is listed on the National Register of Historic Places.

3 Turn Verein
3349 J Street *1925*

Sacramento's chapter of Turn Verein was established by German immigrants in 1854. Although
the male social and athletic club (Turn Verein
translates to "gymnastics union") can be found
most places where Germans settled,
Sacramento's is the oldest on the Pacific Coast
and the only one that is member-owned. The
hall features handball/racquetball courts, a gym,
meeting rooms and kitchen facilities, and is
available for weddings and receptions. The terra cotta entrance medallion, featuring a discus thrower, was fashioned by Gladding, McBean & Co.

4 Church of the Sacred Heart
39th and J Streets, Harry Devine, Sr. *1930*

This fine Romanesque Revival church features stained glass work by Harry
Clarke, one of the best of the Irish stained glass craftsmen. Stained glass had
been a lost art in Ireland since the Elizabethan period, but the craft was revived
in Dublin in the early 20th century.

5 East Lawn Cemetery
Folsom Boulevard, between 42nd and 46th Streets

East Lawn was established in 1904 and is located in a serene neighborhood setting. The cemetery features a mausoleum built in 1924 at a cost of $400,000.

6 Fabulous Forties
bordered by 40th, 47th and J Streets and Folsom Boulevard

The Fabulous Forties is Sacramento's grandest residential area. The neighborhood, particularly on 45th and 46th Streets, is distinguished by its generous lots,
wide streets and spacious
English Revival, Spanish
Colonial Revival, Renaissance
Revival and Colonial Revival
homes. It is a neighborhood of
rock-ribbed Republicans that
once counted Ronald and
Nancy Reagan among its residents. The Reagans lived at
1341 45th Street (Dean &
Dean, built for George Pollack,
engineer of the Tower
Building) between 1967-75.
The Reagans' Hollywood
friends such as Jack Benny,

REAGAN RESIDENCE

Dean Martin and Red Skelton would entertain at the Reagans' annual reception
for legislators. Neighborhood children were welcome to come over, stick their
feet in the pool and check out the fun as well.

OAK PARK

Oak Park is Sacramento's first suburb, established in 1889. Previously the area had been the site of stockyards, fields, orchards and vineyards. The area was annexed by the City of Sacramento in 1911 — by that time, residential growth had reached approximately 7,000 persons, primarily blue collar families of English, Irish and German origin. An eight-route electric trolley system connected Oak Park to downtown Sacramento and other areas. Ironically, this area that had offered the benefits of suburban living to an earlier generation suffered as a result of the development of further-flung suburbs (and the community-destroying effects of theHighway 99 freeway) after World War II. Despite its rough edges, Oak Park is making steady improvements, as indicated by the landscaped median on Broadway that runs through the neighborhood's historic business district.

TOUR 15 – OAK PARK

1 James McClatchy Park
Between 5th and 6th Avenues and 33rd and 35th Streets *1927*

This amenity was originally the site of an amusement park built by investors in 1889 to lure residents to the new suburb of Oak Park. The street car system brought Sacramentans directly into the park. The park was turned over to new management in 1913 and renamed "Joyland." Featuring a bandstand, zoo, ballpark and amusement rides, Joyland was a popular community attraction that fit in well with the adjacent business district. A fire in 1920 destroyed the park, and although it was rebuilt, Joyland never regained the same popularity. Mr. and Mrs. Valentine McClatchy purchased the park in 1927 and dedicated it to James McClatchy, father of Valentine and editor of *The Sacramento Bee*. The McClatchys donated the park to the city and today shady McClatchy Park is a venue for summer concerts.

2 Oak Park Business District
Bordered by 33rd Street, 35th Street, 5th Avenue and Broadway

Once the site of a vineyard, this area was subdivided for commercial development in 1902. For many years the district thrived, with neighborhood amenities such as a barber shop, bowling alley, movie theatre, drug store, meat market, shoe store and grocer. Upon the area's decline following construction of the Highway 99 freeway, the Sacramento Housing and Redevelopment Agency cleared away some of the district to build housing. The area has never climbed out of its decline, although former NBA star Kevin Johnson, a native son, has indicated ambitious plans to invest in various commercial ventures to revive the old business district.

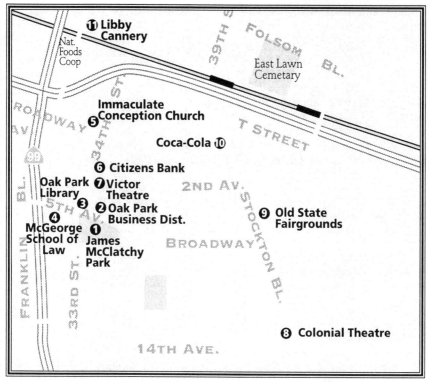

3 Oak Park Library
3301 5th Avenue, Charles F. Dean *1931*

This tidy brick library building was displaced by a larger Oak Park library in 1987. It is now known as the George Fuller Memorial Hall and has charming original interior murals.

4 McGeorge School of Law
3200 5th Avenue

A branch of the University of the Pacific, McGeorge is where U.S. Supreme Court Justice Anthony Kennedy taught until 1987. Justice Kennedy was nominated by President Reagan after the president's previous nominations of Robert Bork and Douglas Ginsberg failed to receive Senate confirmation. Originally exclusively a night school, McGeorge has expanded to a fully accredited law school with day and evening programs under the stewardship of the late Gordon Schaber.

5 Immaculate Conception Church
3263 1st Avenue *1916*

This Tudor church features six stained glass windows that were installed to commemorate the church's 50th anniversary. The stained glass represents events in the life of the Virgin Mary and was fabricated by Clark Studios of Dublin, Ireland.

6 Citizens Bank

3418 Broadway *1914*

The bank building conforms to its triangular shaped lot, with the columned entry jutting out at the corner. Listed in the National Register of Historic Places.

7 Victor Theatre

2830 35th Street *1907*

Now known as the Guild Theatre, the Victor opened its doors the year before the first full-length film was completed in California. The theatre's name was changed to the Oak Park Theatre in 1926 and the building was outfitted with a neon marquee, the first in Northern California. The theatre was reborn as a venue for art films in the 1950s and was renamed the Guild Theatre. After an unseemly period as a pornographic film house, the theatre finally closed in 1969. There have been subsequent efforts to put the building back into use, but so far without lasting results.

8 Colonial Theatre

3522 Stockton Boulevard, Herb Goodpastor *1940*

This art deco movie palace reopened in 1993 and books a combination of films and live events.

9 Old State Fairgrounds

Bordered by Stockton Boulevard, Broadway, 49th Street and V Street, George B. McDougall, supervising architect

Site of the State Fair from 1909 to 1967, the area now is used by the University of California, Davis and the County of Sacramento. Some of the original brick fair buildings remain.

10 Coca-Cola Bottling Plant

2200 Stockton Boulevard, Harry J. Devine, Sr. *1936*

This classic-looking brick Romanesque Revival building, still used to bottle the world's most popular soft drink.

11 Libby, McNeill, Libby Cannery Building
1724 Stockton Boulevard *1913*

This 250,000 square foot cannery was one of Sacramento's largest employers, with up to 1,900 workers. The company built 50 employee cottages and established a day care center to make it possible for large numbers of women to work in the facility. The cannery closed in 1982 and was converted to offices.

CURTIS PARK

The Curtis Park neighborhood is Sacramento's second oldest suburb, settled in the early 1900s. The neighborhood has a charming assortment of Craftsman, Tudor and Mediterranean style homes. Ancient Valley Oak trees stand in the middle of Markham Way and 3rd Avenue, despite having nearly the entire area within their drip lines paved over since the 1920s.

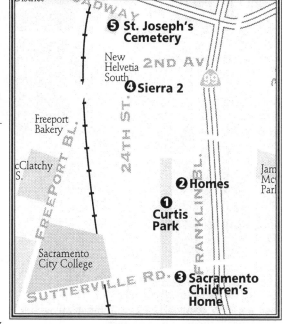

TOUR 16 – CURTIS PARK

1 Curtis Park
Bordered by W. Curtis, E. Curtis and Donner Ways and by Sutterville Road

Curtis Park is named after William Curtis, a successful dairy farmer who arrived in California in 1852 and went on to establish a successful dairy farm in the area. The park's distinctive oval-shape comes from its early use as Sacramento's first horse racing track, known as the Louisiana Racetrack, which was developed by Curtis for trotting events in the 1860s.

2 Homes
Curtis Park, settled mostly in the 1910 to 1930 era, has homes with an exceptional variety of architectural styles, including Mediterranean, Craftsman and Colonial Revival. Perhaps Sacramento's greatest piece of folk art is the **Tile House** located

at 2816 22nd Street. Nearly every square inch of the home's exterior is covered in handcrafted art tile, depicting gargoyles, a Chinese dragon, a growling tiger and various whimsical creatures.

3 The Sacramento Children's Home
2750 Sutterville Road *ca. 1913*
Cottages and laundry, Charles F. Dean *1930*

This Tudor structure was once known as the Sacramento Children's Home and Orphanage.

4 Sierra 2
24th Street, between Castro Way and 4th Avenue

This former elementary school has been transformed into a unique community resource, offering space to dozens of community organizations. The 24th Street Theatre provides an intimate venue for dance, symphony and theatrical performances.

5 St. Joseph's Cemetery
21st Street, between 2nd Avenue and Broadway *1865*

St. Joseph's is the second oldest cemetery in the city. The cemetery was purchased in 1864 by the congregation of St. Rose Catholic Church, which once was located at 7th and K Streets, now the site of St. Rose of Lima Park. The cemetery was consecrated in May 1865.

LAND PARK

Developed between the 1920s and 1940s, Land Park is considered one of Sacramento's best residential areas. Tree-lined Land Park Drive is the neighborhood's spine, winding past well-tended homes and through William Land Park.

TOUR 17 – LAND PARK

1 William Land Park
Bordered by Riverside and Freeport Boulevards, 11th and 13th Avenues and Sutterville Road *1914*

Pioneer William Land served as mayor and was the owner of the Western Hotel, once one of the

city's finest hostelries and ultimately sacrificed to the Interstate 5 freeway. In his will, Land left $250,000 to the city for a regional park. The city established the 236-acre William Land Park in 1914. Stuffed with great urban amenities and mature landscaping, Land Park is the most popular outdoor area in the city. Among the park's features are the 15-acre **Sacramento Zoo**, with 150 exotic species in a pleasant and compact setting; **Funderland**, which offers amusement rides for small children; **Fairy Tale Town**, a children's park based on the themes of familiar fairy tales; **William S. Land Amphitheater** (Harry Devine, Sr., 1958) adjacent to a large duck pond and the site for summertime Shakespeare in the Park performances; the **Botanical Garden**, a Works Progress Administration project that has blossomed under the tireless care of city parks employee Daisy Mah; and a nine-hole **golf course**, built in 1929 and working overtime with 70,000 rounds played annually. The park also has plenty of ball diamonds, fields and picnic areas. The *Swanston Fountain* (north side of zoo, west of Land Park Drive, Ralph Stackpole, 1924), with its granite statue of a pioneer gold miner,

was erected by George Swanston as a tribute to his father, Charles Swanston. The elder Swanston owned most of the property now occupied by the Land Park neighborhood.

2 Homes

The most impressive homes are found just north of William Land Park in the area that includes 13th Avenue, College Drive, Brockway Court, East Lincoln and West Lincoln. U.S. Supreme Court Justice Anthony Kennedy lived at 3641 East Lincoln before he was nominated in 1987 by President Reagan to serve on the U.S. Supreme Court.

3 Tower District
Broadway, between 15th and 19th Streets

Anchored by the Tower Theatre (William David, 1938) the Tower District later gave birth to international retail giant Tower Records. On the north side of the

theatre, above the Tower Cafe, is the original Tower Records sign. The record store was established by Russ Solomon in 1960 in the back of his dad's pharmacy. Tower Records world head-quarters is located in nearby West Sacramento. The Tower District has emerged as a popular community gathering place, combining

GENESIS OF THE TOWER RECORDS EMPIRE

the theatre with restaurants, cafes, nightclubs and small shops.

4 Joe Marty's El Chico
1500 Broadway *1938*

El Chico was Sacramento's first sports bar, opened in 1938 by Joe Marty (1913-1984). Marty played baseball alongside Joe DiMaggio for the Pacific Coast League's San Francisco Seals and later went on to play for the Chicago Cubs. One day at Chicago's Wrigley Field, Marty graciously posed for a picture with a boy and his father. Unbeknownst to Marty, the father was Al Capone. When the photo was published in *The Chicago Tribune* the next day, the Commissioner of Baseball warned that another mistake like that would result in Marty's being kicked out of baseball. Although Sacramento has produced scores of professional baseball players, Marty is the only native Sacramentan to hit a World Series home run. The late Sacramento sportswriter Bill Conlon fondly remembered Marty's 20 years of bartending at El Chico: "Our friend spilled enough Scotch toward the end of a shift to flood Edinburgh." Marty sold the place a few years before his death, with the stipulation that the bar's collection of old baseball memorabilia remained unchanged.

5 Edmonds Field Site
Riverside Boulevard and Broadway

Now the site of a Target store, this corner housed a number of ballparks occupied by the Sacramento Solons of the Pacific Coast League from 1910-1960. Impressed by Sacramento's strong attendance figures, *The Sporting News* in 1928 called Sacramento "possibly the best baseball city for its size in the country."

6 Old Sacramento City Cemetery
Entrance at 10th Street and Broadway *1850*

When an outbreak of cholera took the lives of 600 Sacramentans in 1850, city officials pleaded with John Sutter to donate a burial site. Sutter, already feeling beleaguered by miners sponging off his land, crops and livestock, turned over this site to the city, quipping that he would donate additional

acreage if the city filled it with those who were taking advantage of him. The cholera victims were buried in shallow trenches, sometimes 50 to a grave. The cemetery features a pioneer section and is the final resting place of seminal figures in California history: Albert M. Winn, Sacramento's first mayor and the founder of Native Sons of the Golden West, a nativist fraternal organization with halls throughout California; Mark Hopkins, one of the Central Pacific Railroad's Big Four who is buried in a pink granite vault; Governors Newton Booth, John Bigler and William Irwin; and John Sutter, Jr., founder and planner of the City of Sacramento. Flowers for the ceme-

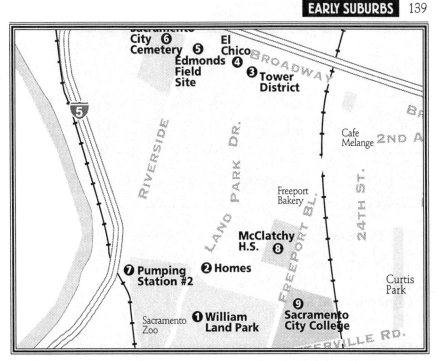

tery were provided for many years by the nearby Bell Conservatory, once located on the block bordered by 9th, 10th, V and W Streets. The conservatory was a smaller replica of the ornate conservatory in San Francisco's Golden Gate Park. Mrs. E.B. Crocker purchased the structure for $38,000 in 1881, reportedly because she did not want San Francisco to have something that Sacramento did not have. The Bell Conservatory was closed in 1944 and was later demolished to make room for a Safeway. Free guide brochures to the Old Sacramento City Cemetery are available at the Broadway entrance. Hours 7 a.m. - 4:30 p.m.

7 Pumping Station #2
915 11th Avenue *1914*

Tucked back from Riverside Boulevard is this old station, pumping water from the Sacramento River for the use of city residents. In contrast to the utilitarian structures that today serve a similar function, Pumping Station #2 fits in well with the residential area. Once located adjacent to the station were the indoor Riverside Swimming Baths and, later, the outdoor Land Park Plunge.

8 McClatchy High School
3066 Freeport Boulevard, Leonard Starks
1937

Financed in part by a Public Works Administration (PWA) grant, this fine art deco/Spanish Colonial Revival melange, with its massive entry columns, has a dignity and

style often missing from modern school buildings. The high school includes a 953-seat theatre.

9 Sacramento City College
3835 Freeport Boulevard

Established in 1916, Sacramento City College is one of the oldest public community colleges in California. The city purchased this location for the college in 1922. Notable on the campus are the PWA Moderne buildings (Gymnasium, Auditorium, Engineering Technology and Aeronautics Addition) built between 1936-39 and designed by Sacramento architect Harry Devine, Sr.

NORTH SACRAMENTO

North Sacramento is a former city that was annexed by the City of Sacramento in the 1960s. Long a troubled area, North Sacramento sees itself as Sacramento's neglected stepchild, adopted by an unnurturing parent.

The neighborhood is located on the site of Rancho Del Paso, a 44,374-acre Mexican land grant made in 1844 by Mexican Governor Manuel Micheltorena to Eliab Grimes. James Ben Ali Haggin took ownership in 1866 and turned the area into an internationally famous breeding ground for thoroughbred racehorses. Haggin sold the ranch in 1910 to developers who were planning to build a new town on the north side of the American River. Promotional material boasted that the area was served by a streetcar and was ideally located for homes. North Sacramento incorporated as a city in 1924.

North Sacramento was a healthy, working-class neighbor of Sacramento through the 1950s. Then hard times struck: cheap housing and new highways

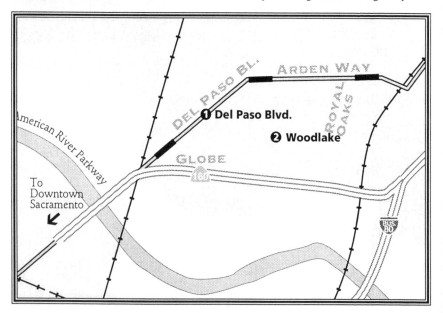

lured young families to the suburbs, Highway 160 split the town in half and the opening of nearby Arden Fair Mall drew customers away from North Sacramento businesses. Desperate to turn the situation around, North Sacramento voters in 1964 narrowly approved a referendum to annex to the City of Sacramento.

Rather than saving North Sacramento, consolidation simply depleted the area's political representation and led to further deterioration. In recent years, however, North Sacramento has mounted an effort to revive its deteriorated business district by recruiting new businesses, promoting artists' lofts and building better transportation connections.

TOUR 18 – NORTH SACRAMENTO

1 Del Paso Boulevard

The heart of North Sacramento's business district is Del Paso Boulevard. When North Sacramento was first subdivided, Del Paso Boulevard boasted more than 2,000 palm and ornamental shade trees. The 1934 widening of the bridge connecting North Sacramento to the capital city on the other side of the American River allowed Del Paso to become one of the region's busiest thoroughfares. North Sacramento's subsequent decline can still be seen in the vacant lots and empty buildings of Del Paso Boulevard, although lately the area has seen some improvements. One of the most notable structures on Del Paso Boulevard is **Iceland** (1430 Del Paso Boulevard, Charles F. Dean, 1940), an ice-skating rink in a Streamline Moderne style.

2 Woodlake

Bordered by Del Paso Boulevard, Globe Avenue, Highway 160 and Royal Oaks Drive

Woodlake is North Sacramento's affluent neighborhood. The winding, tree-lined streets and Tudor-style homes make Woodlake one of Sacramento's best residential areas.

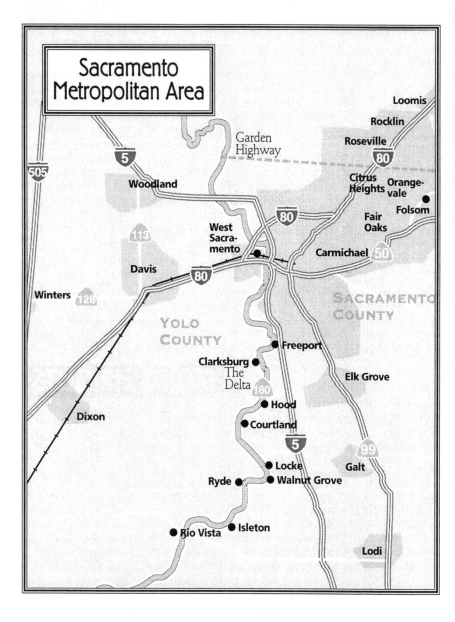

PART V
BEYOND SACRAMENTO
CARMICHAEL

Carmichael is named after Daniel W. Carmichael, who in 1909 subdivided 2000 acres into 10-acre lots in the area, selling the parcels for $1,500 each. This unincorporated chunk of Sacramento County was the epitome of the American Dream in the great suburban boom after World War II. Residents lived in comfortable ranch-style homes, kept horses in spacious front yards, shopped at early malls and took horseback rides along the American River. Even today, with the boulevards choked by frustrated commuters, many parts of Carmichael have a country club aura. Tree-lined Fair Oaks Boulevard winds through the area, passing through the "gourmet gulch" surrounding Pavilions and Loehmann's Plaza, as well as the mansions on Crocker and Hopkins Streets in the Sierra Oaks neighborhood. Supporters of former Governor Ronald Reagan built a Governor's Mansion in Carmichael along the American River near the end of Reagan's term in 1974. Incoming Governor Jerry Brown, who urged "lower expectations," declined to move into the opulent residence. The Legislature subsequently sold the mansion, forcing each subsequent governor to live in a comparatively modest home in one of Carmichael's many well-kept neighborhoods.

CITRUS HEIGHTS

Citrus Heights was known as the Sylvan District beginning in 1862, a reference to the oak groves once common to the area. Real estate promoter Alfred Trainor christened the area Citrus Heights in 1910, hoping to attract buyers to 10-acre lots. A typically florid advertisement lured potential buyers to visit a land "where the sun shines 300 days in the year, where you may work in the open fields any day in the year — in the very heart of California, enclosed by mountain ranges and transversed by noble rivers, where every ten acres is supplied by Free Water Rights, Electric Lights, Telephone and Mail Service." Citrus Heights' fruit industry grew rapidly until the trees were delivered a death blow by a severe freeze in December 1932. Farming and ranching continued in the area, however, until families started flocking to Citrus Heights' one-to five-acre lots after World War II. The area's population increased from 3,000 in 1946 to 21,685 in 1959. The construction of Sunrise Mall in 1970 transformed the Sunrise Boulevard-Greenback Lane region from open fields to a traffic-choked mess, spurring development that eradicated the identities of the surrounding communities. Concern over explosive growth and a lack of responsiveness from Sacramento County officials led Citrus Heights to vote to incorporate in 1996. **Rusch Park** (Antelope Road at Auburn Boulevard), the city's largest at 51 acres, boasts a well-used swimming pool as well as one of the oldest homes in the city, **Rusch Home** (Rosswood Drive off Antelope Road). The 1916 Craftsman bungalow, a state site of historical interest, was once part of a 480-acre ranch purchased by the pioneer Rusch family in 1858. **Citrus Heights Community Club** (6921 Sylvan Road), a community meeting hall, was the original Sylvan School, an 1862 one-room schoolhouse previously located at another location. **Sylvan Cemetery** (Auburn Boulevard between Old Auburn Road and Antelope Road), also established in 1862, contains a section of pioneer grave sites.

DAVIS

This vibrant college town takes its name from Jerome and Mary Davis, who sold their 2,000-acre ranch to the Central Pacific Railroad for $40 per acre in 1868. Later that year, the railroad established a depot and laid out lots on a section of the former ranch, and the new town was dubbed Davisville ("ville" was dropped in 1907 to prevent mail from ending up in Danville). By the end of 1869, 400 residents, 200 homes, a large store and a hotel had been attracted to the site bounded by First, Fifth, B and J Streets. Davis grew slowly as a small agricultural community, but a marked shift in the town's character began in 1905 when the Legislature approved the establishment of a farm for the University of California's College of Agriculture. This farm evolved into the largest campus of

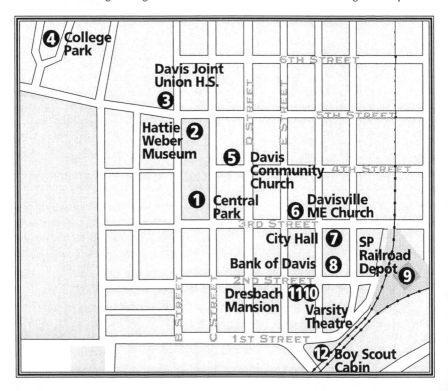

the U.C. system, which has had a profound impact evident even today. About half of Davis' 55,000 residents are enrolled in the university, and much of the rest of the population is employed by, or provides services to, the campus. The city is known for its progressive politics, characterized by strong support for energy conservation, growth management and, above all, bicycles. More than 50,000 two-wheelers use the miles of bike paths provided by the town and the university. Among the town's best attractions are the pleasant downtown shopping district, Wednesday and Saturday farmers' markets, red double-decker buses imported from London (call Unitrans at 530/752-2877 for schedules and routes), the Palms Public Playhouse and plentiful public art.

TOUR 19 – CENTRAL DAVIS

1 Central Park
Bounded by 3rd, 5th, B and C Streets

Central Park is the primary outdoor gathering place for the citizens of Davis, particularly at the farmers' market held on Wednesdays and Saturdays, year round. In addition to the park's playgrounds, children love the pedal-powered *Flying Carousel of the Delta Breeze* (1995) as well as the ground-level fountain near 4th and C Streets (*Source and Resource*, Jeffrey Reed and Kathleen Kaspar-Noonan, 1994).

2 Hattie Weber Museum
445 C Street *1911*
Renovation, Richard Berteaux *1991*

This Davis history museum (open Wednesdays and Saturdays, 530/758-5637) is located in the city's former library, which was the first library in Yolo County. The structure was moved to this location from 117 F Street and is named after the city's first librarian.

3 Davis Joint Union High School
23 Russell Boulevard *1927*

Converted to City Hall in the early 1980s, the former Davis Joint Union High School is a handsome, Mission Revival brick structure. The council chamber includes the acrylic painting *Davis Greetings* (Darrell Forney, c. 1970s) as well as a tapestry entitled *The Valley* (Birgitta Olsen, 1982).

4 College Park
North side of Russell Boulevard between Oak Avenue and Miller Drive *1924*

A homeowner's association sold lots in College Park for $475 to $500 in 1924. The stately neighborhood is the site of the Chancellor's House (16 College Park) and the Art Deco International House (10 College Park). The shady streets feature 19 landmark trees.

5 Davis Community Church
412 C Street *1926*

This church was designed to serve a wide number of community uses when the original Presbyterian congregation became interdenominational in 1926. The Spanish Colonial building is among the city's proudest structures of the period. The cypresses flanking the front entrance were grown from seeds brought from the Garden of Gethsemane.

6 Davisville Methodist Episcopal Church
305 E Street *1874*
Remodeled *1905*

This structure is one of the oldest buildings in the city. The church disbanded in 1895 and sold the building that year to Joseph Henle. Henle converted the former church to his family home, adding a porch and bay window in 1905.

7 City Hall
226 F Street, P.L. Dragon and C.R. Schmidts *1938*

This Mission-style building was designed to handle all city administrative offices as well as the fire department. At the time the city's population was about 1,600. Growth of the city and its government eventually overwhelmed the limited space available, and the last city tenant, the Davis Police Department, moved out in 2001. A heated controversy broke out when the city installed *The Joggers* (Tony Natsoulas, 1986), a sculpture featuring two joggers running in opposite directions. Some city officials were concerned that the pointed finger of one of the joggers might poke the eye of an unwary pedestrian.

8 Bank of Davis
203 G Street *1914*

The Bank of Davis was founded by J.B. Anderson, the city's first mayor. The Sullivanesque building is a dominant structure at this downtown corner. The bank was sold to the Bank of Sacramento in 1964 and later to Security Pacific Bank. The building housed doctors, lawyers and dentists on the second floor.

9 Southern Pacific Railroad Depot
Second and H Streets, SPRR Architectural Bureau *1913*

Davis owes its existence to the Central Pacific Railroad's decision to build a depot at this site to serve a new branch line in 1868. The original wood-frame station was replaced in 1913 by Southern Pacific. The attractive structure is a fine example of Mission Revival architecture, with warm stucco walls, an arcade and round arches. Note the nearby Water Tower, built in the same style during the same period. The sculpture at the entry of the depot parking lot (*Solar Intersections*, Robert Behrens, 1989) is a jarring modern counterpoint to the depot's romantic style.

10 Varsity Theatre
616 Second Street *1950*
Renovated, SH2A Architects *1992*

This Streamline Moderne moviehouse no longer shows movies in this age of multiplexes. These days the Varsity is a venue for live events.

11 Dresbach Mansion
604 Second Street *1875*

Davis founder William Dresbach had the good timing to convert Jerome Davis' large home into a hotel just a year before the Central Pacific Railroad built a nearby depot. Dresbach called the new town Davisville. Dresbach served as the town's first postmaster and later built this 12-room Stick-Italianate mansion. The home exhibits the fancy woodwork common to the Victorian era. The mansion now houses city government offices.

12 Boy Scout Cabin
First and F Streets *1927*
Restored *1982*

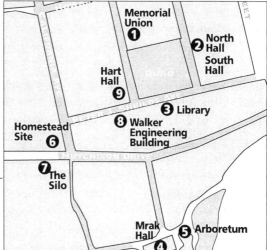

Local Rotarians constructed the cabin using wooden power poles donated by Pacific Gas and Electric Company. The community pitched in to restore the dilapidated structure in 1982 and upgraded the landscaping in 1999.

TOUR 20 – UNIVERSITY

1 Memorial Union
North Quad, Confer & Willis *1955*

The bustling Memorial Union houses a multitude of student organizations and services, including the the UCD Bookstore and the popular Coffeehouse.

2 North Hall and South Hall
East Quad *1908 - 1912*

These Shingle-style buildings were the campus' first residence halls. Construction of larger housing facilities led to the buildings' being converted to offices after 1960. The much larger Dutton Hall (1999), designed in the same style, sits between the two structures.

3 Library
Peter J. Shields Avenue, Starks and Flanders *1940*

The north side of the library was designed in an Art Deco style by the Sacramento firm of Starks and Flanders. Iridescent light fixtures similar to what one might find in a movie theatre of the period hang from the ceiling of the second floor reading room.

4 Mrak Hall
Mrak Hall Drive

Imposing Mrak Hall, an administration building named after former campus Chancellor Emil Mrak, is set formally on a tree-lined pedestrian mall to the north, with a traffic circle to the south.

5 Arboretum

The 120-acre Arboretum features a large lake, native plants, bicycle paths and benches in a peaceful park-like setting on Putah Creek.

6 Jerome and Mary Davis Homestead Site
Northwest intersection of California Avenue and Hutchinson Drive

The ancient olive and fig trees are the only surviving remnants of Jerome and Mary Davis' homestead, which they had built into a 13,000 acre ranch by 1864.

7 The Silo
Southwest intersection of California Avenue and Hutchinson Drive, Cunningham and Politeo *1908*
Remodel, Clifford C. Jay

Originally part of a dairy barn, the Silo was gutted and now features a bar, restaurant, fast food and meeting rooms.

8 Walker Engineering Building
Peter J. Shields Avenue *1927*

This Mission Revival structure was one of the first permanent campus department buildings.

9 Hart Hall
Peter J. Shields Avenue *1928*
Renovated *1992*

This Mission Revival building was named for George Hart, the first dean of the university's School of Veterinary Medicine.

DELTA

The Sacramento-San Joaquin Delta is a fascinating area filled with pear orchards, Victorian farmhouses, historic towns, bascule bridges and unpretentious restaurants. The Delta is about as close as you can get to the Deep South in California, convincing enough for Hollywood to use the area as the setting for *All the King's Men* and *Cool Hand Luke*. Residents generally do not have much use for the political games occurring a few miles north under the Capitol dome. What you get here are people who like the simple, scenic beauty and leisurely pace of this unique California region. In the Delta, you are on "Delta Time."

The Delta is formed by the Sacramento, San Joaquin and Mokelumne Rivers' draining into a triangular chunk of fertile real estate, with the cities of Sacramento, Stockton and Antioch being the points of the triangle. Archeologists believe the area was occupied by Plains Miwok tribes beginning in about 1500 B.C. These Native Americans lived in conical houses made of poles and thatched with tules, subsisting on the bountiful game, fish and vegetation in the Delta. Like other native peoples in California, the Plains Miwok were decimated by the arrival of foreign explorers and settlers, especially as the result of an 1833 epidemic that killed 75 percent of the Native Americans in the Sacramento Valley.

After the California gold rush, a few former miners settled in the Delta, determined to find a way to reclaim the land. Between 1855 and 1878, the state legislature provided incentives for others to buy Delta land for just $1.25 per acre if the buyer would reclaim the land within five years. Completion of the Central Pacific Railroad in 1869 brought thousands of surplus Chinese laborers to the Delta to build levees for dollar-a-day wages. The laborers used horse-drawn scrapers to pile the soil, but these levees regularly failed against the power of the Sacramento River. The development of the long-boom clamshell dredge in 1876 revolutionized levee building and began a period in which huge tracts of swamp land were reclaimed for agricultural purposes.

The Delta contains more than 1,000 miles of waterways, making the area a magnet for boating, fishing and wildlife viewing. The Delta also figures prominently in California's famous water wars, with much debate focused on the extent to which Delta water will be divided among agricultural, wildlife and urban users.

FREEPORT

Freeport sits just nine miles from the State Capitol, yet this peaceful town feels much more remote. The town was built by investors in 1863 to avoid paying a Sacramento tax on goods brought into the city by boat and transferred to rail. The shipping of supplies to the mines kept Freeport bustling during the Gold Rush. A.J. Bump built the first store in 1863, located at 8259 Freeport Boulevard. The Freeport Bridge (1929) is a bascule bridge of the type common to the Delta. Large 200,000-pound counterweights effectuate the opening of the bridge for vessels plying the river. These bridges replaced most of the ferries that were essential transportation links in the Delta's early development.

 CLARKSBURG

Robert Christopher Clark, a Sacramento lawyer from Kentucky, purchased land in the area where Clarksburg is located in 1856. Clark went on to serve in the legislature and as a county judge. The town proper is located four miles south of the Freeport Bridge. Just north of the bridge, in the area once known as the Lisbon district, sits **St. Joseph's Catholic Church** (32890 South River Road, 1924). Just before entering the town of Clarksburg on Netherlands Avenue one notices a vacant, Mission Style structure (36510 South River Road) that was once the home of **Lawlor's Store**, a longtime business that first opened in 1879. **Clarksburg Community Church** (52910 Netherlands Avenue, William Raymond Yelland, 1937) was a primary community gathering place, hosting meetings by the Garden Club, Farm Bureau Women and Clarksburg Ladies Fellowship. Further west on Netherlands Avenue are the Spanish style **Clarksburg Elementary School** (52870 Netherlands Avenue, 1923) and **Delta High School** (52810 Netherlands Avenue, 1928).

HOOD

The Southern Pacific Railroad ran a spur to this small town, which was named in 1909 after William Hood, the SP's chief construction engineer in the 1880s. North of the town is the **Rosebud Mansion** (Nathaniel Goodell, c. 1870s), a grand Italianate home built for William Johnson, a state senator. The mansion is on the National Register of Historic Places.

 COURTLAND

James V. Sims established Courtland in 1870. The town once boasted a sizable Chinatown and a robust economy fueled by fish canneries, pears and asparagus. Courtland still is the center of the nation's most productive pear region, which the town celebrates at the two-day Pear Fair held each July. Courtland's most imposing building can be seen from the levee, the Classical Revival **Bank of Courtland** (1920) which went belly up after the stock market crash of 1929.

You can feel history's grip as you wander around tiny Locke, America's only remaining rural Chinese town. The heirs of George Locke allowed Chinese workers to build a settlement on the Locke family property beginning in 1914, at a time when persons of Chinese ancestry were prohibited from owning property by state law. Locke was a bawdy, wide-open town during the 1920s-1940s, with five brothels, five gambling houses and several bars servicing a population that would reach a seasonal peak of 1,600 persons. During Prohibition the town attracted plenty of Caucasians looking for booze, gambling and sex. For five decades the town was occupied solely by Chinese from the Chung-San district.

Locke became the only Chinatown in the Delta to escape catastrophic fire, through the vigilance of a night watchman hired by local citizens. In the late 1970s, a Hong Kong developer purchased the entire town with a plan to develop condos and a Chinese theme park. The scheme was thwarted by the Sacramento County Board of Supervisors, who passed a zoning ordinance to protect Locke's historic character. Today nearly all the Chinese have left Locke, and there are just a handful of people tending to the town. Dilapidated wooden buildings, their paint almost completely faded away, sag forlornly on the quiet, one-lane Main Street, although a few of the storefronts remain occupied.

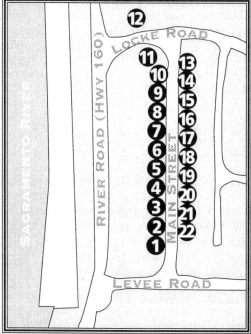

TOUR 21 - MAIN STREET

1 Restaurant Building
1915

This building had a hardwood floor installed specifically for dancing, beginning in about 1928. The building has housed a restaurant, dry goods store and antique shop.

2 Hing Lee Building
1915

One of the first buildings to be constructed in Locke, by one of the town's co-founders, Lee "Charlie" Bing. The building has a general store that carried dry goods, hardware, household items and herb medicines.

3 Tenderloin 12
1915

This building is known as T-12 among the locals. A barber shop was located here and the barber's family lived upstairs.

4 The Yellow Building
1915

The Yellow Building housed one of Locke's original gambling halls. A Caucasian moonshiner by the name of Tuffy Leamons operated a bar here during Prohibition. Gambling returned to the building in the early 1940s, but was eventually driven out by law enforcement.

5 Dry Goods Store
1915

Originally a dry goods store, this building later offered groceries, pool tables, ice cream and a restaurant. The building now houses the River Road Gallery.

6 Star Theatre
1915

The faded arch over the foot of the stairway on the north side of the Star Theatre directed patrons to the entrance to the theatre atop the levee on River Road. The theatre name and Chinese characters on the River Road facade have long since faded away. The theatre featured Chinese and American films as well as Chinese theatre groups from San Francisco. The theatre later was used for prostitution and gambling.

7 Gambling Hall
1915

This building featured gambling for a short period and then became a restaurant in the 1920s. A popular Japanese bakery operated for many years on the levee side of the building.

8 Wah Lee Boots & Dry Goods
1915

Wah Lee supplied essential items to the agricultural workers of the area. The store also featured groceries, tobacco and beer, as well as a bakery and lunch counter.

9 Boarding House
1915

This building originally was a rooming house for Chinese men, with rents in the 1920s set at five dollars per month.

10 Yuen Chong Market
1915

The market has operated since 1915, an anchor in a town where every other early business is long gone. George Marr and Stanford King, the now-deceased former owners, were local institutions who dispensed advice and good humor to locals and visitors who passed through the doors. The store features an arched, stucco facade on the levee side of the building.

11 Joe Schoong Chinese School
1926

The school was funded by contributions from local gambling houses. Several generations of young people from Locke and nearby towns received instruction here in several Asian dialects.

12 Boarding House
1915

The building originally housed Chinese agricultural workers, and later served as office space and housing for Mexican workers.

13 Warehouse Building
1915

A fancy arched false front is the dominant feature of this building, which has been used as a warehouse for many years.

14 Residence
1915

This building has been a residence from the time of its construction.

15 Drug Store
1915

This former gambling house, with a residence on the upper floor, later became Locke's best known drug and herbal medicine store.

16 Fish Market
1915

This fish market catered to the high local demand for fresh seafood.

17 Lodge Building
1915

For many years this building served as a lodge for immigrants from one of China's villages.

18 Bing Restaurant
1915

Town co-founder Lee "Charlie" Bing ran a Chinese restaurant here beginning in 1915. Al Adami, a bootlegger from Ryde, purchased the building in 1930 and opened Locke's first Caucasian-owned business, a restaurant famously known as Al the Wop's. The restaurant features a lively bar with dollar bills tacked to the ceiling (hand over a dollar and you'll find out how it's done). Adami kept an upstairs office behind the bar's mural depicting a western round-up. Bar regulars would come in and would call for Al to come down. Adami would look through a peephole (strategically located behind the horse's tail) to determine whether he wished to visit the customer. Al's menu features New York sirloin steaks, which the locals spread with peanut butter.

19 Jan Ying Benevolent Association
1915

For decades this building has been the gathering place for men from China's Chung-San district. Members would come here to speak in their familiar dialect, receive mail, read Chinese newpapers, play games and drink tea.

20 Dai Loy Gambling House
1915

Dai Loy means "a very big welcome." The building was designed to be identical to a successful gambling hall that had burned down in nearby Walnut Grove (consistent with the Chinese belief that one should not mess with good luck and fortune). The gambling house was owned by Lee "Charlie" Bing and operated from 1916 to 1951. The windows were boarded not only to discourage raids and thwart robbers, but also to prevent wives from locating their spouses. The building now is a museum operated by the Sacramento River Delta Historical Society, featuring an interior and exterior that faithfully represents the Dai Loy's rowdier days. The museum is open weekends from April through November.

21 Hing Yick Building
1915

The Hing Yick Building was another gambling house built by Charlie Bing. The business closed down in the 1940s.

22 Foon Hop Co.
1915

This building also was an early gambling house, later becoming the Foon Hop Co. grocery.

WALNUT GROVE

Walnut Grove is the only town south of Red Bluff that occupies both sides of the Sacramento River. East Walnut Grove is primarily commercial, West Walnut Grove residential. The town was founded in 1851 by John Sharp, a farmer and rancher who also operated a general store, ferry, blacksmith shop, post office and hotel. A significant number of Japanese, who had helped build the levees and work the fields, established a community between A, C, Market and Grove Streets. Several bathhouses on B Street served as the primary meeting places for Japanese men to relax and gossip. **Hayashi Company** (1281 B Street, 916/776-1015) has been a purveyor of Japanese groceries and fish since the early 1920s. **Gakuen Hall** on Pine Street, next door to the Buddhist Church, is a Japanese community hall built in 1928. The dilapidated **Grove Theatre** on Market Street operated from the 1920s through the 1960s. A primary town hangout is **Tony's Place** (14157 Market Street, 916/776-1317), a cocktail lounge featuring Portuguese beans and steak dinners on Saturday and Sunday, and lunch during the week. Other popular restaurants close to Walnut Grove include **Giusti's** (14743 Walnut Grove-Thornton Road, 916/776-1808), an Italian restaurant under operation by the Giusti family since 1910 (the original building dates from 1896) and **Wimpy's** (1400 W. Walnut Grove Road, 209/794-2544), a coffee shop and restaurant serving straightforward American food. Walnut Grove's location is easy to spot from miles away due to the close proximity of several television towers that are about twice the height of the Eiffel Tower.

RYDE

Ryde was named by rancher Thomas H. Williams in 1893, after Williams' hometown on the Isle of Wight. The dominant feature of this small settlement is the **Ryde Hotel** (14240 Highway 160, 916/776-1318), an Art Deco structure built in 1927 during the height of Prohibition. The lower level housed a speakeasy that poured bootleg liquor, featured casino gambling and offered jazz music to customers visiting from the riverboats. A trap door in the floor (sealed in 1930) gave access to a tunnel running under the road to the edge of the river. Herbert Hoover, a teetotaler who presumably was unaware of the illicit activity on the lower floor, announced his candidacy for president here in 1928. The hotel recently underwent a significant renovation, and dining is featured on weekends.

GRAND ISLAND MANSION

Grand Island Mansion (take Highway 220 just north of the Ryde Hotel to Grand Island Road, turn left and proceed south for three miles) is the most opulent structure in the Delta. Built in 1917 for German financier Louis Meyers at a cost of $350,000, the mansion boasts 24,000 square feet and 58 rooms. There are 18 bedrooms, 11 bathrooms, a cinema, a bowling alley, a soda fountain and an observatory. The mansion is listed on the California Registry of Historic Homes and is among the largest private homes in the United States. The building is open for Sunday brunch as well as for private events (916/775-1705).

DELTA FERRIES

Many people are unaware that the California Department of Transportation (Caltrans) operates two free delta ferries that will transport you and your vehicle across delta waterways. Just north of the Ryde Hotel, take Highway 220 to Grand Island Road, turn right and go to the Howard Landing Ferry. The ferry boat, called the J-Mack, will take you

and your vehicle across Steamboat Slough to Ryer Island. The diesel-powered J-Mack pulls itself across the slough by a greased cable anchored to the banks on each side. Upon reaching Ryer Island, travel south on Ryer Island Road to the Ryer Island Ferry. The Real McCoy, a free-running, diesel powered vessel built in 1945, takes about five minutes to cross the river. Both ferries run 24-hours with a short break for lunch.

RIO VISTA

In 1857, Colonel N.H. Davis surveyed a town site on land he had purchased for just 15 cents per acre from General John Bidwell. Davis called the town Los Brazos del Rio (arms of the river) because the Sacramento River formed at the location. The name was changed to Rio Vista (river view) in 1860. The entire town was swept away by flood in 1861-2, which led to its relocation on higher ground donated by two ranchers, Joseph Bruning and T.J. McWorthy. Salmon fishing was the leading industry in Rio Vista's early years, and the town was an important shipping hub for Delta crops. Rio Vista features Victorian-era homes on Second Street ("Millionaire's Row"), located in the hills overlooking the town. The city's most unusual attraction is **Foster's Big Horn** (143 Main Street, 707/374-2511), a bar and restaurant that contains more than 300 wild game trophies. Original owner Bill Foster, who died in 1963, shot 95 percent of the animals himself, in a series of safaris that began in 1928. The collection includes a full grown elephant, the largest mammal trophy in the world, as well as a giraffe, hippopotamus, rhinoceros, lion and buffalo. Rio Vista also is known worldwide for its **Bass Derby Festival**, which attracts 50,000 visitors the second weekend in October. The **Rio Vista Museum** (16 N. Front Street, 707/374-5169), located in an old blacksmith's shop, offers visitors exhibits on Rio Vista history each weekend afternoon. **Sandy Beach County Park**, located at the southern end of the town on Beach Drive, sports a scenic location on the Sacramento River. Three miles out of town is the **Brannan Island State Recreation Area** (17645 Highway 160, 916/777-6671), which includes campsites, picnic areas, swimming and interpretive displays.

ISLETON

Isleton is the smallest incorporated area in Sacramento County, founded in 1874 by Dr. Josiah Poole. The town once featured a sizable Chinatown, which was lost to fires in 1915 and 1926. New buildings were put up with corrugated tin siding, asbestos shingles and brick, helping deter future conflagrations. Many of these buildings still stand on the north end of Isleton's historic Main Street. The town featured three large canneries by the 1920s and was known as the Asparagus Capitol of the World. Gambling, booze and prostitution formed the basis of Isleton's economy during Prohibition. The Depression marked the beginning of Isleton's decline, as riverboat traffic decreased, the canneries

foundered and railroads expanded elsewhere. **Isleton's Crawdad Festival** attracts 200,000 people each Father's Day weekend for food, music and crafts.

DIXON

Dixon's first residents and even buildings were moved from a settlement known as Silveyville, located three miles east of Dixon The town of Dixon sprang up in 1868 when Thomas Dickson donated 10 acres for a town site and train depot to the Central Pacific Railroad. Dickson made the donation with the understanding that the new town would be named after him, but the railroad misspelled the station name as "Dixon." To compound the insult, the hearing-impaired Dickson was walking near the tracks one day and was nearly killed by one of the trains he helped bring to the town. Dixon long has had an agricultural economy, with sheep one of the principle commodities. The two major community celebrations include the **May Fair**, California's oldest state-affiliated fair, and the August **Lambtown USA Festival**.

ELK GROVE

A businessman opened a hotel called the Elk Grove in 1850, taking the name from his hometown in Missouri. The Central Pacific Railroad later adopted the name for its station nearby. Elk Grove was a quiet small town for generations, even with some residential development in the 1960s and 1970s. Growth really kicked in with the 1980s and 1990s. Local unhappiness with county planning decisions spurred several citizen attempts at incorporation, which ultimately succeeded in March 2000. Elk Grove features a tiny old town and a large regional park, **Elk Grove County Park**, at Elk Grove-Florin Road, east of Highway 99. Elk Grove's city limits also include the growing Laguna area. Laguna gets its name from Laguna Creek, which meanders through this area between Interstate 5 and Highway 99. Laguna received national attention in the late 1980s when local developer and later California State Treasurer Phil Angelides opened up an ambitious residential area (Laguna West) that incorporated details similar in some respects to

those of Sacramento's Land Park neighborhood, where Angelides grew up: traditional architecture, ample landscaping, front porches, garages placed at the rear of the lot and no cul-de-sacs. Residents say that the neighborhood is more sociable than the typical suburban neighborhood. The area also has landed major electronics firms, Apple Computer and JVC, and enjoys the accouterments of a robust suburb: cinema multiplexes, big box retailers and chain restaurants. The nearby **Stone Lakes National Wildlife Refuge** offers the opportunity to view wildlife in a natural habitat.

FAIR OAKS

The Howard and Wilson Publishing Company of Chicago purchased 6,000 acres of the old Rancho San Juan land grant in 1895. The company immediately subdivided the land and advertised the property to prospective Eastern buyers. Landowner E.H. Howard called the area Fairoaks, named after a Virginia settlement where Howard had been wounded during the Civil War. Buyers were lured with the promise that Fairoaks (the name was changed to two words in 1931) had water rights, fine weather, excellent fruit-growing acreage and an anti-saloon clause. The first 150 prospective buyers arrived in November 1895, and many stayed to plant orchards of orange, olive and almond trees. By 1901 there were 1200 acres of orchards and the growers established a fruit cooperative, packing house and olive mill. During the Great Depression, when many growers were barely able to survive the hard economic times, severe freezes killed off almost all the fruit trees. These days, Fair Oaks is among the most desirable Sacramento suburbs, with large lots, plenty of shade trees and easy access to the American River Parkway. In the middle of the now-sprawling area is **Fair Oaks Village** (Fair Oaks Boulevard at California Avenue), the early center of the community. The village includes several older commercial buildings containing shops, restaurants and offices. The village Plaza Park is the site of many community festivals such as the **Fair Oaks Fiesta** in May. The nearby **Fair Oaks Cemetery** (7780 Olive Drive), established 1903, is the final resting place for many of the community's pioneers.

FOLSOM

Folsom is on the site is a former Mexican land grant, adjacent to the property Mexico had deeded to Sacramento founder John Sutter. Joseph L. Folsom purchased most of the land grant in 1855. Theodore Judah selected the town as the eastern terminus of California's first railroad, connecting Folsom to Sacramento. This route, known as the Sacramento Valley Railroad, eventually became the first segment of the Central Pacific Railroad. **Folsom State Prison** (Prison Road off Natoma Street) was established in 1880 to relieve overcrowding at San Quentin. Constructed of blue granite quarried on the site, the prison's turreted guard tower, arched entries and prison buildings are one of California's most massive examples of the Richardsonian Romanesque style. Inmates referred to the prison as "the end of the world." **Folsom Prison Museum** (916/985-2561, ext. 4589) is open daily and contains a number of exhibits about life in the prison's earlier years. **Folsom Dam** (Dam Road off of Folsom-Auburn Road, tours Tuesday-Saturday, 10 a.m. and 1 p.m., 916/989-7275) was constructed in 1955. The dam is a critical component of the Sacramento area's flood control system and the resulting **Folsom Lake State Recreational Area** (see listing under Parks in Activities chapter) is one of the most popular recreation areas in the state. **Sutter Street** is the heart of Folsom's historic district, with plenty of restored 19th-Century buildings housing shops, museums, restaurants and nightclubs. Look for the **Folsom Children's Museum** (912 Sutter Street, 916/353-0961), with interactive displays and exhibits, and the **Folsom History Museum** (823 Sutter Street, 916/985-2707), with exhibits on Folsom's history spanning the Maidu Indian era, the first explorers, Gold Rush, Central Pacific Railroad and more. Folsom's population soared by 65 percent between 1990 and 2000, driven by expansion of Folsom Prison and the recruitment of major high tech firms such as Intel and Hewlett-Packard. The growth has occurred in sprawling, generally upscale subdivisions over the rolling hills surrounding the historic central district.

TOUR 22 – HISTORIC FOLSOM

1 Wells Fargo Assay Office
823 Sutter Street *1860*

Now the home of the Folsom History Museum, this assay office building was demolished in 1959 to make way for a service station. Concerned citizens saved the granite block facade and steel shutters. The building also served as the western terminus of the Pony Express from 1860-61.

2 Southern Pacific Railroad Depot
200 Wool Street *1906*

Now the location of the Folsom Chamber of Commerce, the depot is located on the site of the terminus of the Sacramento Valley Railroad that was completed by Theodore Judah in 1856.

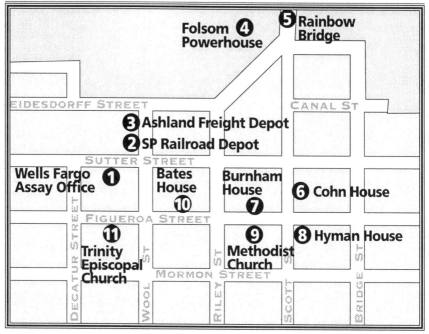

Folsom ④ Powerhouse

⑤ Rainbow Bridge

EIDESDORFF STREET

CANAL ST

❸ Ashland Freight Depot

❷ SP Railroad Depot

SUTTER STREET

Wells Fargo Assay Office ❶

Bates House ⑩

Burnham House ❼

❻ Cohn House

FIGUEROA STREET

⑪ Trinity Episcopal Church

⑨ Methodist Church

❽ Hyman House

MORMON STREET

DECATUR STREET · WOOL ST · RILEY ST · SCOTT ST · BRIDGE ST

3 Ashland Freight Depot
200 Wool Street *1858*

Next to the SPRR depot is the oldest standing train station west of the Mississippi. The Ashland Freight Depot was moved to the present location from Greenback Lane and Auburn-Folsom Road. Displayed inside the unpainted wooden station are antique buggies, a railroad freight cart, tools and a 1920 fire engine. Surrounding the depot are farming and mining equipment, a replica of a blacksmith's shop, SP rolling stock and a miner's cabin.

4 Folsom Powerhouse
Scott and Leidesdorff Streets *1895*

This National Historic Landmark ushered in the age of large electrical transmissions in North America. On July 13, 1895, the powerhouse sent electrical power 22 miles away to light up the City of Sacramento and provide power to that city's street cars. The Pacific Gas and Electric Company closed the plant in 1952 when construction commenced on Folsom Dam. The utility donated the powerhouse to the state in 1958, and today the powerhouse is the only such 19th-century facility in the nation that is open to the public. Visitors can observe the intact forebays, canal system and transformers, operated and maintained with the assistance of volunteers (916/989-3924 for group tours).

5 Rainbow Bridge
1918

The first bridge was built here in 1861. The picturesque, arched concrete structure crossing Lake Natoma is the fourth bridge at this site. The bridge replaced the nearby steel truss bridge that now carries pedestrians and bicyclists. That bridge, built in 1893, was moved to the Klamath River in Siskiyou County from 1930 until the 1990s. Folsom brought the bridge back and restored it in 2000.

6 Cohn House
307 Scott Street *1865*

Built for Simon Cohn, an early Folsom merchant, this impressive Queen Anne home remained in the Cohn family for more than 100 years.

7 Burnham House
602 Figueroa Street *c. 1890*

James Burnham was a Wells, Fargo and Co. employee in the 1870s who later became an insurance agent. A fire in 1974 destroyed the round turret and the rest of the second level of this Queen Anne home.

8 Hyman House
603 Figueroa Street *1881*

The Jacob Hyman family lived in this Italianate home until the 1940s. The house features large bay windows and Corinthian columns.

9 Methodist Church
609 Figueroa Street *1860*

This Gothic Revival church has served Methodist, Presbyterian and Baptist congregations. The building also provided space for Folsom High School and other area schools from 1922 to the mid-1930s.

10 Bates House
714 Figueroa Street *c. 1858*

This house is the oldest private dwelling in Folsom. Dr. Leman Bates, a dentist, came to Folsom when the town was established in 1855.

11 Trinity Episcopal Church

803 Figueroa Street *1858*

The wooden Trinity Episcopal Church is Folsom's oldest church building that has been in continuous use. The oldest church that has not been in continuous use is the 1857 St. John the Baptist Catholic Church, located a few blocks away at the corner of Sibley and Natoma Streets. St. John's also includes a pioneer cemetery with headstones of pioneer Irish immigrants.

GALT

Galt's founder was Dr. Obed Harvey, a dapper landowner who in 1869 convinced the Central Pacific Railroad to run track by his property in Southern Sacramento County. The railroad soon laid out a town along the right-of-way and Harvey asked his farmer friend, John MacFarland, to come up with a name for the new town. MacFarland chose Galt, after a Canadian town that he had lived in for a short period. Many of Galt's first buildings were moved from the defunct town of Liberty, which was located one mile south. The dominant employers in Galt's early years were agriculture and the railroad. In the early 20th Century the coast-to-coast Lincoln Highway ran through the town, shifting Galt's commercial center away from the railroad depot that once stood along the tracks. The Sacramento County Fair was held in Galt from 1932 to 1959, and local farmers and miscellaneous vendors still sell produce and other goods at the **Galt Market** on the old fairgrounds site (890 Caroline Avenue, 209/745-2537; Tuesday and Wednesday beginning at 6 a.m.). After years of dissatisfaction with county governance, Galt incorporated in 1946. Some of Galt's early structures still exist, including **Dr. Harvey's Guest House/Office** (2nd and C Streets, c. 1870); the first post office building, later the **I.O.O.F. Hall** (4th and C Streets, 1869); **St. Luke's Episcopal Church** (3rd and B Streets, 1884); **St. Christopher's Catholic Church** (3rd and F Streets, 1885); and the **Galt Christian Church**, which had been moved from the town of Liberty (7th and B Streets, 1857). The old water tower at 6th and D Streets is a beloved town landmark. Galt attractions include the nearby **Cosumnes River Preserve** (13501 Franklin Boulevard, 916/684-2816), which includes a three-mile nature trail open during daylight hours; **Galt Historical Museum** (204 Oak Avenue, 209/745-0951), open two Saturday afternoons per month in the historic Rae House; and **Liberty Cemetery** (U.S. Highway 99 at Liberty Road, south of Galt), the only remnant of the pioneer town of Liberty.

LODI

Lodi is yet another town that sprang up in the wake of the Central Pacific Railroad in the late 1860s. The town was first known as Mokelumne Station, but confusion with the spelling and delivery of mail (two nearby communities were Mokelumne City and Mokelumne Hill) led to residents to change the name to Lodi after just a few years. Why Lodi was selected has been the subject of speculation every since. The most colorful account is that Lodi was the name of a champion racehorse much admired in this town known for its fondness

for gambling. Others say that some of the town's early families named it after their hometown of Lodi, Illinois. Still others say that the name derives from the Bridge of Lodi in Italy where Napoleon claimed his first military victory. Regardless of the origins, the name change was approved by the Legislature in 1874. Lodi was known as a prolific watermelon producer from the 1880s to 1900, until the market became saturated and prices dropped. Fortunately Lodi's sandy loam and hot summers were ideally suited to the tokay grape, which had high demand as a table grape and for producing inexpensive wine and brandy. The local wine industry accounted for 25 percent of California's wine production by 1900 and became the foundation for Lodi's economy. The town established a three-day Tokay Carnival in 1907, building a beautiful Mission style **Gateway Arch** (Pine Street east of Sacramento Street, E.B. Brown, 1907) that remains a community symbol. Lodi since has moved beyond tokay to become California's top producer of the five most popular varietals (see Wine Country Touring in Activities). Trivia buffs will note that A&W root beer was invented here in 1919 by drugstore owner Roy Allen, who gave away the concoction to celebrants at a World War I victory parade through the city. Lodi features a large population of German ancestry, the legacy from a wave of immigration from South Dakota in the 1890s. The town's charming attributes belie the "Nowheresville" reputation it obtained when John Fogerty sang, "Oh Lord, I'm stuck in Lodi again," a 1969 B-side hit for Creedence Clearwater Revival. The city features the 101-acre **Lodi Lake Park and Nature Area**, a gorgeous regional park that includes trails along the Mokelumne River; **Micke Grove Park**, a 65-acre park that includes a zoo, rose garden, amusement park and the San Joaquin Historical Society and Museum (11793 North Micke Grove Road); a delightful **historic downtown district**, offering shops, bakeries and restaurants; the **Lodi Street Faire** the first Sunday in May and October; the **Lodi Grape Festival** and the **Harvest Fair** in September.

LOOMIS

This small Placer County town was named after Jim Loomis, a pioneer saloon keeper who also served as postmaster, railroad agent and express agent. Town lots were established in 1885, with fruit sheds and stone quarries the principle early industries. Current Loomis residents highly prize the town's spacious lots, rural character and community spirit.

ORANGEVALE

Orangevale has a citrus-based agricultural heritage that dates to 1888. Prominent Sacramento business leaders such as Val McClatchy of the famous newspaper family and Harris Weinstock of the venerable department store were among the directors trying to sell 10-acre tracts in the area through the Orange Vale Colonization Company. One of the few survivors from this era is **The Villa** (9281 Oak Avenue), an 1889 guest house for prospective buyers. The recently renovated Eastlake structure, with its prominent eaves and large porch, provided welcome shade and hospitality to those considering investing in the new area. The Villa originally was perched on a bluff overlooking the American River, but has been moved twice and is now the home of Serve Our Seniors, Inc. The citrus industry became a victim of a severe freeze during the Depression. Today Orangevale offers a mix of neighborhoods dating from the 1950s forward.

ROCKLIN

Rocklin, as the name implies, began as a quarry town. The State Capitol Building features walls partially constructed from Rocklin granite (the lighter blocks are from Rocklin, the darker blocks are from Folsom). The town was established in 1866 when the railroad located a roundhouse and shops there. The Southern Pacific began expanding the railyards in 1905-06, but then abruptly decided to move the whole operation to Roseville. Rocklin also came in second place when the State of California decided in 1868 that Folsom was a preferable site for a new state prison. Today the quarries are still around, but Rocklin has evolved into a sprawling city. One notable feature at the entrance to Rocklin from Interstate 80 is the **Finnish Temperance Hall**, an early frame structure located on Rocklin Road.

ROSEVILLE

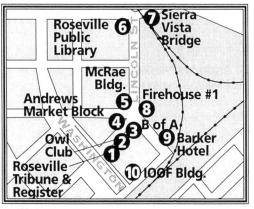

Roseville was known beginning in 1864 as Junction, because it was the site where the Central Pacific Railroad crossed over a small rail line linking the towns of Folsom and Lincoln. When the Southern Pacific (the C.P.'s successor) relocated its roundhouse and shops from Rocklin, Junction became incorporated as Roseville. Railroading still is a prominent component of Roseville's identity, with the railyard now the western headquarters of the Union Pacific Railroad (the S.P.'s successor). On its 100th anniversary in 1964, Roseville's small town charms earned the honor of "All American City" by the editors of Look Magazine. Although struggling to revitalize, downtown Roseville offers plenty of antique shops and interesting structures. The city center has shifted in recent years to the east side of Interstate 80, in the vicinity of Douglas Boulevard. The new community gathering spots include the postmodern **Rocky Ridge Town Center** (Douglas Boulevard at Rocky Ridge Drive), which features Borders Books and Music and the popular Macaroni Grill, and the **Century Theatre complex** (Eureka Road at Lead Hill Boulevard), a magnet that attracted prominent eateries such as Cafe Bernardo, River Rock Cafe and Mikuni. One of

Roseville's most enduring institutions is **Denio's Roseville Farmers Market** (1551 Vineyard Road, 916/782-2704), a massive swap meet that has operated since 1947.

TOUR 23 – HISTORIC ROSEVILLE NORTH

1 Roseville Tribune and Register
117 Church Street *1915*

A typical commercial building from the early 20th Century, this rusticated-block structure housed the predecessor to the current daily newspaper, the *Roseville Press Tribune*.

2 The Owl Club
109 Church Street *1921*

The Owl Club began pouring drinks right after Prohibition ended in 1934. Prior to that period this building housed a grocery on the ground floor and a Chinese restaurant on the second floor.

3 Bank of America Building
341 Lincoln Street *1927*

The Bank of America Building occupies the site of Roseville's first formal bank, which was built in 1907. B of A built this Neo-Classical structure in 1927 and remained in the building until 1966. Thereafter the building has been the home of the *Roseville Press Tribune* and a variety of other businesses.

4 Andrews Market Block
101 Main Street *1916-1924*

Fred Miller ran the Andrews Market in this building from 1926 to 1978. A sports bar now occupies the ground floor.

5 McRae Building
108 Main Street *1908*

The upper floor of this building offered the McRae Opera House, which was an important community gathering spot for meetings, dances and plays. A series of town meetings in the building led to the decision to incorporate Roseville as a city. The post office occupied the ground floor from 1919 to 1924.

6 Roseville Public Library
557 Lincoln Street *1912*

A.B. McRae donated the land for Roseville's first public library, which was funded in part by Andrew Carnegie. The Neo-Classical building features granite from Rocklin and brick and terra cotta from Gladding, McBean. The library moved out of the building in 1979, and today the building houses the **Roseville Historical Museum**, where you can learn all about the city's past (916/773-3003).

7 Sierra Vista Bridge
1929

The Sierra Vista Bridge, a crooked structure that links historic Roseville with the Sierra Vista Park subdivision, is also known as Rainbow Bridge for its arched concrete supports.

8 Fire House No. 1
400 Lincoln Street *1926*

Fire House No. 1 replaced a hose cart house that was located at this site. The tiny building now is occupied by a cable access television studio.

9 Barker Hotel
302 Lincoln Street *1911*

The original Roseville Hotel first located at this site in 1869. This building was later replaced by other hotels (the Western, the Ross House), until C. Henry Barker erected the current structure. The Barker Hotel once was one of Roseville's finest places to lodge.

10 I.O.O.F. Building
100 block of Pacific Street *1878*

This lodge for the Independent Order of Odd Fellows is Roseville's oldest building. The now-empty I.O.O.F. Building is typical of early Western architecture, with 18-inch thick walls, steel shutters and a shed roof.

TOUR 24 – HISTORIC ROSEVILLE SOUTH

1 Seawell Underpass
Washington Boulevard between Pacific and Vernon Streets *1950*

A segment of the old Southern Pacific Railroad separates historic Roseville's north and south sides, which created a significant traffic bottleneck at the Lincoln Street railroad crossing prior to 1950. State Senator Jerry Seawell secured state funding to allow Washington Boulevard to dip below the tracks, allowing vehicles and pedestrians to travel between the two downtown sections unimpeded by the railroad traffic.

2 Mural
Washington Boulevard between Vernon and Atlantic Streets, Juanishi Orozsco and Juan Cervantes *1992*

The mural blends views of Roseville's past and present, using sly humor and bold color.

3 Masonic Temple/Roseville Theatre Building
241 Vernon Street *1925*

The upper level of this building, occupied by the local Masonic order, features a row of large arched windows. The theatre on the ground level has a colorful tile entry and a tile fountain in the lobby. These days live music and plays are performed on the theatre stage.

4 Royer Park
Bounded by Judah, Oak, Royer and Lincoln Streets; Douglas Boulevard and Park Drive *1917*

Royer Park was Roseville's first major park, located on land sold to the city by the Royer family. Mature trees and gentle Dry Creek beautify this traditional city park. Entering the park from Washington Boulevard one encounters a steel-framed footbridge crossing over Dry Creek. The 1925 **P.F.E. Footbridge** once was located on lower Vernon Street and was used by employees of the Pacific Fruit Express Ice Plant to cross over the Southern Pacific Tracks. Next to the bridge is the **Veterans' Memorial Building**, a Mediterranean structure built in 1930. Quaint Period Revival houses, mainly built in the 1920s, face the park on the east side of Park Drive.

5 Haman House
424 Oak Street *1909*
Renovated, *1992*

The Roseville Arts Center has been the occupant of this Victorian home since 1976. Original owner William Haman was the manager of the Placer County Winery, a member of the first Roseville City Council and a member of the Placer County Board of Supervisors. A private zoo once occupied a portion of the grounds.

6 Tower Theatre
415 Vernon Street *1940*

Painted in luminous shades of aqua and with a large neon sign, the art deco Tower Theatre was the dominant Roseville entertainment venue for a couple of decades after its opening. Movies ended in the late 1970s and the building now houses the Roseville Arts Center.

7 Roseville Post Office

330 Vernon Street *1935*
Remodeled, *1970s*

The post office received an unfortunate 1970s remodel that stuck gaudy blue awnings over the arched windows and entry, with an ungainly ramp along the front of the building.

8 Roseville City Hall

316 Vernon Street, Charles F. Dean *1935*

Roseville's City Council held meetings in this building for more than five decades, after which overcrowding forced elected officials across the street to a former Bank of America building.

WEST SACRAMENTO

West Sacramento, which sits across the Sacramento River from the capital, is an outgrowth of the pioneer town of Washington. Margaret McDowell, a widower whose husband was murdered in a Sacramento saloon, laid out the town in 1850 on George Washington's birthday. Mrs. McDowell hoped that the town would one day rival the prominence of Sacramento. Washington later was named Broderick, after David Broderick, a former U.S. Senator and ardent abolitionist who was killed in a Sacramento duel in 1859. Broderick's early population was composed of rivermen and gamblers, according to a 1940 history of Yolo County; and the town never did reach the stature envisioned by its founder. In the late 1940s the town became the beneficiary of a deep water shipping channel, an engineering feat that allowed huge ships to dock 85 miles from the sea. Broderick was folded into West Sacramento when that city incorporated in 1987. West Sacramento has since worked to recruit businesses, build luxury housing, provide new infrastructure and redevelop blighted West Capitol Boulevard. The city's most prominent building is the ziggurat-shaped former **Money Store Headquarters** (Ed Kado, 1997), located on the Sacramento River across from Old Sacramento. Some have criticized the massive building for being insensitive to the quaint 1850s architecture of Old Sacramento. Others like the building's audacity, particularly how it transforms into an apparently translucent landmark at night. A well-appointed riverwalk was constructed on the east side of the building in 1999, providing a connection between West Sacramento and Old Sacramento via the Tower Bridge and I Street Bridge. West Sacramento also is the home of the new **Raley Field** (just across the Tower Bridge from Old Sacramento), where the Pacific Coast League's River Cats have brought Triple A professional baseball to the Sacramento area for the first time since the 1970s.

WINTERS

Winters is named after Theodore Winters, a stockman and racehorse breeder. The town started out in 1875 as an agricultural village, its leading business people lured from Eastern states by the promise of gold. The flat terrain pushes up against rolling hills on the west and the emerald Putah Creek on the south. Creedence Clearwater Revival's 1970 song "Green River" was inspired by John Fogerty's boyhood memories of summer vacations along Winters' Putah Creek. Although the town has grown considerably in recent years, the description of Winters in the 1940 History of Yolo County still could apply today: "the situation, climate, environment, soil, easy access to larger places and natural resources, in combination with a warm-hearted, friendly citizenry, render the community an attractive home town." Winters possesses a small central business district, with several quaint commercial buildings from the late 19th and early 20th centuries.

WOODLAND

Woodland derives its name from the vast oak forest that originally covered the area. The name was coined by the spouse of city founder Frank Freeman. Freeman purchased an agricultural supply store and 160 acres in 1857, and dreamt of transforming his property into the trading center of Yolo County. He established a post office in 1861, lured businessmen by building shops and offered free lots to those wishing to build homes. Freeman's promotional efforts were aided by the great floods of 1862, which forced the Yolo County seat from the town of Washington (now West Sacramento) to the higher ground of Woodland. Freeman filed a town plat in 1863 and donated a city block for the county courthouse. Woodland emerged as Yolo County's most important commercial center by the mid-1860s, fueled by the prosperity of local farmers and business people. The arrival of the railroad in 1869 led to further economic growth, and Woodland formally was incorporated as a city in 1871. By 1888 Woodland had the highest per capita wealth in the nation, which is reflected in the number of fine Victorian homes still gracing the city's older neighborhoods.

An 1892 fire in Woodland's Chinese section of Dead Cat Alley destroyed many of Main Street's commercial buildings, but the town quickly rebuilt. Woodland's Main Street has suffered from competition with discount retailers on the outskirts of town, but the city has taken some steps to improve the old commercial district. Among Woodland's attractions are the **Hays' Antique Truck Museum** (1962

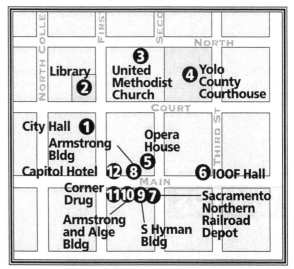

Hays Lane, 530/666-1044), which possesses the largest collection of antique trucks in the country, and the **Yolo County Historical Museum** (512 Gibson Road, 530/666-1045), housed in a Greek Revival mansion that, although remodeled on numerous occasions, dates to 1849. Some of the most interesting neighborhoods are located within the area bounded by Lincoln Avenue, Bartlett Avenue, College Street and Second Street.

TOUR 25 – MAIN STREET AND CIVIC CENTER

1 City Hall

300 First Street, Harry J. Devine, Sr. *1936*
Firehouse and Jail,
Charles Dean *1932*
Police Station *1961*
Addition and Remodel, Schaefer and Wirth *1976*

The city hall complex sits on the site of Woodland's first city hall, built in 1892. Despite its development over a 45-year period with five different architects, the complex represents a coherent example of the Spanish Colonial Revival style.

2 Woodland Public Library

250 First Street, George Dodge and John Dolliver *1905*
West Wing *1915*
North Wing *1929*
Expansion and Restoration *1985*

Established with the financial support of Andrew Carnegie, the Woodland Public Library has been an important civic asset for nearly a century. The building enjoys a park-like setting, with a forest of thick palms planted on the entrance side of the building. Voters approved $2.5 million to pay for various improvements to the library in 1985, which include a restored fireplace in the main reading room.

3 United Methodist Church

212 Second Street, Ronald S. Tuttle *1925*

The United Methodist Church has been located at this site since 1883, although the church's beginnings in Woodland date back to 1852. The Spanish Colonial Revival building features a handsome bell tower.

4 Yolo County Courthouse

725 Court Street, William H. Weeks *1917*

The Yolo County Courthouse is the most majestic public building in the county. The Renaissance Revival building reflects the City Beautiful period of municipal design, when public buildings reflected the high ideals of progressive reformers. Terra cotta embellishments, which include Roman soldiers and female figures above the entrance, Corinthian pilasters and columns and a granite-like finish, are the work of Gladding, McBean & Co. The building is listed on the National Register of Historic Places.

5 Woodland Opera House
340 Second Street *1895*
Restored, *1981-89*

The Woodland Opera House is one of only two opera houses from the late 19th Century that survive in California (the other is in Napa). The building replaced an 1885 opera house that was almost completely destroyed by fire. David Hershey rebuilt the structure in 1895, providing the largest stage north of San Francisco. The building hosted plays, vaudeville and silent movies until 1913, when a woman fell from the entrance, breaking her leg. The Hershey family closed the building rather than pay a $2,000 judgment to the injured woman. The deteriorating building was saved from demolition in 1971, and, after a nine-year restoration effort, re-opened as a 500-seat venue for the performing arts.

6 I.O.O.F. Hall
723 Main Street *1905*

The International Order of Odd Fellows Hall is built in a modified Mission style, with three towers rising from the south and east sides.

7 Sacramento Northern Railroad Depot
626 Main Street *c. 1912*

Electric interurban trains provided convenient service between Sacramento and Woodland beginning in 1912. The trains would enter this Mission Revival building through the corner arch, which since has been enclosed.

8 Armstrong Building
617 Main Street *1893*

Nearly identical to the buildings to the west, this commercial/office structure features an historic advertisement on the east side for Levi Strauss overalls.

9 S. Hyman Building
608 Main Street *1890*

This Italianate commercial building reportedly was first used as a drug store.

10 Armstrong and Alge Building
604-606 Main Street *1890*

This Italianate building is nearly identical to the S. Hyman building next door, although twice as wide. The ground floor originally was used for a butcher shop and delicatessen, while the owner's family and a rental occupied the second floor.

11 Corner Drug-Physician's Building
602 Main Street *1889*

This building has housed Corner Drug continuously for more than a century. The front of the building boasts a quartrefoil decoration typical of the Mission style. Neon signage dates from 1948.

12 Capitol Hotel
601 Main Street, Michael O'Connell *1868*

Once an important hotel in Woodland, this Renaissance Revival structure later served as a rooming house.

TOUR 26 – FIRST STREET

1 Mulcahay's Frozen Food Lockers
443 First Street *1935*

This sleek Streamline Moderne commercial building features a banded oval tower.

2 Thomas House
515 First Street, John Hudson Thomas *1920*

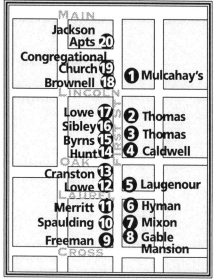

This unusual Dutch Colonial residence was designed by famed Berkeley architect John Hudson Thomas. Thomas, along with Bernard Maybeck, Julia Morgan and other East Bay innovators, was a leader of the architectural style known as First Bay Tradition. The style combined features of California Craftsman, Prairie School, Early American and English Renaissance styles. The house was built for Charles Thomas (no relation to the architect), a prominent businessman who

built many of the city's early commercial structures. Main features of the house include the gambrel roof, shuttered windows and central brick chimney. An 1861 ice house attached to the main house and a carriage house located at 520 Second Street are remnants of Charles Thomas' Victorian mansion that previously occupied the site.

3 Thomas House
525 First Street *c. 1882*

Prior to moving to the lot to the north, Charles Thomas lived in this comparatively modest Italianate home. The entrance features ornate Corinthian columns.

4 Caldwell House

547 First Street *1882*

Samuel Caldwell and his wife purchased the property for this home from
Charles Thomas in 1881. The Caldwells built this Italianate home the following
year, then sold the home two years later to Thomas and Elizabeth Muegge. The
Muegges went to the expense of converting the original squared portico into a
rounded portico, but retained the cast iron Corinthian capitals.

5 Laugenour House

627 First Street *1874*

This Cottage Victorian was built for John and Emma Langenour. Mr. Langenour
was a partner of Charles Thomas in a successful grain warehouse. Mrs.
Langenour was prominent in her own right as a leader in the Women's Christian
Temperance Union and the Women's Suffrage Movement.

6 Hyman House

639 First Street *1909*

This late Queen Anne residence was built for William and Gertrude Hyman.
William Hyman was the principal of Woodland High School from 1909 to 1928.

7 Mixon House

645 First Street *1906*

William Mixon was publisher and editor of *The Mail of Woodland*, a morning
newspaper, and served on the Woodland Board of Trustees. He lived in this
Colonial Revival structure until 1929.

8 Gable Mansion

659 First Street *1885*

This glorious Italianate and Stick style mansion is the most prominent home in

Central Woodland. Set
on an oversized lot, the
house features ornate
bracketed cornices, plen-
tiful balconies and an
expansive porch. This
State Historical
Landmark was built for
Amos and Harvey Gable,
two brothers who
amassed substantial farm
acreage in the Woodland
area. "Mother's Day"
founder Harriet Lee once
rented an apartment on
the second floor for
many years. The home
remained in the Gable family until 1973, when it was sold to Robert McWhirk
and restored.

9 Freeman House
666 First Street *1873*

City Founder Frank Freeman is believed to have had this Victorian cottage constructed as a rental property. The magnolia tree was planted more than 100 years ago by Margaret Day Stephens, the daughter-in-law of Bank of Woodland President Lawrence Stephens.

10 Spaulding House
638 First Street *c.1893*

This Queen Anne Eclectic house features rounded archways on the expansive front porch, a pyramidal porch roof and a central open balcony. The structure was restored after being damaged in a 1981 fire. It was built by T.S. Spaulding, a grocery store owner.

11 Merritt House
632 First Street *1886*

A.J. Steiner, a store owner, personally inspected each piece of hardware and lumber that went into the construction of this Eastlake residence. George Merritt, president of the Bank of Yolo, lived in it from 1897-1921.

12 Lowe House
618 First Street, Meyer and O'Brien *1905*

This Georgian style house was built for Mr. and Mrs. Thomas R. Lowe. Lowe, in partnership with his brother William, was a successful farmer. The brothers were the sons of Edmund Lowe, the director of the Bank of Yolo in the late 19th Century.

13 Cranston House
610 First Street *1906*

This Queen Anne Eclectic structure exhibits a number of interesting features, including the sunburst pattern on the porch gable, delicate scrollwork on the upper floor gables and a polygonal central turret. The dwelling was built for Reuben B. Cranston, who chose not to include fireplaces because he considered them old fashioned. Cranston established a hardware store in downtown Woodland in 1898 that is still in business at 618 Main Street.

14 Hunt House
546 First Street *1875*

This Italianate house originally was owned by William G. Hunt, a Missourian who came to Placerville in 1849. Hunt was the president of the Yolo County Winery, a major Bank of Woodland shareholder and a member of the City Board of Trustees.

15 Byrns House
536 First Street *1870*
Remodeled *1912*

The dwelling originally was a Victorian, built for John Byrns, a farmer, rancher and livery operator. Asa Morris remodeled the building in the Mission Revival style popular in the early 20th Century. Morris was a dairyman who owned a cow that produced a world's record 28,066 pounds of milk in one year.

16 Sibley House
526 First Street *c.1870*

James Sibley, a landowner, built this simplified Italianate house with a bay window, second-floor balcony and bracketed cornice.

17 Lowe House
458 First Street *1890*

This beautiful Queen Anne/Shingle style house was built for Edmund R. Lowe, who was the director of the Bank of Yolo. It is in outstanding condition and is distinguished by a bell-shaped turret.

18 Brownell House
516 First Street *c.1868*

This structure was moved from its original site at First and Lincoln Streets in 1902. The Italianate design features a bracketed and boxed cornice and a balcony over the porch. William Brownell operated a mercantile business in Knight's Landing before joining with John Languenour to run a profitable grain business.

19 Woodland Congregational Church
450 First Street *1874*

This Gothic Revival church was built under the direction of William H. Winne, a contractor and builder who had fought for the Union during the Civil War. The interior was remodeled in 1974. Now owned by the First Church of Christ, Scientist, the building still has its original pews and other furniture.

20 Jackson Apartments
426 First Street *1891*

This unusual Victorian apartment building has a bullet-shaped corner tower and a veranda encircling the second story. The building houses one of Woodland's best restaurants, Morrison's Upstairs, as well as the fine First Street Deli.

BED AND BREAKFAST INNS

Amber House Amber House is actually three houses, all located on a peaceful Midtown street. Each of the homes features a theme (music, art or poetry), with each distinctive room named for a famous figure. Innkeepers Mike Richardson and Jane Ramey have outfitted every room with private marble-tiled Jacuzzi, cable TV, VCR and modem-ready telephones. Amber House will lend you a bicycle (even a tandem for you romantics) and the gourmet breakfast can be served in your room at a time of your choice. *1315 22nd Street, Sacramento; 916/444-8085 and 800/755-6526; www.amberhouse.com*

Davis Bed and Breakfast Inn This cheerful, 1919 Craftsman bungalow was built from a kit from Sears, Roebuck and Co. for a former UC Davis professor. Although located right across the street from the university grounds, the inn is on a relatively quiet street. Watch the bicycling citizens of Davis from the comfy front porch or from one of the upstairs rooms with a balcony. The Davis Bed and Breakfast Inn features nine rooms, all with private bath, telephone and TV. The country-style breakfast is served in the dining room. *422 A Street, Davis; 800/211-4455; www.davisbedandbreakfast.com*

Hartley House This 1906 Colonial Revival home in Boulevard Park was origi-nally owned by the great-grandfather of the innkeeper, Randy Hartley. Randy is a delightful person who has striven to offer top-of-the-line European hotel ambiance. The home features lovely gardens, inlaid hardwood floors and original brass light fixtures (converted from gas). Each of the five rooms includes a TV, VCR, speakerphones and modem-ready phone jacks. Hartley House offers breakfast cooked-to-order, and the inn also features a full dinner menu. *700 22nd Street, Sacramento; 916/447-7829 and 800/831-5806; www.hartleyhouse.com*

On The Bluffs B&Bs often are located in older homes in central urban areas. On The Bluffs breaks the mold — it is a B&B located in a contemporary subur-ban area right on the American River. There are three rooms to choose from, and the inn offers a special rate if two of the rooms are rented together as a suite. The inn features great river views from the common areas, several decks and the River View room. On The Bluffs also has a pool and Jacuzzi, and the inn will loan you a bike to get out onto the bikepath along the American River Parkway. *9735 Mira Del Rio Drive, Sacramento, 866/807-9104 or 916/363-9933; www.onthebluffs.com*

Savoyard This 1925 Italian Renaissance home is located across the street from the McKinley Park rose garden in the East Sacramento neighborhood. Two of the rooms look out onto the rose garden from the front of the house, and the other two other rooms look out onto the backyard's private garden. Savoyard is filled with evidence that innkeepers Bruce and Pat Ansell are longtime world travelers. Pat painted the European-style ceiling frescos. The rooms are richly furnished in antiques and offer TV, private bath and telephone. Breakfast is served in the dining room. *3322 H Street, Sacramento; 916/442-6709 and 800/772-8692; www.savoyard.com*

HOTELS

Delta King Sacramento's only floating hotel, the Delta King is a 1926 riverboat that once transported passengers between Sacramento and San Francisco. Now permanently docked in Old Sacramento, the ship received a thorough restoration in 1984. The 43 staterooms (double the size of the original cabins) are furnished in nautical mahogany and rattan, and feature a view of the river or Old Sacramento. The rooms also offer private bath with clawfoot tubs and antique sinks. Big shots and honeymooners may want to consider reserving the Captain's Quarters, a spacious upper-deck room in the former wheelhouse. The boat's river location brings welcome summer-evening breezes and the occasional horn from the Tower and I Street Bridges. *1000 Front Street, Sacramento; 916/444-KING; www.deltaking.com*

Hyatt Regency at Capitol Park The Hyatt is across the street from the State Capitol and next to the Convention Center. Many of the 500 rooms have nice views of the Capitol Dome, Capitol Park or downtown. The rooms include all the amenities one would expect from a full-service hotel, even televised legislative hearings. The lobby is appointed with decorative iron railings commissioned from a local artist. The Hyatt offers two restaurants (including the well-regarded Dawson's American Bistro and Martini Bar), a nightclub, a lobby lounge, a large swimming pool, airport transportation and expansive banquet/conference facilities. *1209 L Street, Sacramento; 916/443-1234 and 800/233-1234; www.sacramento.hyatt.com*

Lake Natoma Inn The Lake Natoma Inn is located near Folsom's old town. The deluxe Lakeside Suites offer a view of Lake Natoma, a wood-burning fireplace, a Jacuzzi and separate living room and bedroom area. The less-expensive rooms are smaller and offer a view either of historic Folsom or the wooded area surrounding the lake. The hotel features a lakeside restaurant, swimming pool and whirlpool spa, sauna rooms, a nine-hole putting green, volleyball court, 1/2 basketball court, fitness center, massage service and body treatments. *702 Gold Lake Drive, Folsom; 916/351-1500 and 800/808-5253; www.lakenatomainn.com*

Larkspur Landing There are plenty of suite-style hotels, but Larkspur Landing stands out for its amenities and pampering of the business traveler. The hotels provide an Arts-and-Crafts architectural style, original artwork, richly furnished rooms with desks and dataports, a fully equipped business center, meeting rooms and a library. There is a complete kitchen in the room and complimentary grocery shopping service. *121 Iron Point Road, Folsom; 916/355-1616; 1931 Taylor Road, Roseville; 916/773-1717; 800/877-LARKSPUR; www.larkspurhotels.com*

Ryde Hotel This Art Deco former speakeasy was built along the Sacramento River Delta in 1927. In its heyday the Ryde attracted movie stars, presidents, mobsters and the like. Today the newly refurbished hotel offers rooms with Jacuzzis and river views, a compact nine-hole golf course, a swimming pool and the leisurely pace that comes with the Delta. *14340 Highway 160, Ryde; 916/776-1318 and 888/717-RYDE; www.rydehotel.com*

Sheraton Grand The new Sheraton Grand offers first-rate accomodations right next to the Convention Center. The hotel lobby is located in the renovated Public Market Building designed by Julia Morgan. The hotel's 503 rooms are located in the 26-story tower adjacent to the lobby, offering great views of the central city. Amenities include a deli, a restaurant (Morgan's Central Valley Bistro), a swimming pool, a fitness center, a lounge (the popular Public Market Bar in the lobby) and plentiful meeting and conference facilities. *1230 J Street, Sacramento; 916/447-1700; www.sheraton.com/sacramento*

Sterling Hotel This luxury hotel is located in a renovated Victorian mansion two blocks from the Convention Center. All 17 rooms are tastefully furnished, with Italian marble Jacuzzi baths, fresh flowers and bath robes. Some of the rooms have balconies. The Sterling also has a large ballroom for receptions, conferences and business meetings, as well as a high-end restaurant. *1300 H Street, Sacramento; 916/448-1300 and 800/365-7660; www.sterlinghotel.com*

HOSTEL

Sacramento International Hostel It is possible to sleep in a beautifully restored Victorian in downtown Sacramento for less than $20 per person per night. This 1885 Victorian, the former Llewellyn Williams Mansion, is one of the most elegant hostels in the nation. The ornate spiral staircase and oak and mahogany interior have impressed international visitors who are used to more humble hostel accomodations. Sacramento's hostel is spotlessly clean and offers both dormitory-style and private accommodations. A pending relocation of the building to a lot across the street will close the hostel for an eight-month period. As with all hostels, any member of International Youth Hostel or American Youth Hostel is welcome, regardless of age. Nonmembers can stay for an extra $3 per night. If you want to meet people from all over the world and don't mind shared cooking facilities and bathrooms, assisting with chores and occupying yourself while the hostel is closed from 10 a.m. to 5 p.m., then the Sacramento International Hostel is the way to go. *900 H Street , Sacramento; (916) 443-1691; www.norcalhostels.org*

INFORMATION

Visitor Information The **Visitor Information Center** (1101 2nd Street, 916/442-2183) and the **Sacramento Convention and Visitors Bureau** (1303 J Street, 916/264-7777; www.sacramentocvb.org) offer regional information. Information is also available from the friendly **Downtown Guides**, with bright yellow uniforms, who patrol the streets of Sacramento's central business district

Newspapers, Magazines and Websites The Sacramento Bee (www.sacbee.com) offers the largest daily circulation in the region and is published in the morning, **Sacramento News and Review** (www.newsreview.com) is a free weekly (published on Thursdays) that focuses on local and state news and entertainment, **Sacramento Observer** (www.sacobserver.com) is a weekly newspaper (published on Thursdays) on African-American news, **Sacramento Business Journal** (sacramento.bcentral.com/sacramento) provides weekly information (published on Friday) on the local business scene, **MGW** (www.mgwnews.com) is a free bi-monthly newspaper that covers gay and lesbian news, **Outword** (www.outword.com) is a free bi-monthly newspaper that covers gay and lesbian news, **Sacramento Magazine** (www.sacmag.com) is an upscale monthly that does a good job of covering the monthly cultural and events calendar, and **Inside the City** (www.insidepublications.com) is a free monthly providing a neighborhood and small business perspective. Of the major area news websites, **Sacramento Citysearch** (sacramento.citysearch.com) is part of a national guide operated by Ticketmaster, while **Sacramento.com** is the locally grown product driven by the considerable resources of *The Sacramento Bee*.

ARRIVING AND LEAVING

Automobile Most people arrive in Sacramento from one of the four major freeways that intersect less than one mile from the State Capitol Building (Business 80 and U.S. 50 run east-west, Interstate 5 and U.S. 99 run north-south). Winter fog can sock in the entire Central Valley, temporarily closing Interstate 5 and U.S. 99. California State Automobile Association maps are available from AAA offices: 4333 Florin Road, Sacramento, 916/422-6511; 15 Bicentennial Circle, Sacramento, 916/381-3355; 4745 Chippendale Drive, Sacramento, 916/331-7610 and 2100 Professional Drive, Roseville, 916/784-3232; www.csaa.com. *Highway conditions 916/445-7623 and 800/427-7623; www.dot.ca.gov/hq/roadinfo*

Air Sacramento International Airport has yet to secure a direct international flight, but the airport does have a shiny new Terminal A worthy of international visitors. Major rental car companies are located at the airport. Cost for transportation between the airport and downtown Sacramento is about $25 by taxi and $10 by **SuperShuttle** (800/258-3826; www.supershuttle.com/sac.htm). **YoloBus** (530/66628-77; www.yolobus.com) offers the least expensive service ($1) on a loop serving Sacramento, Davis and Woodland. (Be sure to check with the driver which direction the bus is headed!) Shuttles may be picked up in front of all airport terminals, in front of the Senator Hotel (12th and L Streets) and at the Holiday Inn (3rd and J Streets). Many hotels and motels offer free shuttles. Other shuttles can take you directly to your destination. A ground transportation agent is located in front of the restaurant building at the airport to provide information about other shuttles. *Sacramento International Airport located 12 miles north of Sacramento off Interstate 5, 916/929-5411; airports.co.sacramento.ca.us/smf*

Amtrak Amtrak's *Capitols* provide service between Sacramento and San Jose, *San Joaquins* to Los Angeles via the Central Valley, *Coast Starlight* to Los Angeles and Seattle via the Pacific Coast and *California Zephyr* to San Francisco and Reno and points east. *501 I Street, Sacramento; 800/USA-RAIL; www.amtrak.com*

Greyhound The Greyhound depot is located in the heart of downtown. *715 L Street; 800/229-9424;www.greyhound.com*

GETTING AROUND

Car rental Eight major rental car companies are located at Sacramento Metropolitan Airport and in various other locations. Your rental rate may increase considerably if you choose to accept the collision damage waiver and other optional services. Check with your insurance agent to find out whether your personal auto policy already protects you from liability for rental vehicle damage before agreeing to accept the rental company's coverage. In addition, many credit cards provide some coverage.

Public Transportation More than 18 miles of light rail lines and an extensive bus system are operated by **Regional Transit** (916/321-BUSS; www.sacrt.com). Service on light rail is at 15-minute intervals, with comparable service on the busier bus routes. Standard system-wide fare is $1.50. Central City fare is 50 cents, valid between C Street and Broadway, 2nd Street and Alhambra Blvd. A Day Pass costs $3.50. There is no central terminal for buses, but many connect with light rail between 7th Street and 10th Street, adjacent to K Street. RT's Downtown Service Center, 808 K Street, offers ticket sales and service information. Routes and scheduling information for the system are posted at every light rail station. If you plan to use public transit extensively, it is a good idea to purchase *Sacramento Bus & Light Rail Timetables* ($1.50), which offers route and schedule information and has a detailed system map attached. The publication is available at most locations where magazines are sold.

Bicycle Although bike lanes are marked throughout the city, you should avoid streets with heavy auto traffic. Bike racks often are hard to find; parking meters and street signs provide functional substitutes. Many parking garages offer bike racks located within the supervision of toll booth operators. Bicycle paths connect Davis, Sacramento and Folsom. There are several places to rent bicycles, including **City Bicycle Works** (2419 K Street, Sacramento; 916/447-2453; www.citybikeworks.com), **Bike Sacramento** (1050 Front Street, Old Sacramento; 916/444-0200), and **The Bike Depot** (1028 Second Street, Old Sacramento; 916/427-5844).

Paratransit Paratransit (916/429-2744 and 916/429-2568 (TDD) provides transportation for persons with disabilities who are unable to use Regional Transit. Call one or two days in advance of the trip.

THE SEASONS

Winter More than half of the city's annual rainfall comes during this season. Dense "tule" fog can severely diminish visibility at the airport and on major highways. It is best to plan arrivals to, and departures from, Sacramento either in the afternoon or in early evening. An overcoat or rain-coat is good to have on hand.

Spring Spring provides a long burst of color as bulbs, trees, shrubs and vines break out of their winter hibernation. Pollen counts are often high, making life difficult for those with allergies.

Summer Although daytime temperatures are often in the 90s-100s F, cool air from the Bay Area shoots up the Sacramento-San Joaquin Delta most summer evenings, often bringing the mercury down into the 60s F.

Autumn Autumn provides a colorful show of hundreds of thousands of deciduous trees. Leaves begin turning in October, peak color comes in late November and the final leaf falls sometime around the new year.

MEDICAL EMERGENCIES

Three of the largest hospitals in Sacramento are **Sutter General Hospital** (2801 L Street, 24-hour Emergency Services, 916/733-8900), **Mercy General Hospital** (4001 J Street, Emergency Room, 916/453-4424), and **UC Davis Medical Center** (2315 Stockton Boulevard, 916/734-2455).

ACKNOWLEDGEMENTS

My deepest appreciation to my bride, Karen, for supporting my pursuit of this on-going project, spending countless hours editing the manuscript, entertaining our boys and not making me feel (too) guilty about any of it.

My continuing gratitude to Richard Tolmach for his creativity, knowledge, and patience in designing the book. He has raised the standard for regional guides and has been most handy with a corkscrew.

Thanks to John Gilroy for editing with his flinty eye for detail, catching errors that would have gotten past my blissful ignorance.

I can't repay my parents for their love and support but I'm trying to emulate their example.

I am indebted to those who reviewed manuscripts along the way, including Paula Boghosian, Larry Castro, Tim Church, Gary Delsohn, Dan Eriksson, Diane Flynn, Tom Kerbs, Christine Kronenberg, Drew Liebert, Gene Masuda, the late Mimi Modisette, Karen Randles, Maria Eriksson, Vito Sgromo, Rosemary Stewart, Richard Tolmach and Bea, Bob and Dan Visnick. Their insights and comments improved the book. The late Jim Browning (pictured with Aggie on p. 181) contributed photography to the first edition.

The Sacramento Public Library, Sacramento Housing and Redevelopment Agency, California State Library, Yolo County Public Library, Solano County Public Library, Placer County Public Library and area chambers of commerce were most helpful. Much of the source materials came from these entities.

A special thanks to the History and Science Division of the Sacramento Archives and Museum Collection Center, particularly the gracious assistance of Archivist Charlene Noyes and Executive Director James Henley. The following photos were obtained from the collection: Sutter portrait, p. 65; Old Sacramento in the 1950s (courtesy of the Rick Denico collection), p. 67; K Street in the 1920s, p. 77; Eisenhower and Warren motorcade, p. 93; aerial view of Capitol Mall, p. 94, and Jerry Brown, p. 98 (all courtesy of Sacramento Bee collection); State Capitol construction (courtesy of the City Library Collection) p. 95. The photo of Governor Reagan on p. 4 is courtesy of Merlino's. The photo of the Capitol reconstruction on p. 96 is courtesy of the California Department of Parks and Recreation (State Capitol Museum Collection). The rafting photo (p. 60) was courtesy of master rafter Corey Brown.

ABOUT THE AUTHOR

Dan Flynn was born in Oxnard, California and has lived in Sacramento since 1986. His mother's genealogical research found that his Sacramento roots date to the Gold Rush, when his Irish great-great grandfather came to California to work in the mines. Flynn is a consultant for a member of the California Legislature. He lives in Land Park with his wife, Karen, and sons John and Jimmy.

REFERENCES

American Association of University Women, *Vanishing Victorians*, Sacramento: American Association of University Women, 1973.

Bachelis, Faren Maree, *Sacramento and the Gold Country*, Gretna, Louisiana: Pelican Publishing, 1987

Boghosian, Paula and Hatley, Mason, *Historic Architecture of Sacramento Walking Tour: Downtown Tour, Alkali Flat Tour and Capitol Tour* (brochures), Sacramento: Sacramento Heritage, Inc. no date

Business Journal, The

Citrus Heights Historical Society, *A Historical Overview of the Evolution of Citrus Heights*, Citrus Heights: Citrus Heights Historical Society, 1998

City of Woodland, Historical Preservation Commission, *Walking Tour of Historic Woodland* (pamphlet), Woodland: City of Woodland, 1982, 1991

City of Woodland, *Woodland Historical Resource Inventory: Final Report*, Woodland: City of Woodland, 1981-82

CitySearch Sacramento

Davis Enterprise

Davis Historical Resource Management Commission, *Davis Historic Bike Tour* (brochure), Davis: City of Davis, no date

Dixon Historical Society, *Dixon History: 125th Anniversary of the Founding of Dixon*, Dixon: Dixon Historical Society, 1993

Davis, Win, J., *Illustrated History of Sacramento County, California*, Chicago: The Lewis Publishing Co., 1890

Donnelly, Robin, *Biking and Hiking the American River Parkway*, Sacramento: The American River Parkway Natural History Association, 1998

Fair Oaks Historical Society, *Fair Oaks: The Early Years*, Fair Oaks: Fair Oaks Historical Society, 1995

Folsom Historical Society, *7 Mile Historical Tour* (brochure), Folsom: Folsom Historical Society, no date

Galt Chamber of Commerce, *Galt: 1869-1994, The First 125 Years*, Galt: Galt Chamber of Commerce, 1994

Gillenkirk, Jeff and Motlow, James, *Bitter Melon: Inside America's Last Rural Chinese Town*, Berkeley: Heydey Books, 1987

Folsom Chamber of Commerce, *Folsom Historic Tour* (pamphlet), Folsom: Folsom Chamber of Commerce, no date

Gebhard, David, et al., *The Guide to Architecture in San Francisco and Northern California*, Salt Lake City: Peregrine Smith Books, 1985

Guinn, J.m., *History of the State of California and Biographical Record of the Sacramento Valley, California*, Chicago: Chapman Publishing Company, 1906

Hart, James D., *A Companion to California*, New York: Oxford University Press, 1978

Historic Environment Consultants, *Nonresidential Building Survey*, Sacramento City Planning Department, 1981

Historic Environment Consultants, *Sacramento Survey No. III*, Sacramento Old City Association and Sacramento Housing and Redevelopment Agency, 1985

Holden, William H., *Sacramento: Excursions Into Its History and Natural World*, Fair Oaks: Two Rivers Publishing Co., 1987

Hoover, Mildred Brooke; Rensch, Hero Eugene; Rensch, Ethel Grace, *Historic Spots in California: Third Edition*, Stanford: Stanford University Press, 1966

Hunt, Margaret, *History of Solano County, California*, Chicago: The S.J. Clarke Publishing Co., 1926.

Inside East Sacramento and *Inside the City*

Jackson Research Projects, *The Old Courthouse Block, H-I-6-7 Streets*, Sacramento 1848-1983, Davis, 1983

Kurutz, Gary, *Architectural Terra Cotta of Gladding, McBean*, Sausalito: Windgate Press, 1989

Lebovich, William I., *Historic American Buildings Survey, America's City Halls*, Washington, D.C., The Preservation Press, 1984

Leland, Dorothy Kupcha, *A Short History of Sacramento*, San Francisco, Lexikos, 1989

Loefland, John, *North Davis: Guide to Walking a Traditional Neighborhood*, Woodland: Yolo County Historical Society, 1999

Martini, Tony, *Climate of Sacramento, California*, National Weather Service, 1993

McGowan, Joseph A., and Willis, Terry R., *Sacramento: Heart of the Golden State*, Woodland Hills, Windsor Publications, 1983

Miller, Robert, *Guide to Old Sacramento*, Sacramento River City Press, 1976

Mills, James R., *A Disorderly House: The Brown-Unruh Years in Sacramento*, Berkeley: Heydey Books, 1987

Mims, Julie Elizabeth and Kevin, *Sacramento: A Pictorial History of California's Capital*, Virginia Beach: The Doring Company, 1981

Neasham, V. Aubrey, *Old Sacramento: A Reference Point in Time*, Sacramento, Sacramento Historic Landmarks Commission, 1972

Old City Guardian, Sacramento Old City Association

Page, Charles Hall & Associates, *Historical/Architectural Survey of Sacramento* (residential buildings), 1976

Press Tribune, The

Reagan, Nancy, with Novak, William, *My Turn: The Memoirs of Nancy Reagan*, New York: Random House, 1989

Reed, G. Walter, Editor, *History of Sacramento County*, Los Angeles: Historical Record Co., 1923

Roseville Chamber of Commerce Revitalization Committee, *Historic Roseville Walking Tour* (pamphlet), Roseville: Roseville Chamber of Commerce, no date

Sacramento Bee, The

Sacramento Bee, The, *Sacramento Guide Book*, Sacramento: The Sacramento Bee, 1939

Sacramento City Directory, 1882-1959

Sacramento.com

Sacramento Magazine

Suttertown News

Sacramento News and Review

Sacramento Union

Samish, Arthur H. and Thomas, Bob, *The Secret Boss of California: The Life and High Times of Art Samish*, New York: Crown Publishers, 1971

Tinkham, George H., *History of San Joaquin County, California*, Los Angeles: Historic Record Company, 1923.

Trainor, Richard, *Sacramento: A Contemporary Portrait*, Woodland Hills: Windsor Pubs, 1991

University of California, Davis, *Self-Guided Walking Tour and Campus Information* (brochure), Davis: University of California, Davis, no date

Walters, Bob E., *Delta: The Cruising Wonderland of California's Sloughs and Rivers*, Fullerton: Cordrey & Walters Publishing, 1983

Walters, Shipley, *Clarksburg: Delta Community*, Woodland: Yolo County Hist. Society, 1988

Walters, Shipley, *Woodland: City of Trees, A History*, Woodland: Yolo County Hist. Society, 1995

Warren, Earl, *The Memoirs of Chief Justice Earl Warren*, New York: Doubleday and Company, 1977

Willis, William I., *History of Sacramento County, California*, Los Angeles: Hist. Record Doc., 1913

Woodbridge, Sally B., *Historic American Buildings Survey, California Architecture*, San Francisco: Chronicle Books, 1988

INDEX

WE NEED YOUR HELP!

We welcome your suggestions, criticisms, additions, and changes to the information in this book; they will be considered for incorporation into subsequent updates. Please complete this questionnaire and send to:

Embarcadero Press
P.O. Box 188325
Sacramento, CA 95818-8325
or e-mail us at sacguide@earthlink.net

Additions and changes

Page #	Change needed

Based on my personal experience, I wish to nominate or disapprove for listing the following establishment: _____

PLEASE DESCRIBE EXPERIENCE, including date of visit.

_____

_____

_____

_____

I do not have a financial interest, directly or indirectly, with the management or ownership of this establishment.

Name _____ Tel # _____

Address _____

City _____ Zip _____

ORDER FORM

The Inside Guide to Sacramento can be purchased by mail!

Pricing is as follows:

	California	Out of State
First Book:	$15 $3.00 tax and shipping **$18**	$15 $2.00 shipping **$17**
Additional Books:	$15 $2.00 shipping **$17**	$15 $2.00 shipping **$17**

California pricing **includes** 7.75 percent sales tax.
Bulk discounts are available. Write to us or call (916) 441-0275 for a discount schedule.

Make check payable to: **Embarcadero Press, Dept F**
P.O. Box 188325
Sacramento, CA 95818

Name

Address

City

State   Zip

Daytime Phone

Payment must accompany order. Please allow up to 4 weeks for delivery.